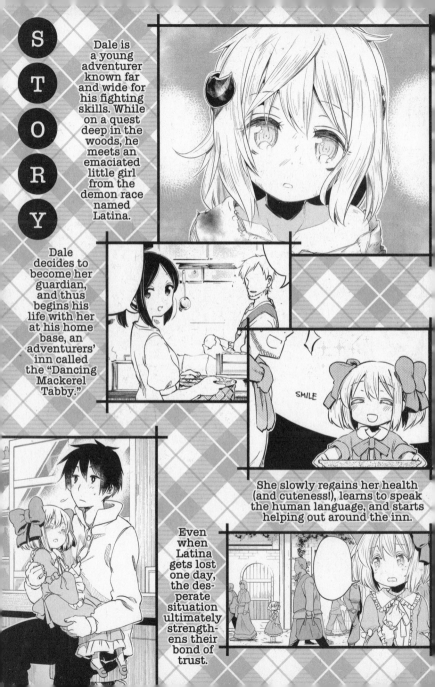

STORY

Dale is a young adventurer known far and wide for his fighting skills. While on a quest deep in the woods, he meets an emaciated little girl from the demon race named Latina.

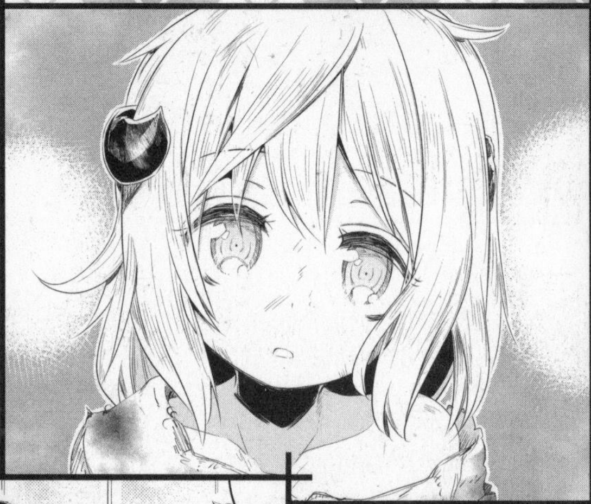

Dale decides to become her guardian, and thus begins his life with her at his home base, an adventurers' inn called the "Dancing Mackerel Tabby."

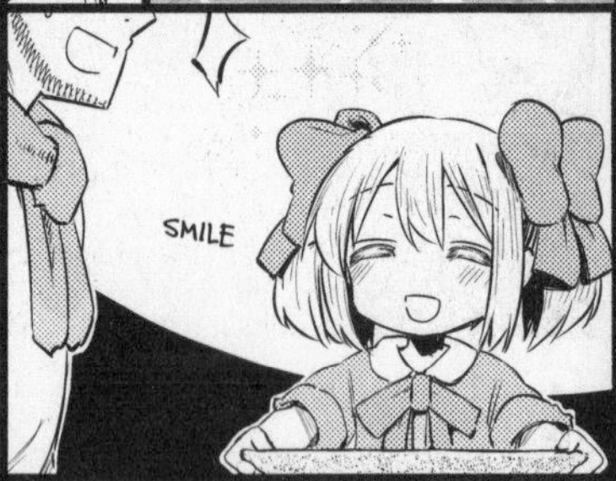
SMILE

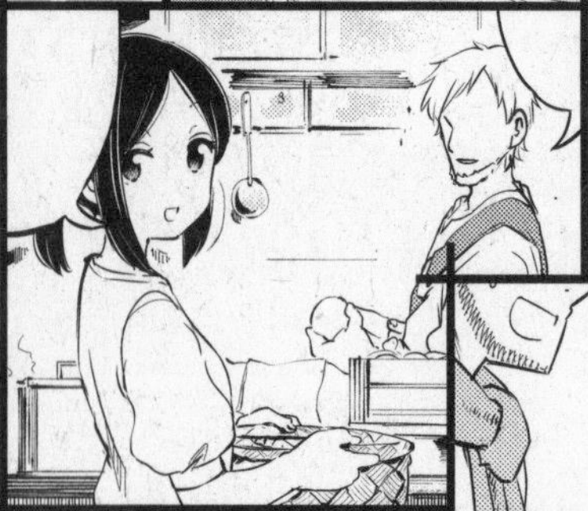

She slowly regains her health (and cuteness!), learns to speak the human language, and starts helping out around the inn.

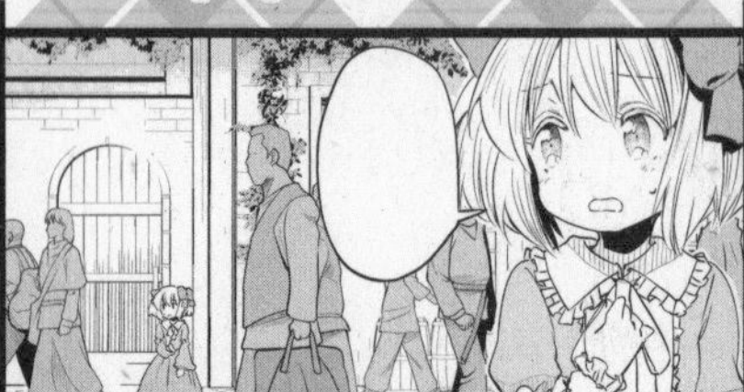

Even when Latina gets lost one day, the desperate situation ultimately strengthens their bond of trust.

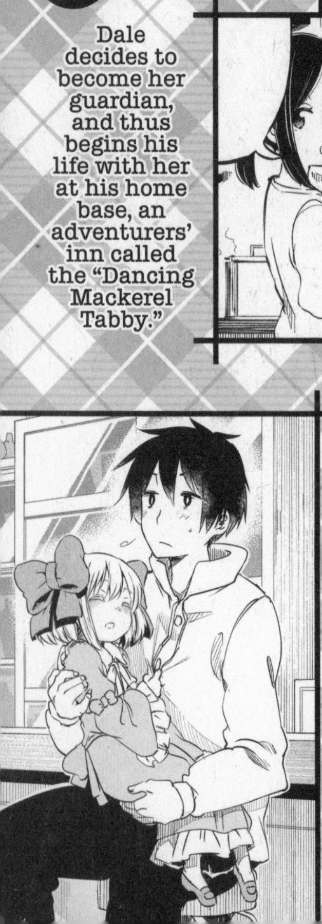

If It's For My Daughter, I'd Even Defeat a Demon Lord.

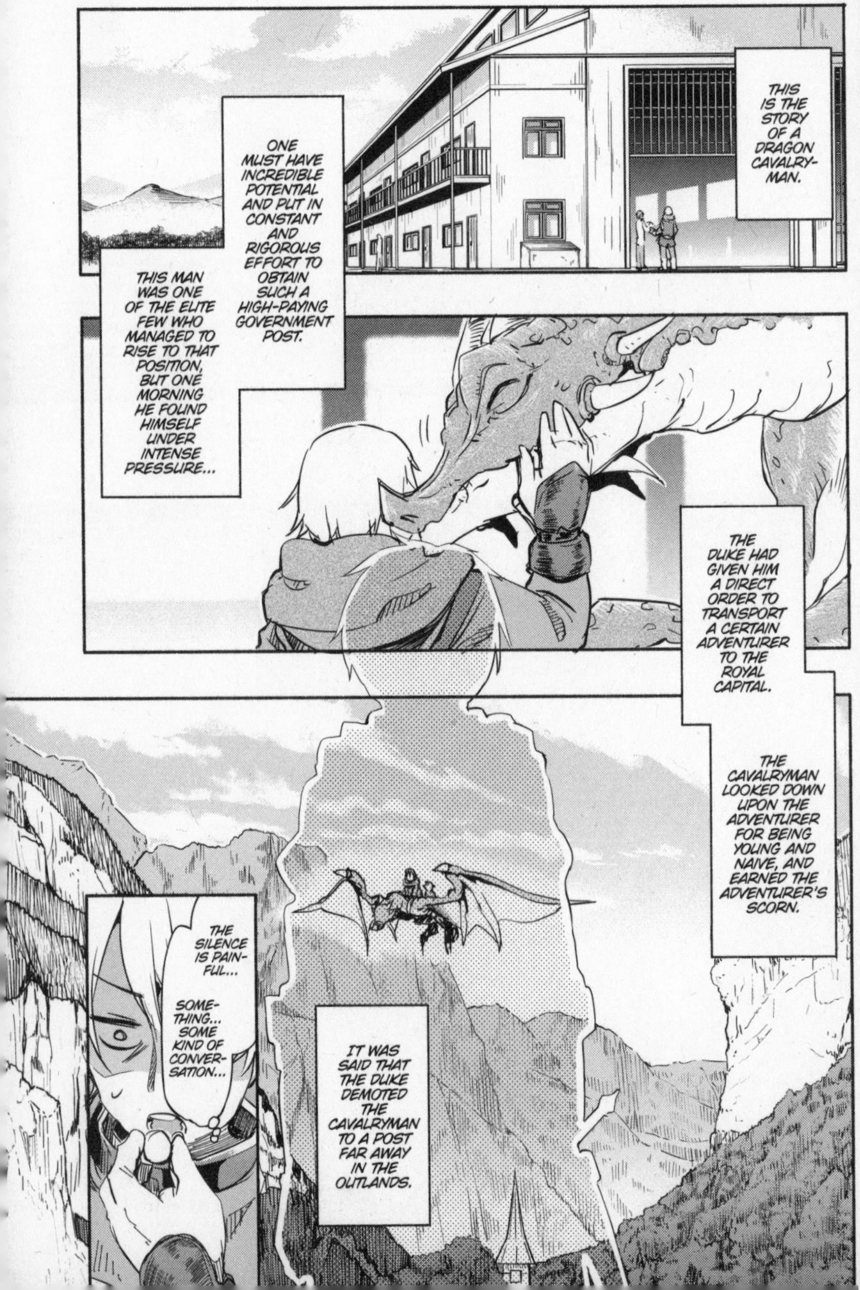
THIS IS THE STORY OF A DRAGON CAVALRYMAN.
ONE MUST HAVE INCREDIBLE POTENTIAL AND PUT IN CONSTANT AND RIGOROUS EFFORT TO OBTAIN SUCH A HIGH-PAYING GOVERNMENT POST.
THIS MAN WAS ONE OF THE ELITE FEW WHO MANAGED TO RISE TO THAT POSITION, BUT ONE MORNING HE FOUND HIMSELF UNDER INTENSE PRESSURE...
THE DUKE HAD GIVEN HIM A DIRECT ORDER TO TRANSPORT A CERTAIN ADVENTURER TO THE ROYAL CAPITAL.
THE CAVALRYMAN LOOKED DOWN UPON THE ADVENTURER FOR BEING YOUNG AND NAIVE, AND EARNED THE ADVENTURER'S SCORN.
THE SILENCE IS PAINFUL...
SOMETHING... SOME KIND OF CONVERSATION...
IT WAS SAID THAT THE DUKE DEMOTED THE CAVALRYMAN TO A POST FAR AWAY IN THE OUTLANDS.

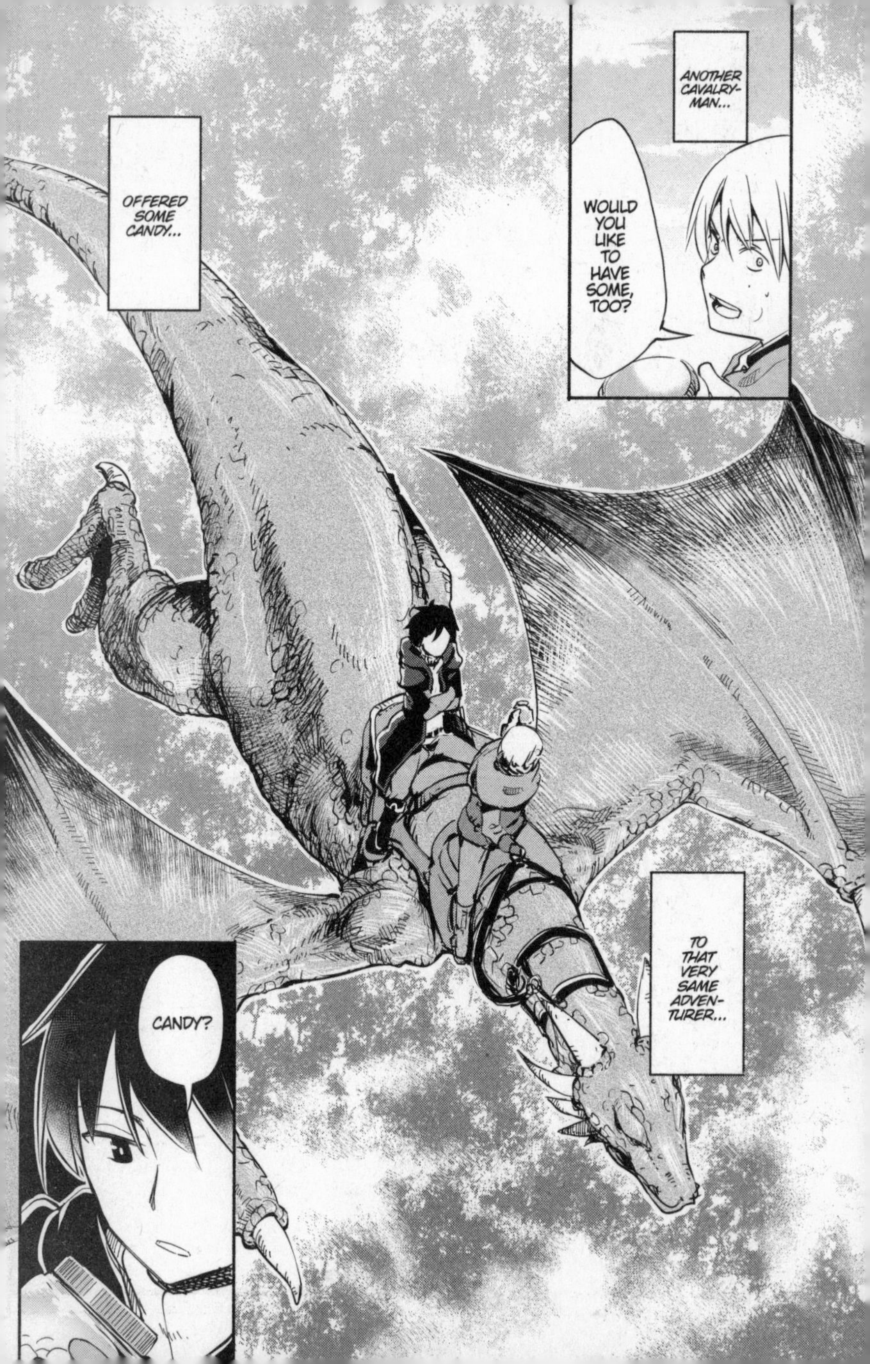
ANOTHER CAVALRY-MAN...
WOULD YOU LIKE TO HAVE SOME, TOO?
TO THAT VERY SAME ADVEN-TURER...
OFFERED SOME CANDY...
CANDY?

7. Youth Away from Home

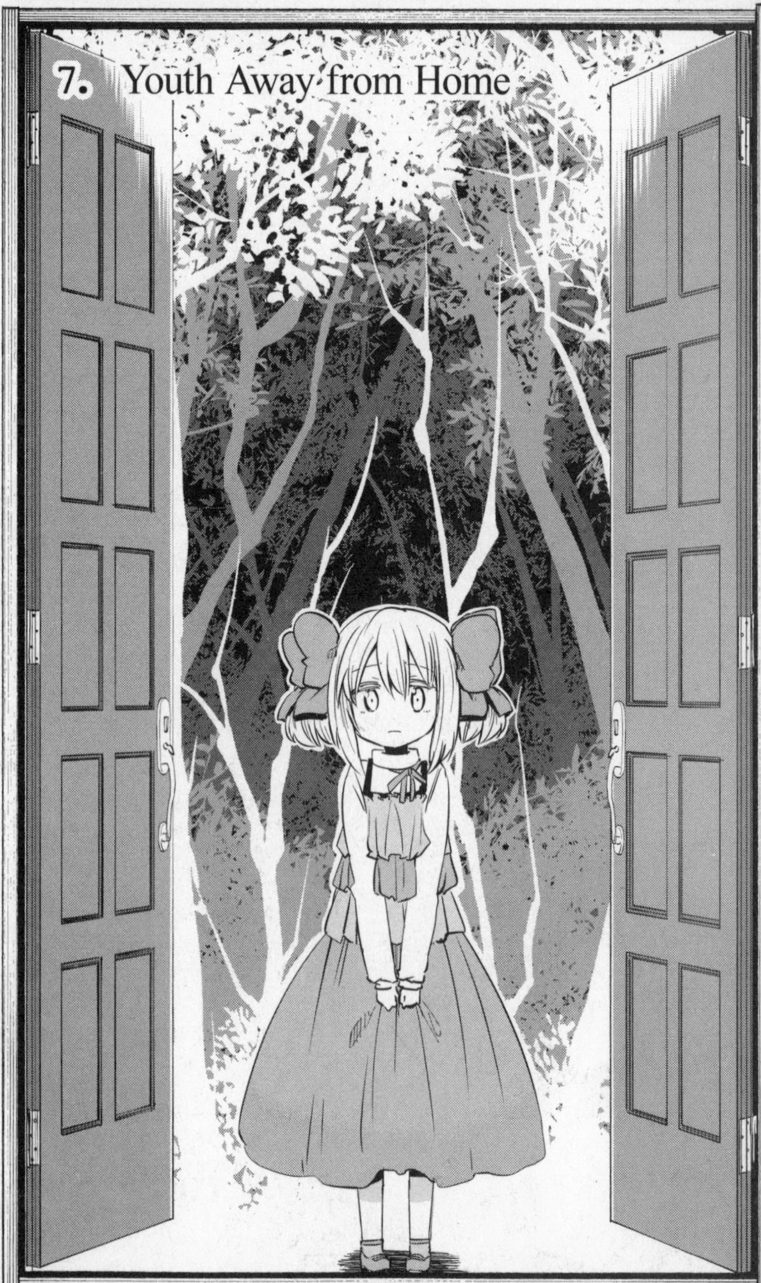

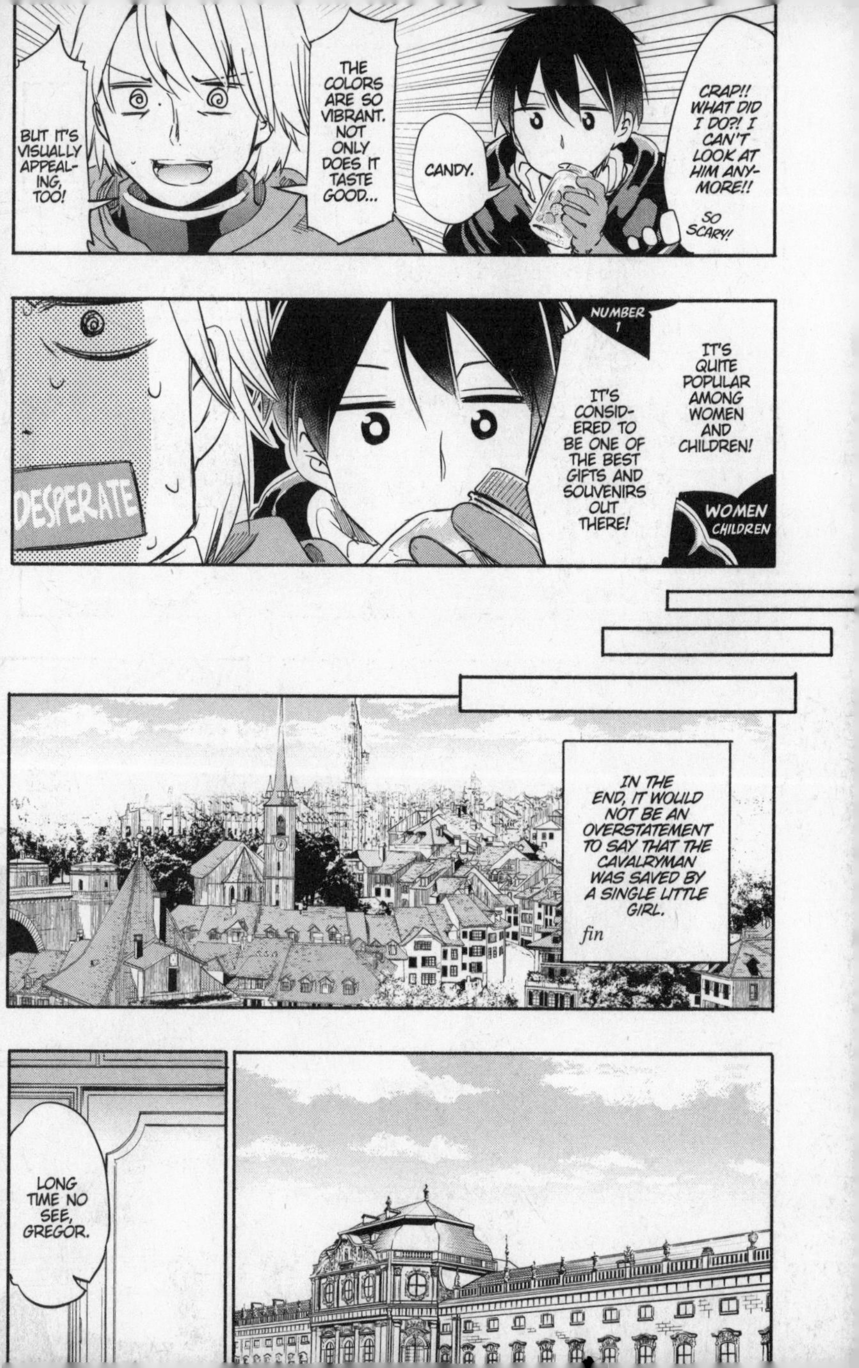
CRAP!! WHAT DID I DO?! I CAN'T LOOK AT HIM ANYMORE!!
SO SCARY!
CANDY.
THE COLORS ARE SO VIBRANT. NOT ONLY DOES IT TASTE GOOD...
BUT IT'S VISUALLY APPEALING, TOO!
NUMBER 1
IT'S QUITE POPULAR AMONG WOMEN AND CHILDREN!
WOMEN
CHILDREN
IT'S CONSIDERED TO BE ONE OF THE BEST GIFTS AND SOUVENIRS OUT THERE!
DESPERATE
IN THE END, IT WOULD NOT BE AN OVERSTATEMENT TO SAY THAT THE CAVALRYMAN WAS SAVED BY A SINGLE LITTLE GIRL.
fin
LONG TIME NO SEE, GREGOR.

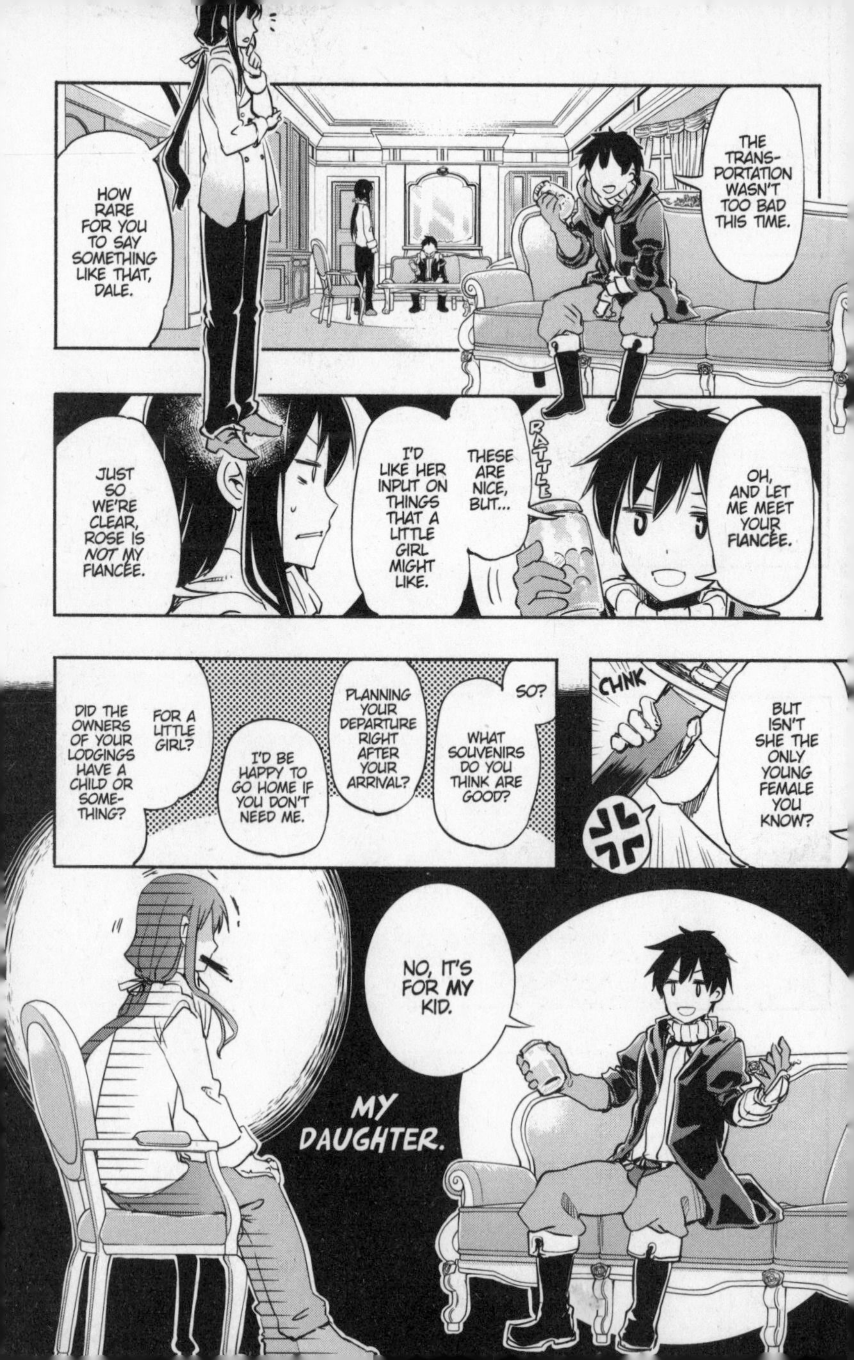
THE TRANSPORTATION WASN'T TOO BAD THIS TIME.
HOW RARE FOR YOU TO SAY SOMETHING LIKE THAT, DALE.
OH, AND LET ME MEET YOUR FIANCÉE.
RATTLE
THESE ARE NICE, BUT...
I'D LIKE HER INPUT ON THINGS THAT A LITTLE GIRL MIGHT LIKE.
JUST SO WE'RE CLEAR, ROSE IS *NOT* MY FIANCÉE.
CHINK
BUT ISN'T SHE THE ONLY YOUNG FEMALE YOU KNOW?
SO?
WHAT SOUVENIRS DO YOU THINK ARE GOOD?
PLANNING YOUR DEPARTURE RIGHT AFTER YOUR ARRIVAL?
I'D BE HAPPY TO GO HOME IF YOU DON'T NEED ME.
FOR A LITTLE GIRL?
DID THE OWNERS OF YOUR LODGINGS HAVE A CHILD OR SOMETHING?
NO, IT'S FOR MY KID.
MY DAUGHTER.

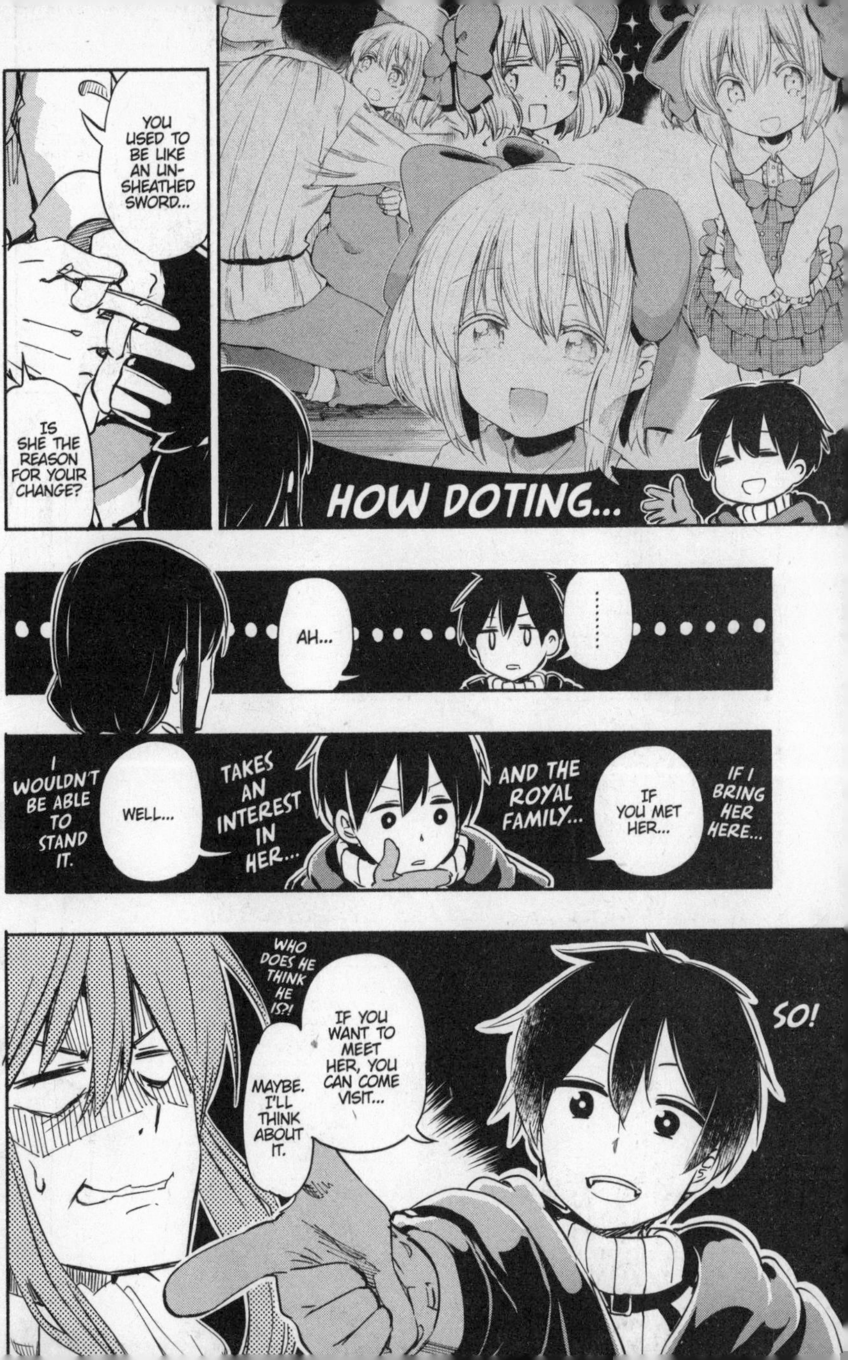
HOW DOTING...
YOU USED TO BE LIKE AN UN-SHEATHED SWORD...
IS SHE THE REASON FOR YOUR CHANGE?
......
AH...
IF I BRING HER HERE...
IF YOU MET HER...
AND THE ROYAL FAMILY...
TAKES AN INTEREST IN HER...
WELL...
I WOULDN'T BE ABLE TO STAND IT.
SO!
IF YOU WANT TO MEET HER, YOU CAN COME VISIT...
WHO DOES HE THINK HE IS?!
MAYBE. I'LL THINK ABOUT IT.

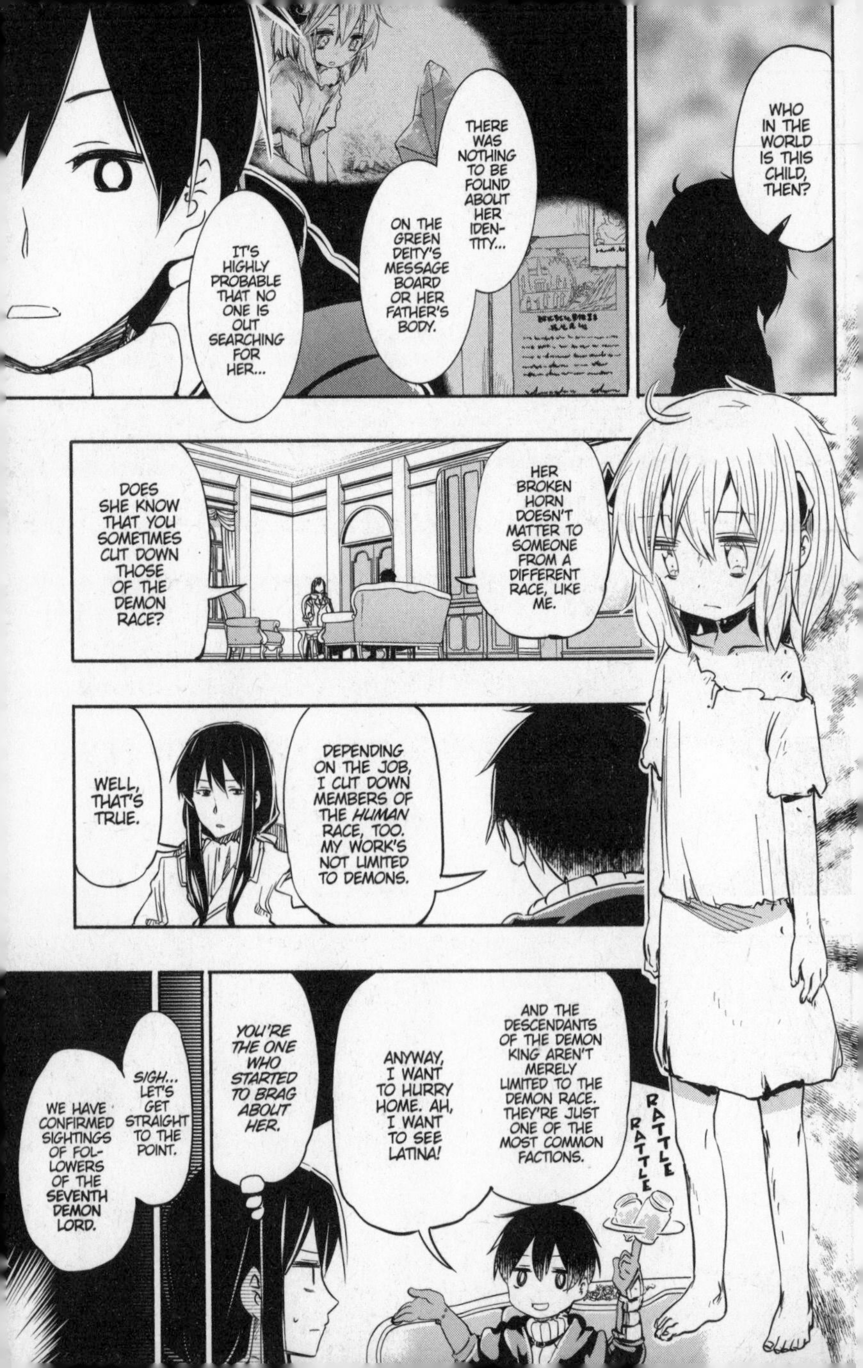
WHO IN THE WORLD IS THIS CHILD, THEN?
THERE WAS NOTHING TO BE FOUND ABOUT HER IDENTITY...
ON THE GREEN DEITY'S MESSAGE BOARD OR HER FATHER'S BODY.
IT'S HIGHLY PROBABLE THAT NO ONE IS OUT SEARCHING FOR HER...
HER BROKEN HORN DOESN'T MATTER TO SOMEONE FROM A DIFFERENT RACE, LIKE ME.
DOES SHE KNOW THAT YOU SOMETIMES CUT DOWN THOSE OF THE DEMON RACE?
DEPENDING ON THE JOB, I CUT DOWN MEMBERS OF THE *HUMAN* RACE, TOO. MY WORK'S NOT LIMITED TO DEMONS.
WELL, THAT'S TRUE.
RATTLE RATTLE
AND THE DESCENDANTS OF THE DEMON KING AREN'T MERELY LIMITED TO THE DEMON RACE. THEY'RE JUST ONE OF THE MOST COMMON FACTIONS.
ANYWAY, I WANT TO HURRY HOME. AH, I WANT TO SEE LATINA!
YOU'RE THE ONE WHO STARTED TO BRAG ABOUT HER.
SIGH... LET'S GET STRAIGHT TO THE POINT.
WE HAVE CONFIRMED SIGHTINGS OF FOL-LOWERS OF THE SEVENTH DEMON LORD.

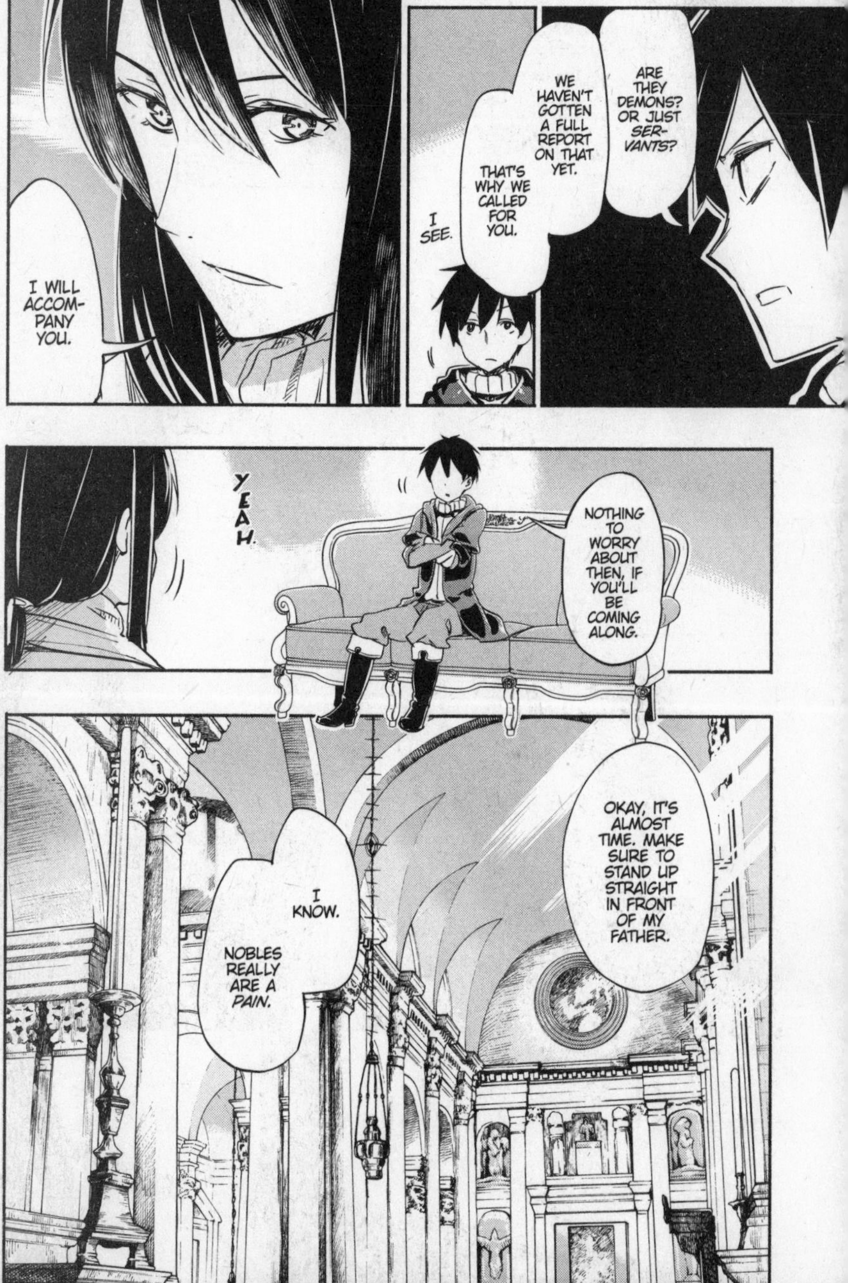
ARE THEY DEMONS? OR JUST *SERVANTS*?
WE HAVEN'T GOTTEN A FULL REPORT ON THAT YET.
THAT'S WHY WE CALLED FOR YOU.
I SEE.
I WILL ACCOMPANY YOU.
NOTHING TO WORRY ABOUT THEN, IF YOU'LL BE COMING ALONG.
YEAH.
OKAY, IT'S ALMOST TIME. MAKE SURE TO STAND UP STRAIGHT IN FRONT OF MY FATHER.
I KNOW.
NOBLES REALLY ARE A *PAIN*.

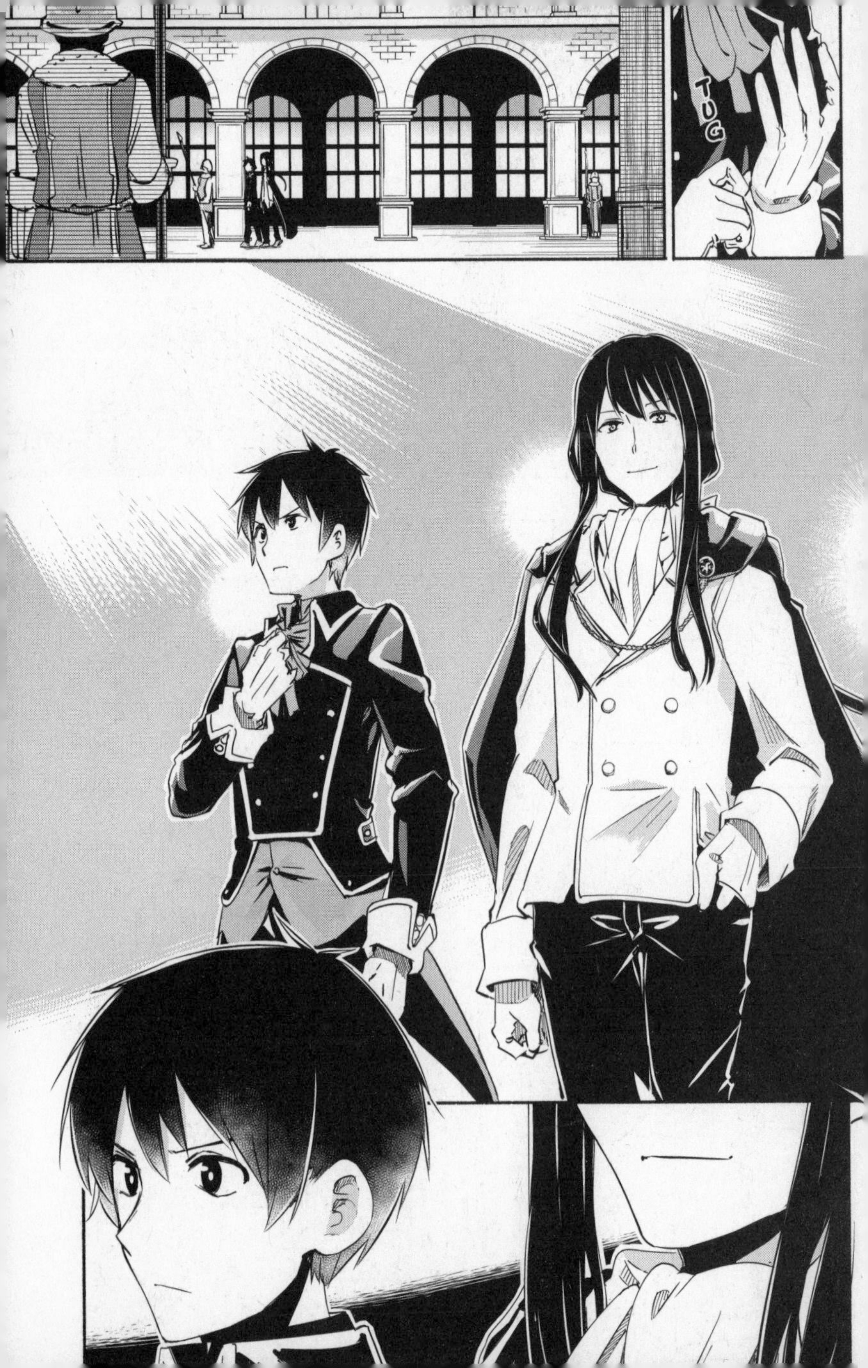
TUG
—

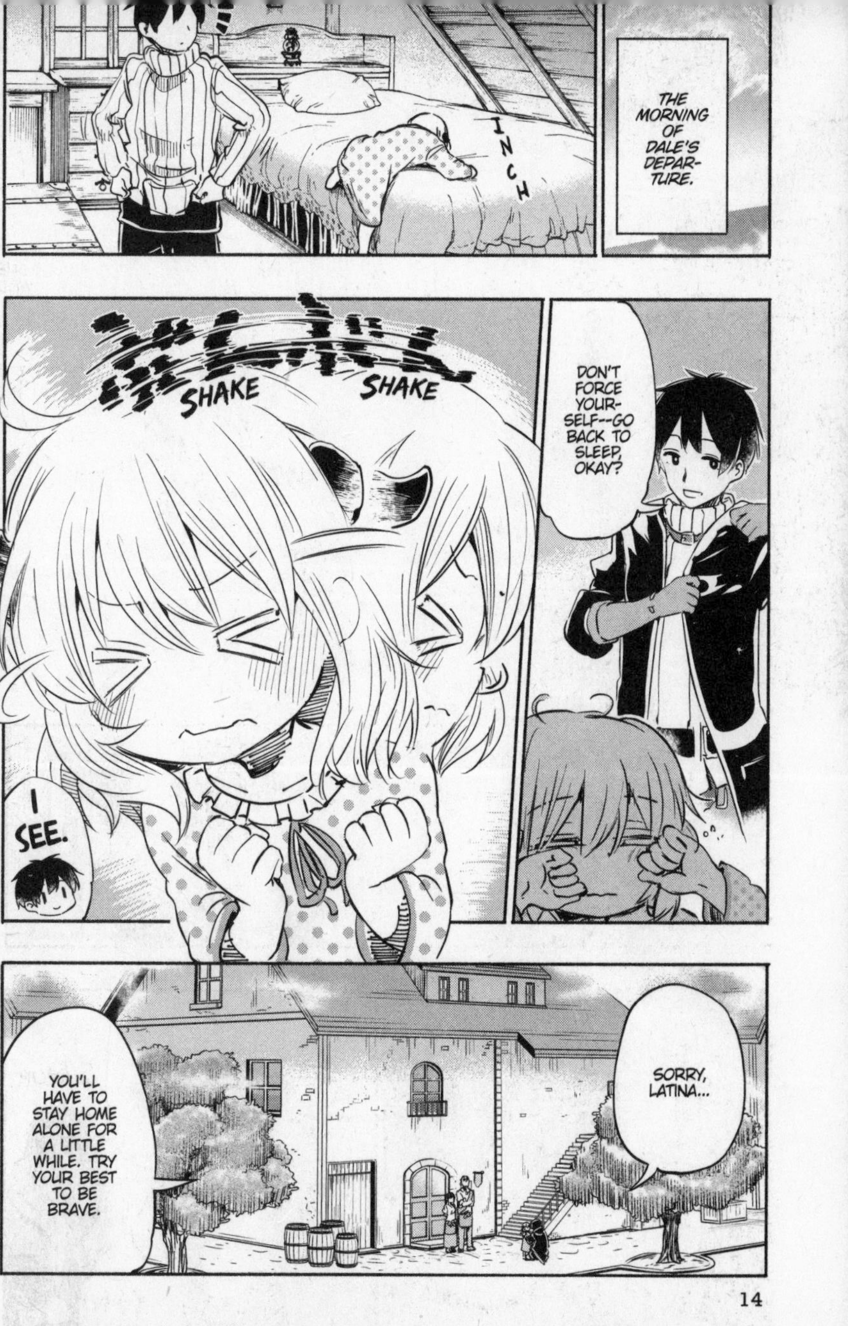
THE MORNING OF DALE'S DEPARTURE.
INCH
DON'T FORCE YOURSELF--GO BACK TO SLEEP, OKAY?
SHAKE SHAKE
I SEE.
SORRY, LATINA...
YOU'LL HAVE TO STAY HOME ALONE FOR A LITTLE WHILE. TRY YOUR BEST TO BE BRAVE.

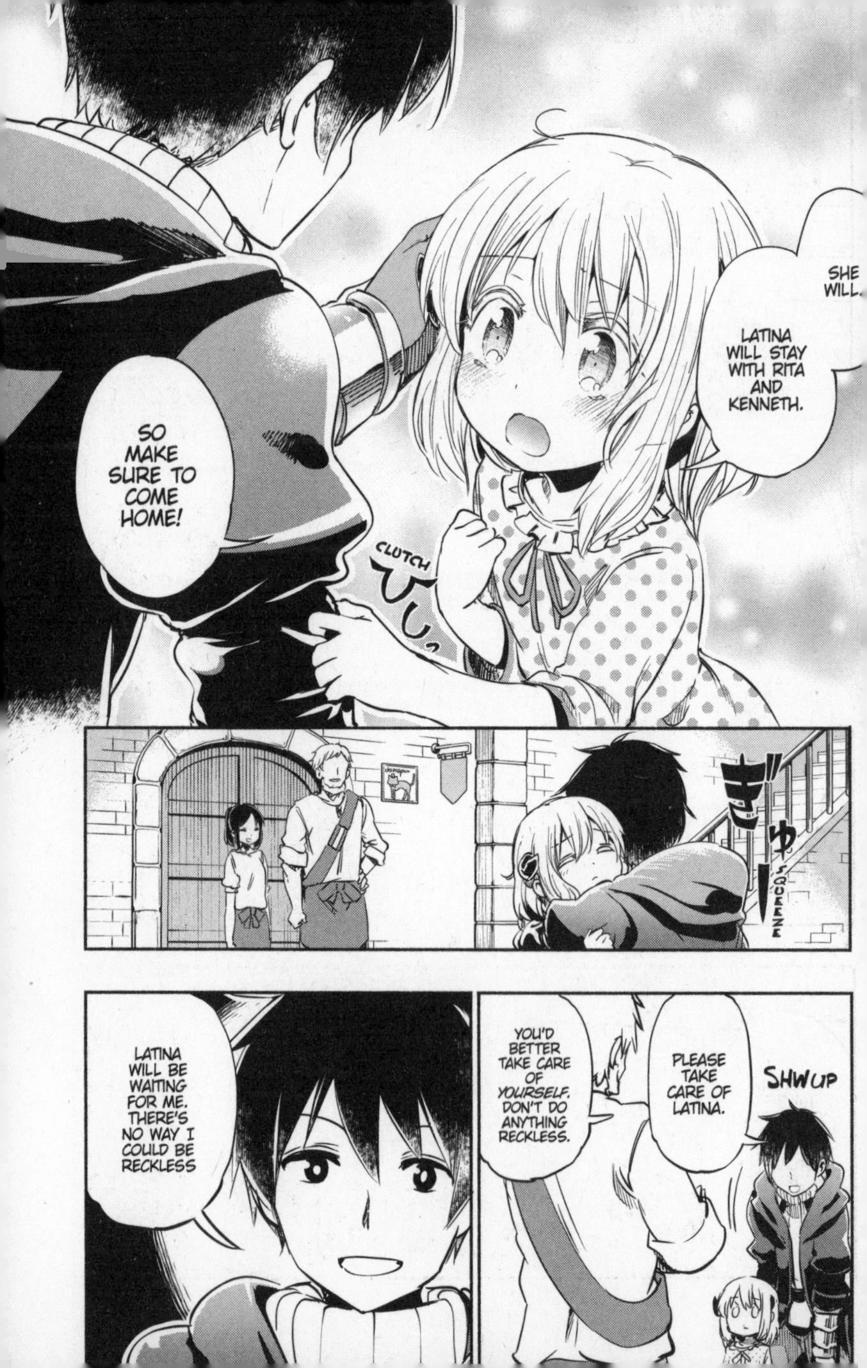
SHE WILL.
LATINA WILL STAY WITH RITA AND KENNETH.
SO MAKE SURE TO COME HOME!
CLUTCH
SQUEEZE
SHWUP
PLEASE TAKE CARE OF LATINA.
YOU'D BETTER TAKE CARE OF *YOURSELF*. DON'T DO ANYTHING RECKLESS.
LATINA WILL BE WAITING FOR ME. THERE'S NO WAY I COULD BE RECKLESS

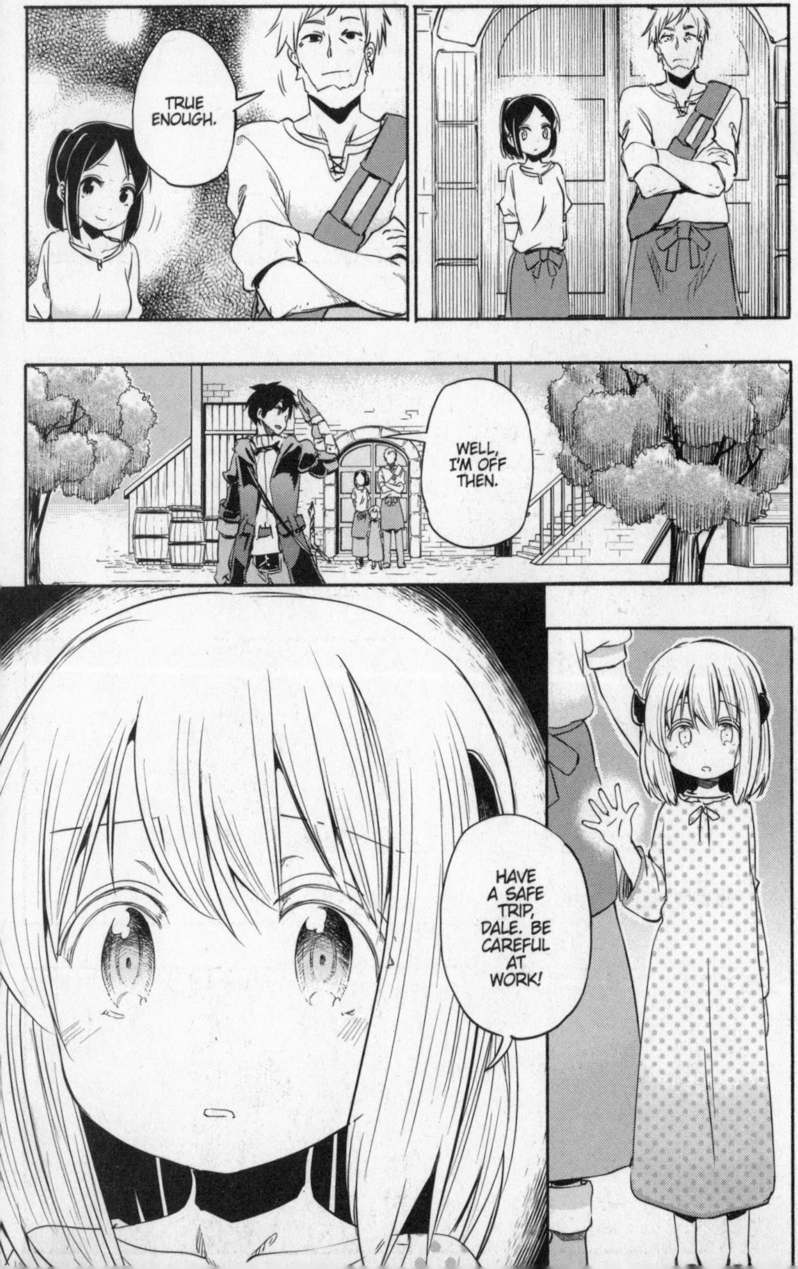
TRUE ENOUGH.
WELL, I'M OFF THEN.
HAVE A SAFE TRIP, DALE. BE CAREFUL AT WORK!

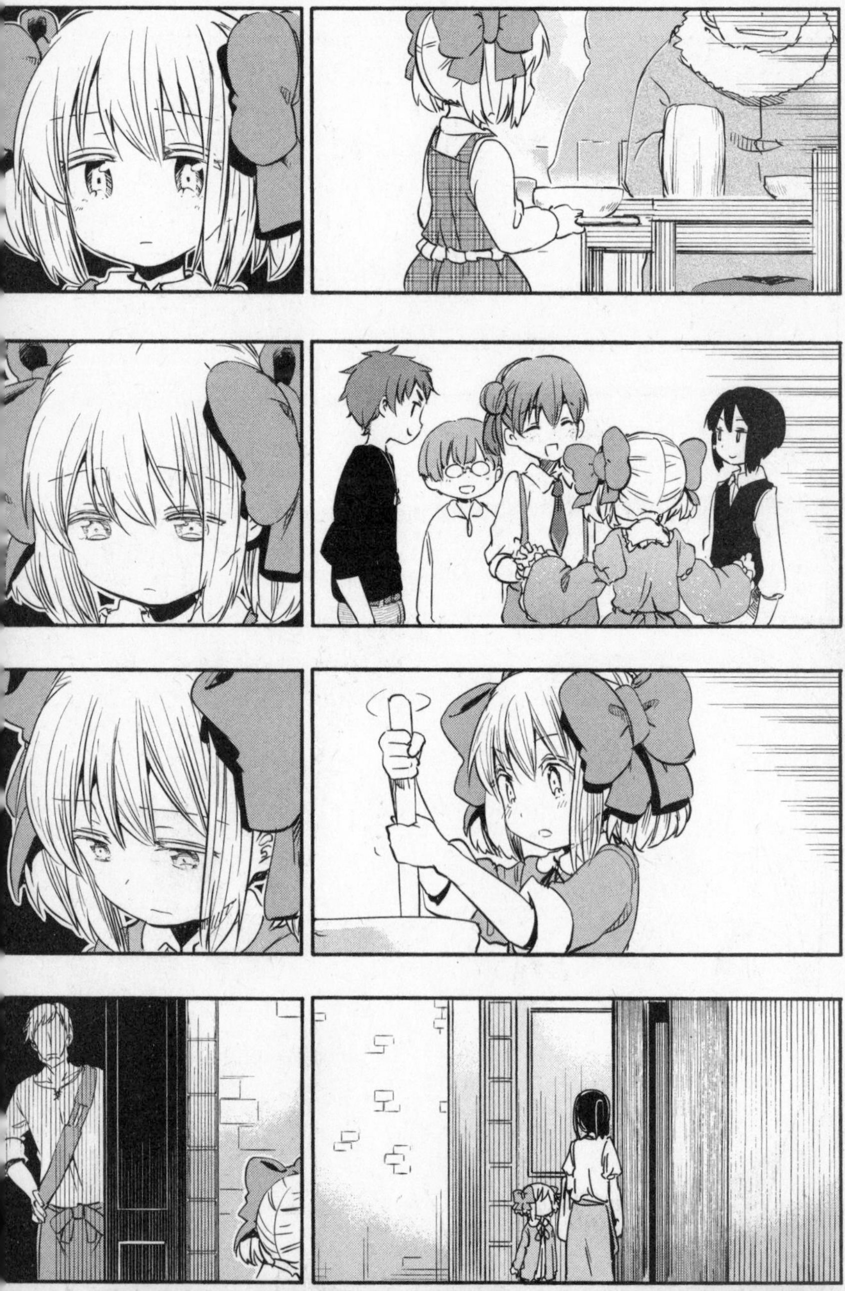

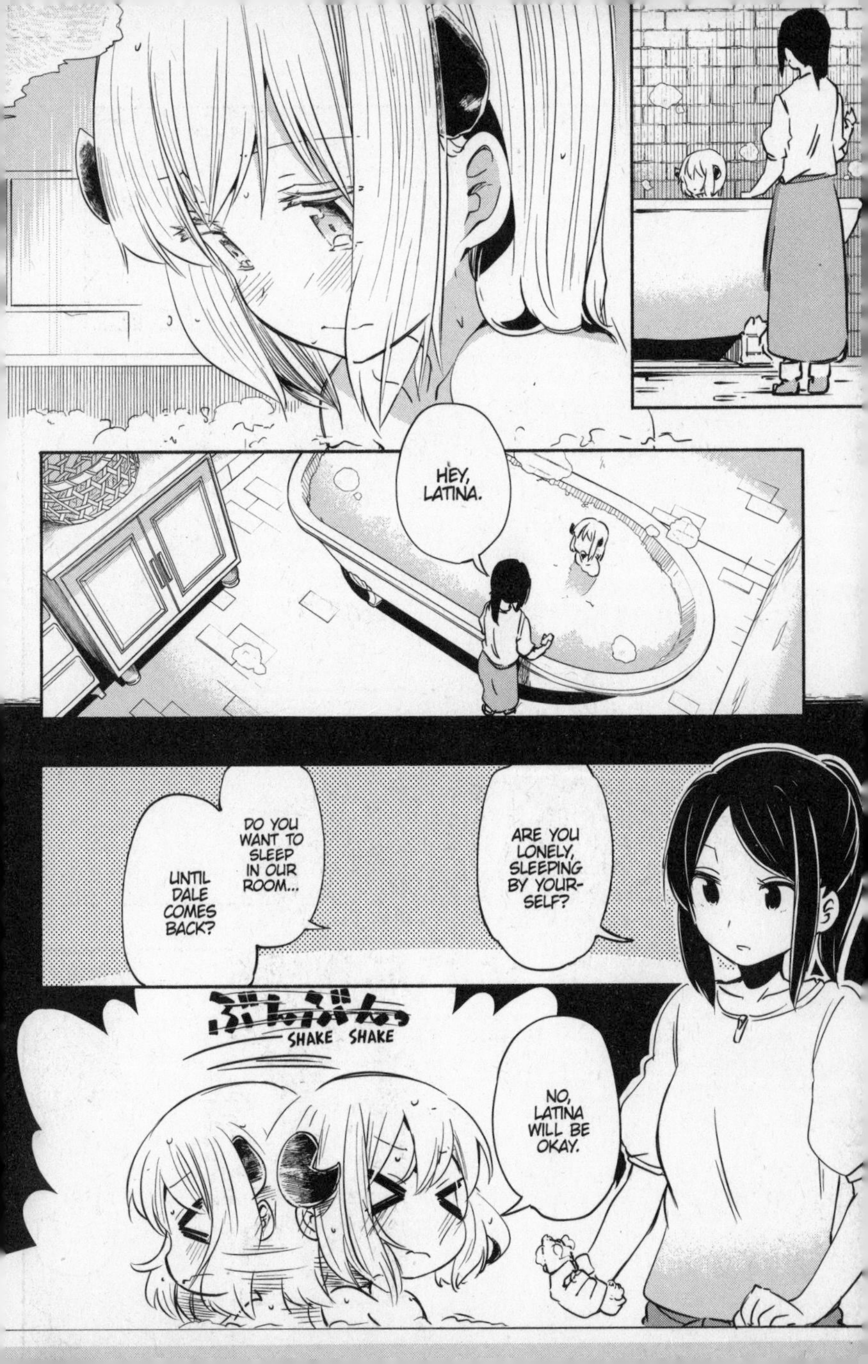
HEY, LATINA.
ARE YOU LONELY, SLEEPING BY YOUR-SELF?
DO YOU WANT TO SLEEP IN OUR ROOM...
UNTIL DALE COMES BACK?
SHAKE SHAKE
NO, LATINA WILL BE OKAY.

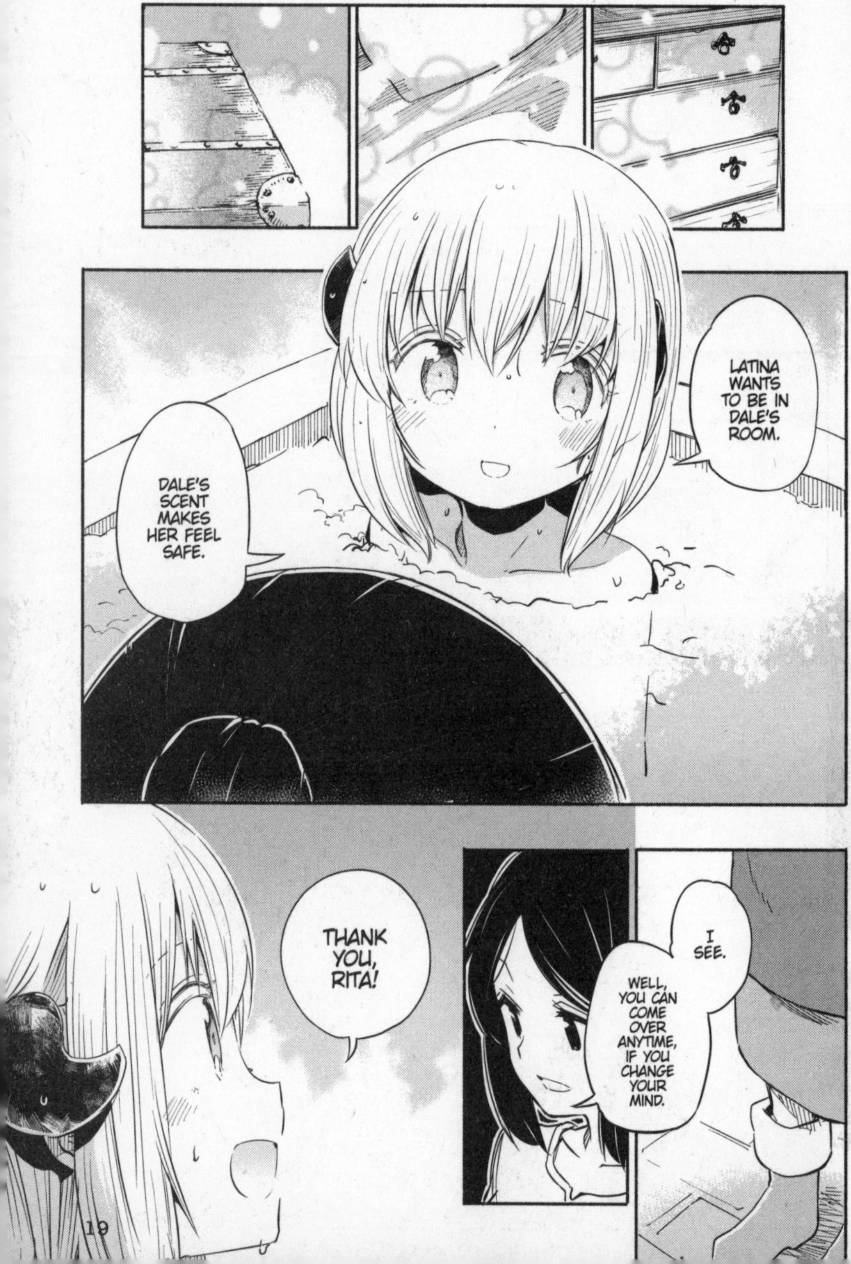
LATINA WANTS TO BE IN DALE'S ROOM.
DALE'S SCENT MAKES HER FEEL SAFE.
I SEE.
WELL, YOU CAN COME OVER ANYTIME, IF YOU CHANGE YOUR MIND.
THANK YOU, RITA!

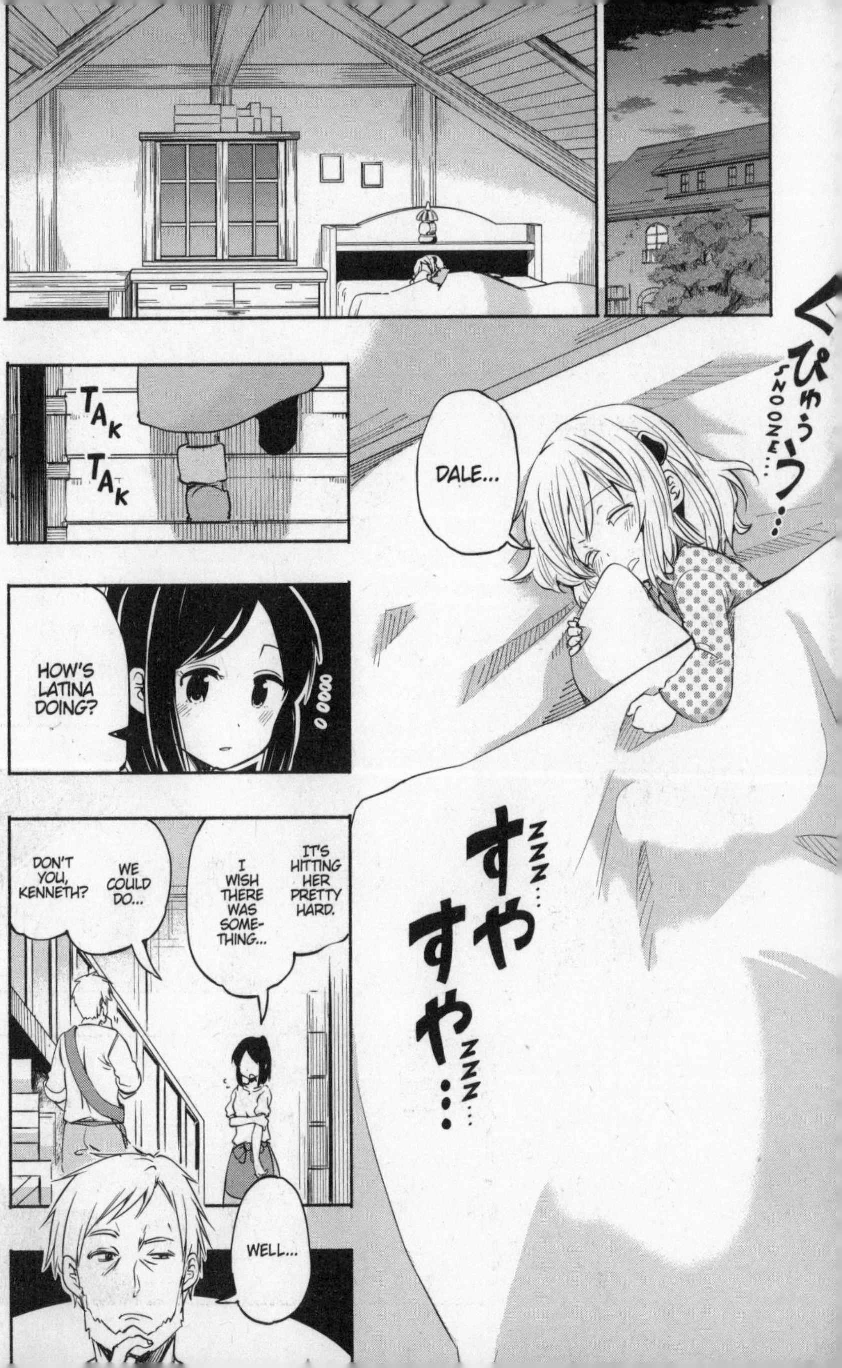
くぴゅう…
SNOOZE…
DALE...
すやすや
ZZZ...
ZZZ...
TAK
TAK
HOW'S LATINA DOING?
IT'S HITTING HER PRETTY HARD.
I WISH THERE WAS SOME-THING...
WE COULD DO...
DON'T YOU, KENNETH?
WELL...

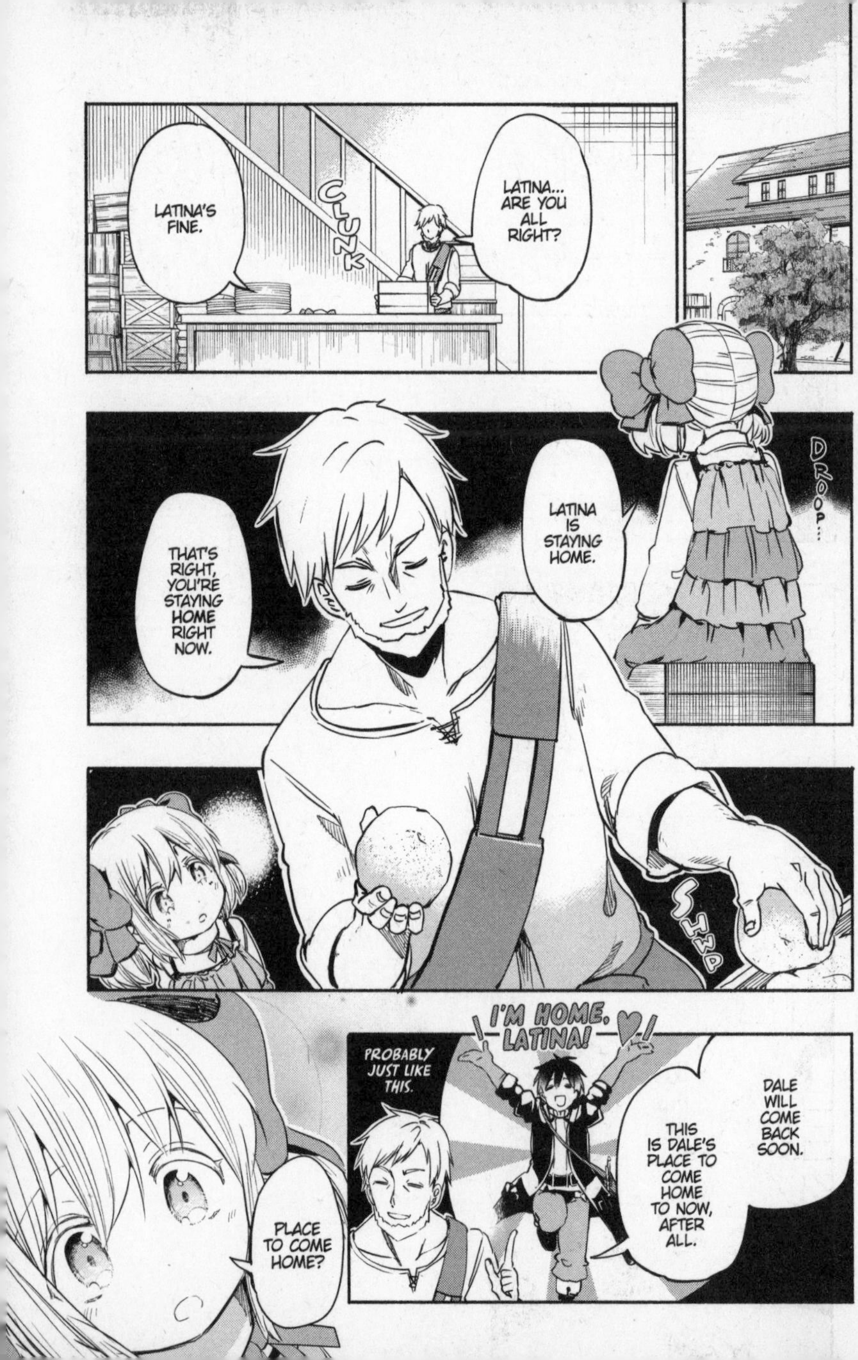
LATINA... ARE YOU ALL RIGHT?
CLUNK
LATINA'S FINE.
DROOP...
LATINA IS STAYING HOME.
THAT'S RIGHT, YOU'RE STAYING HOME RIGHT NOW.
SHWP
DALE WILL COME BACK SOON.
THIS IS DALE'S PLACE TO COME HOME TO NOW, AFTER ALL.
I'M HOME, LATINA!
PROBABLY JUST LIKE THIS.
PLACE TO COME HOME?

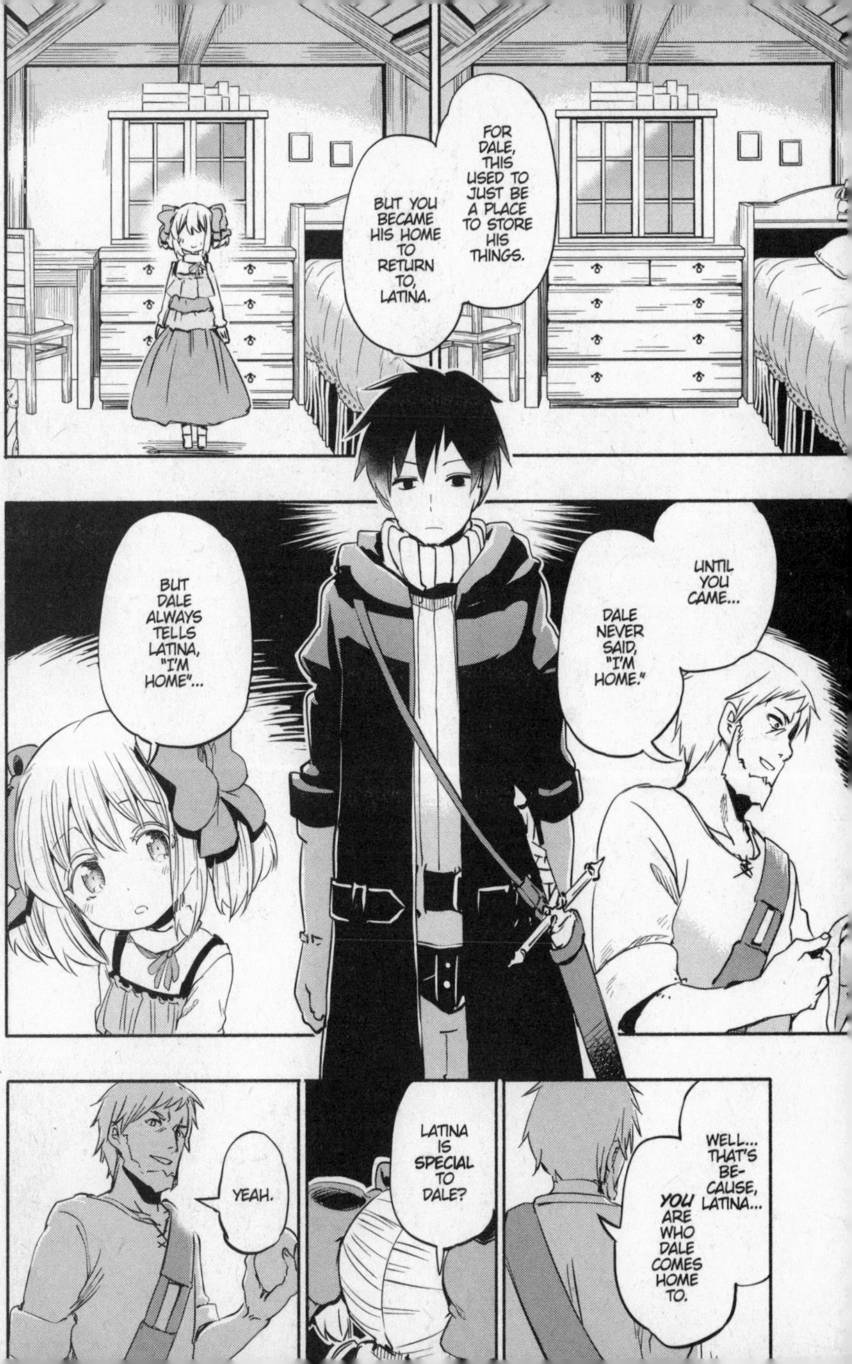
FOR DALE, THIS USED TO JUST BE A PLACE TO STORE HIS THINGS.
BUT YOU BECAME HIS HOME TO RETURN TO, LATINA.
UNTIL YOU CAME...
DALE NEVER SAID, "I'M HOME."
BUT DALE ALWAYS TELLS LATINA, "I'M HOME"...
WELL... THAT'S BE-CAUSE, LATINA...
YOU ARE WHO DALE COMES HOME TO.
LATINA IS SPECIAL TO DALE?
YEAH.

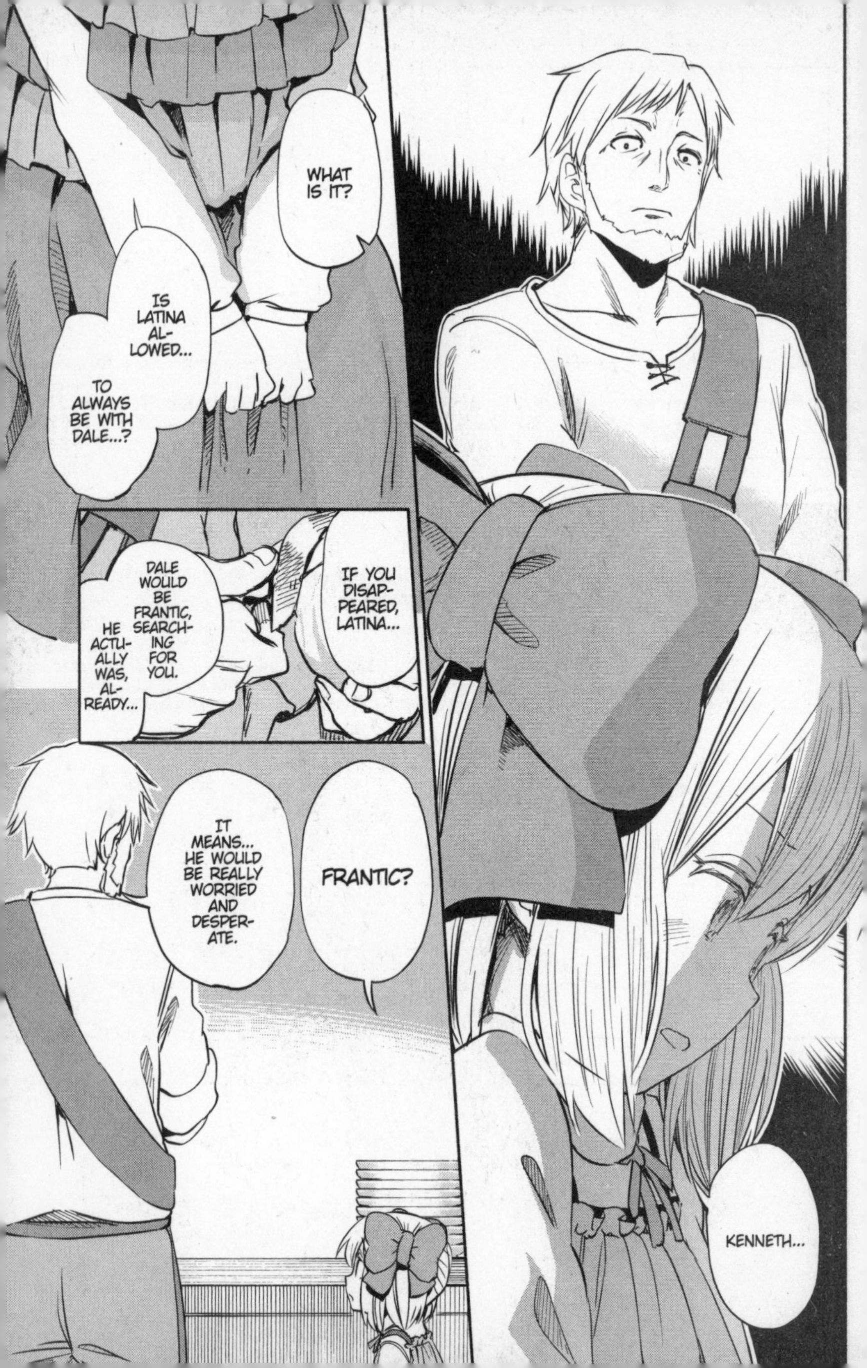
KENNETH...
WHAT IS IT?
IS LATINA ALLOWED...
TO ALWAYS BE WITH DALE...?
IF YOU DISAPPEARED, LATINA...
DALE WOULD BE FRANTIC, SEARCHING FOR YOU.
HE ACTUALLY WAS, ALREADY...
FRANTIC?
IT MEANS... HE WOULD BE REALLY WORRIED AND DESPERATE.

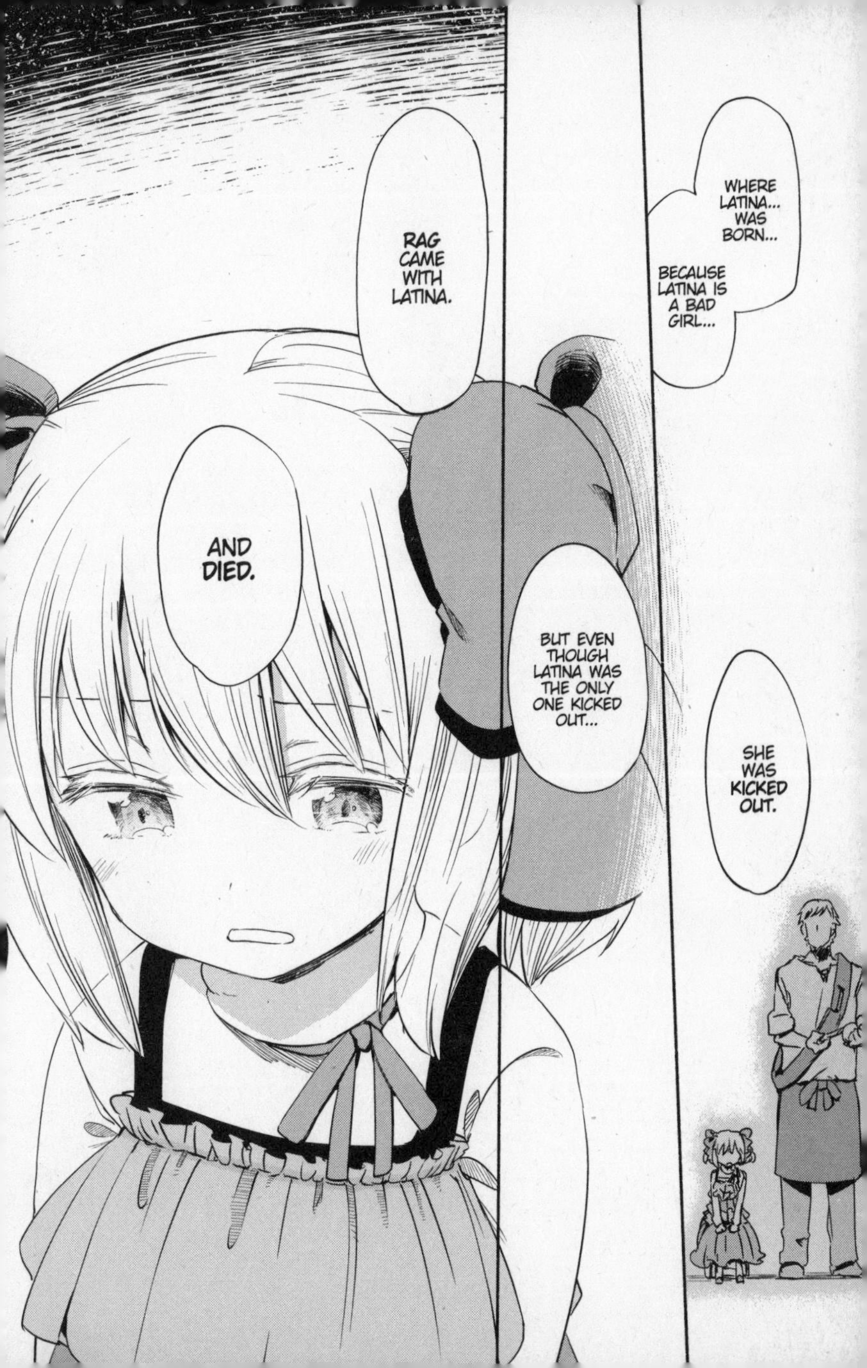
WHERE LATINA... WAS BORN...
BECAUSE LATINA IS A BAD GIRL...
SHE WAS KICKED OUT.
BUT EVEN THOUGH LATINA WAS THE ONLY ONE KICKED OUT...
RAG CAME WITH LATINA.
AND DIED.

IF It's
For My
Daughter
I'd Even Defeat
a **Demon**
Lord

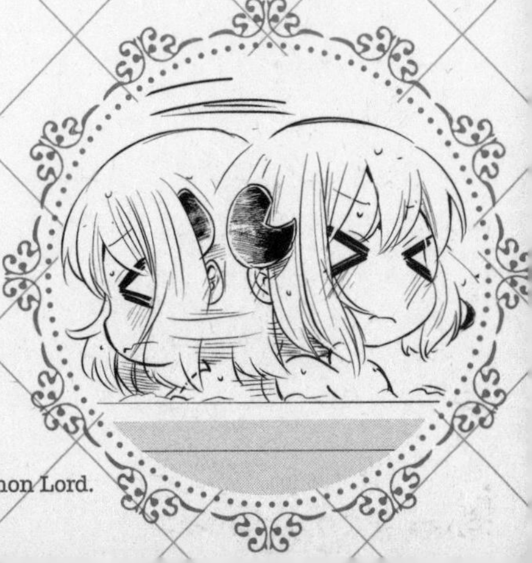

If It's For My Daughter, I'd Even Defeat a Demon Lord.

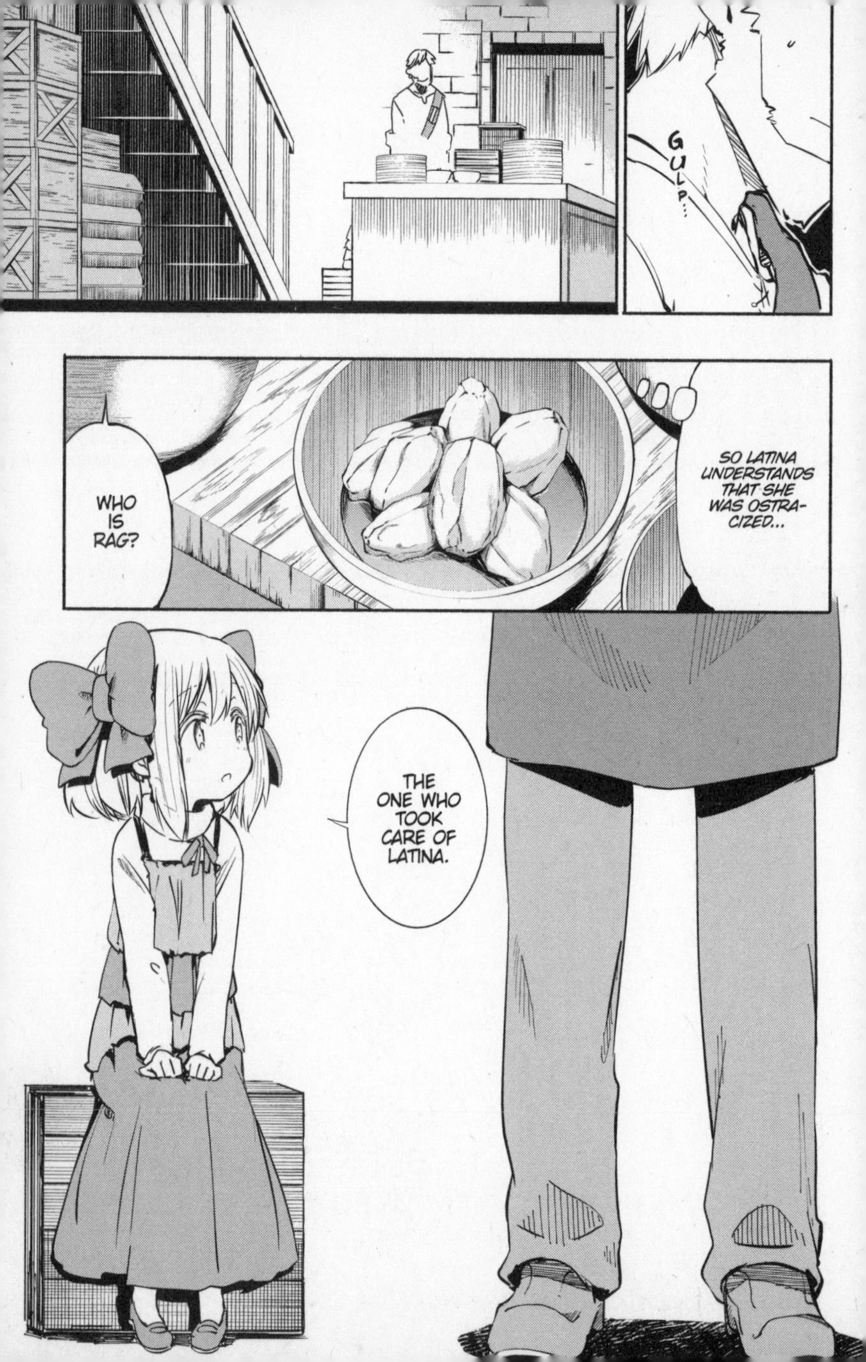
GULP...
SO LATINA UNDERSTANDS THAT SHE WAS OSTRA-CIZED...
WHO IS RAG?
THE ONE WHO TOOK CARE OF LATINA.

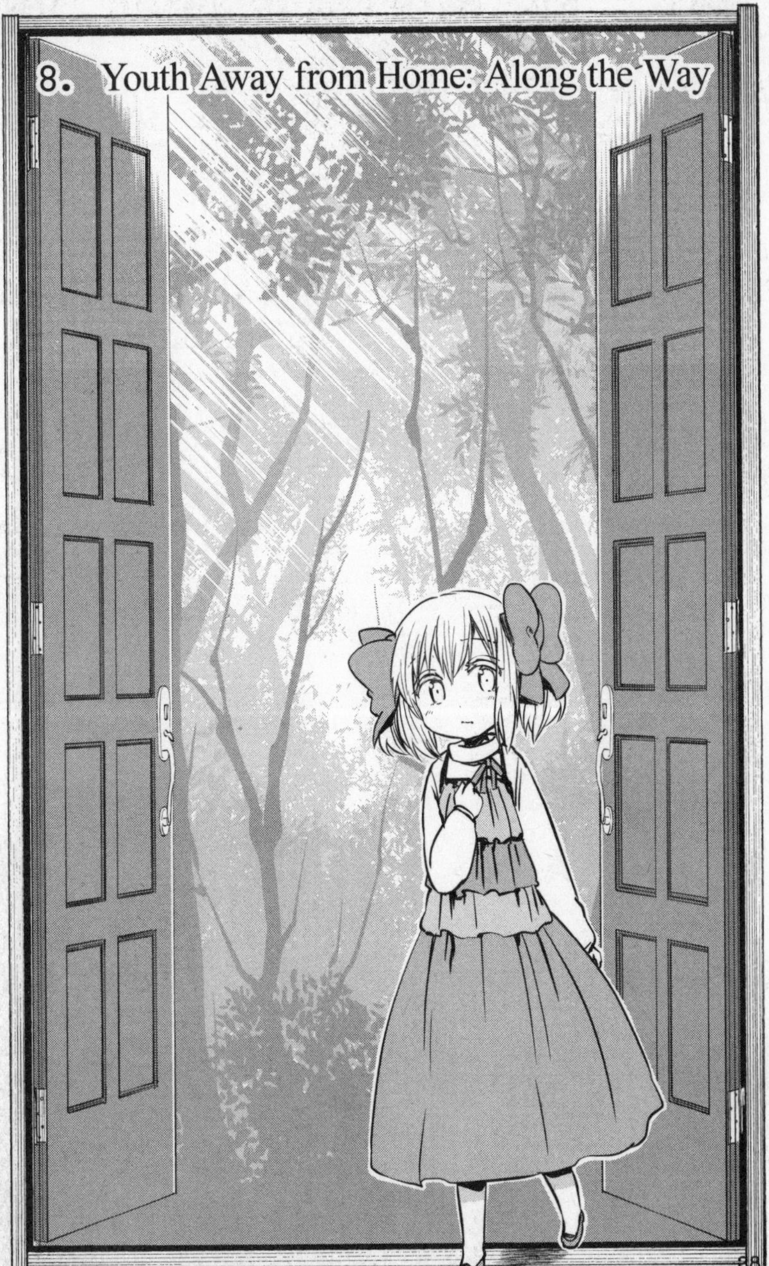
8. Youth Away from Home: Along the Way
28

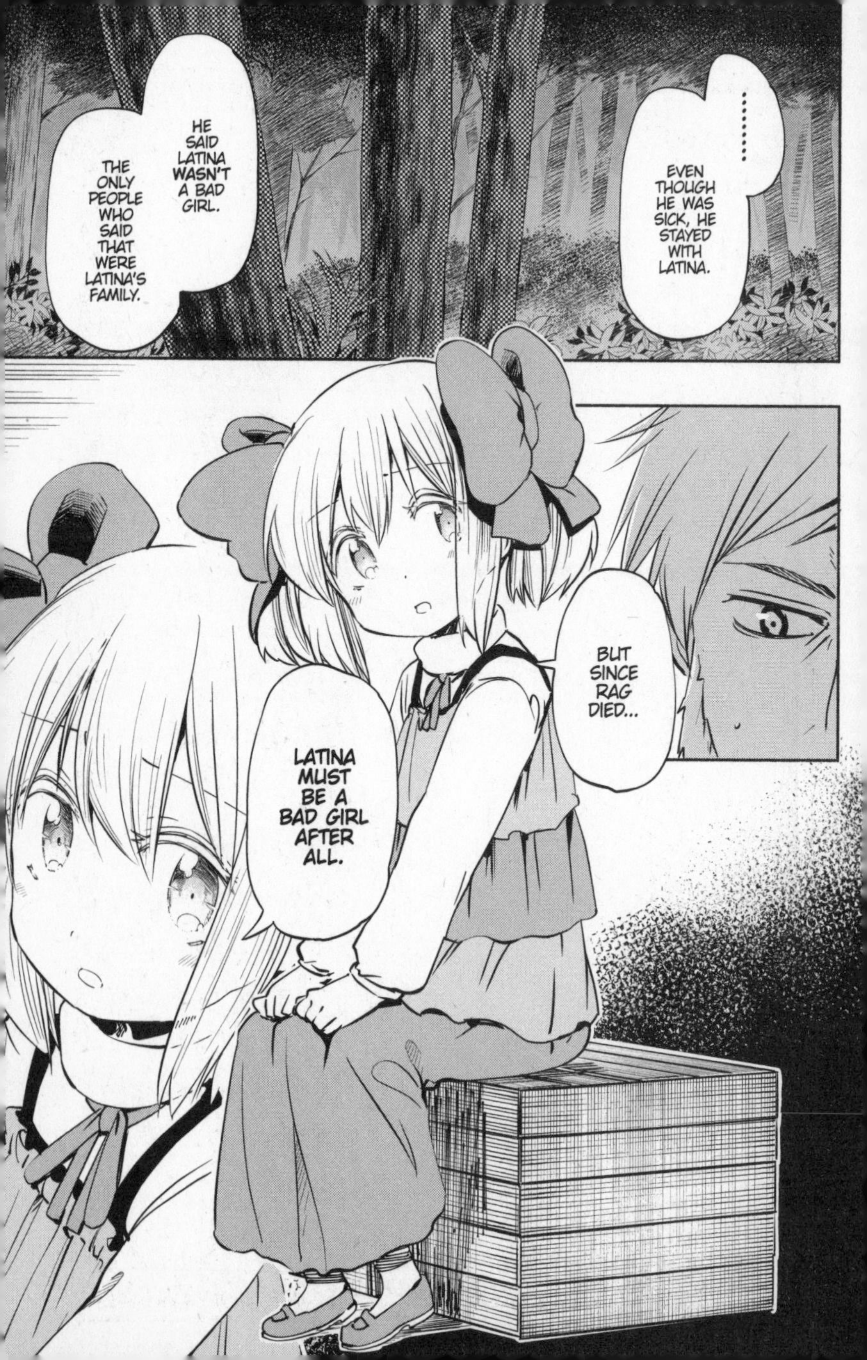
......
EVEN THOUGH HE WAS SICK, HE STAYED WITH LATINA.
HE SAID LATINA WASN'T A BAD GIRL.
THE ONLY PEOPLE WHO SAID THAT WERE LATINA'S FAMILY.
BUT SINCE RAG DIED...
LATINA MUST BE A BAD GIRL AFTER ALL.

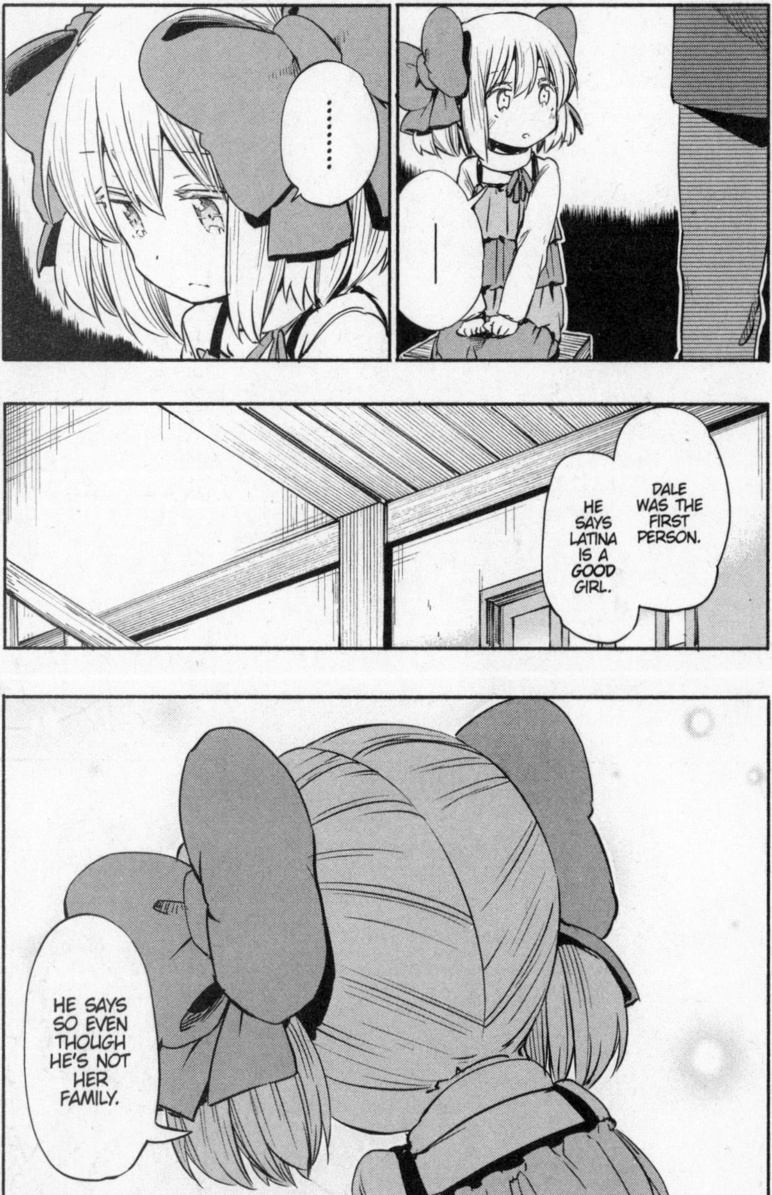
—
......
DALE WAS THE FIRST PERSON.
HE SAYS LATINA IS A GOOD GIRL.
HE SAYS SO EVEN THOUGH HE'S NOT HER FAMILY.

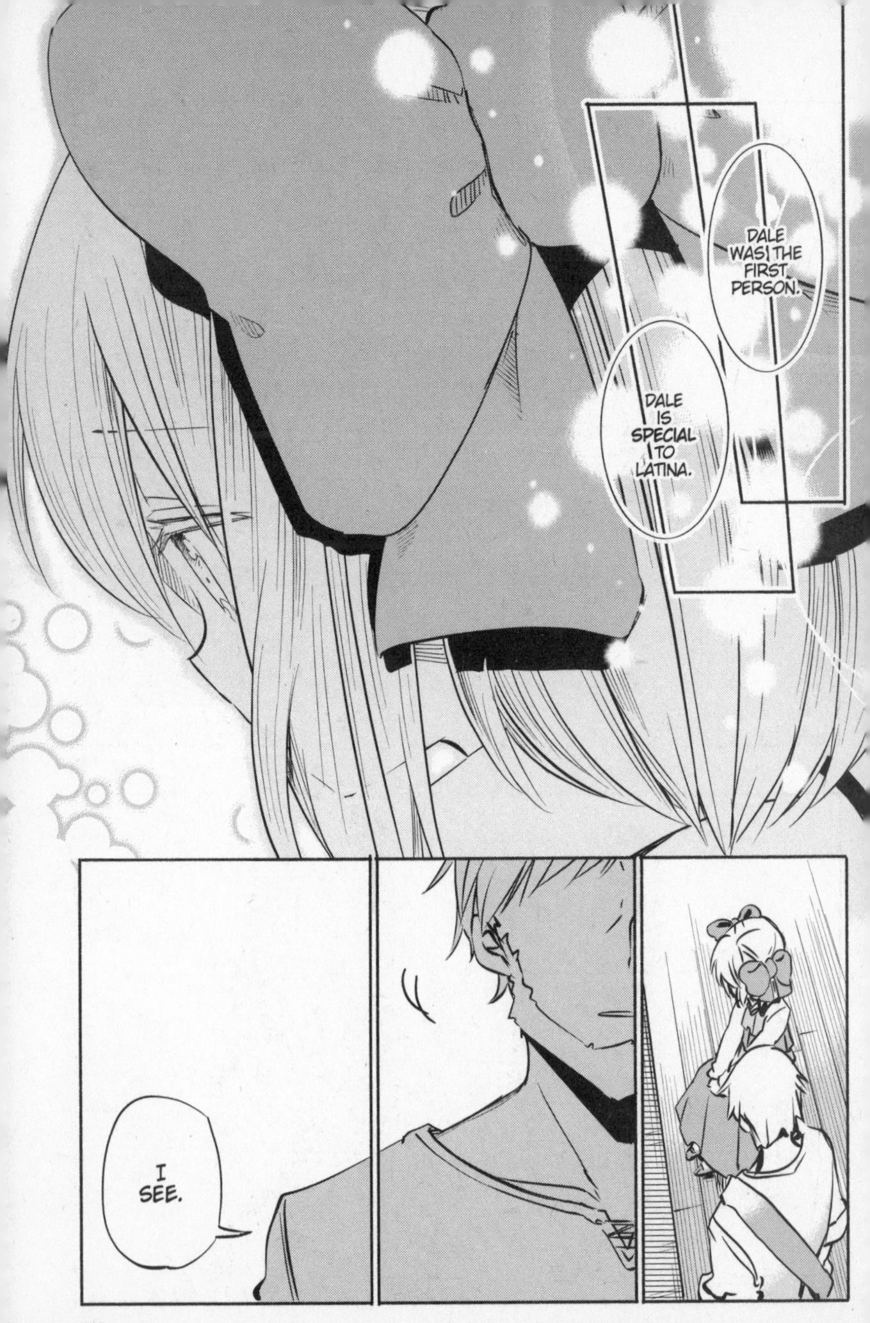
DALE WAS THE FIRST PERSON.
DALE IS SPECIAL TO LATINA.
I SEE.

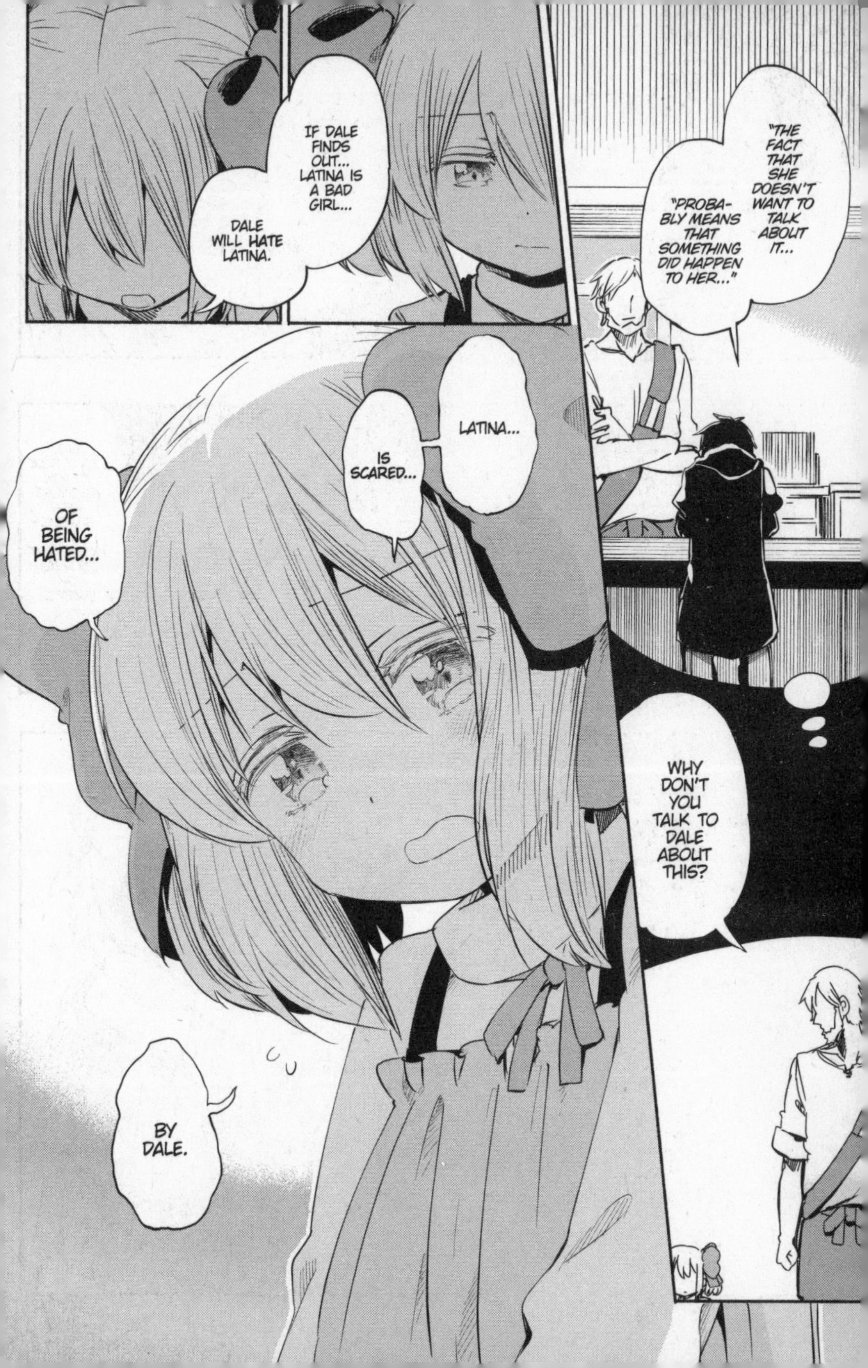
"THE FACT THAT SHE DOESN'T WANT TO TALK ABOUT IT...
"PROBA-BLY MEANS THAT SOMETHING DID HAPPEN TO HER..."
IF DALE FINDS OUT... LATINA IS A BAD GIRL...
DALE WILL HATE LATINA.
WHY DON'T YOU TALK TO DALE ABOUT THIS?
LATINA...
IS SCARED...
OF BEING HATED...
BY DALE.

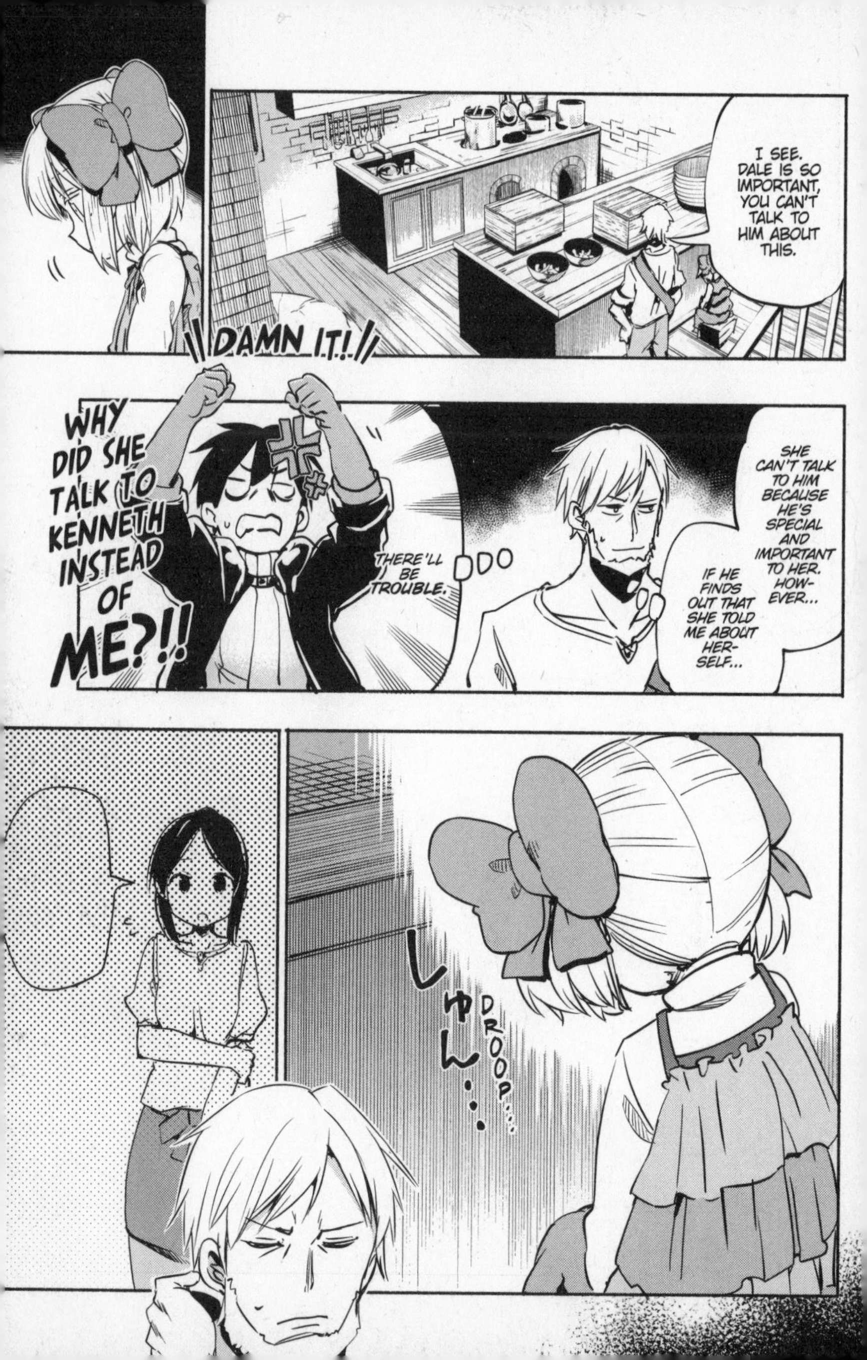

I SEE. DALE IS SO IMPORTANT, YOU CAN'T TALK TO HIM ABOUT THIS.
SHE CAN'T TALK TO HIM BECAUSE HE'S SPECIAL AND IMPORTANT TO HER. HOW-EVER...
IF HE FINDS OUT THAT SHE TOLD ME ABOUT HER-SELF...
THERE'LL BE TROUBLE.
DDO
DAMN IT!!
WHY DID SHE TALK TO KENNETH INSTEAD OF ME?!!
しゅん…
DROOP...

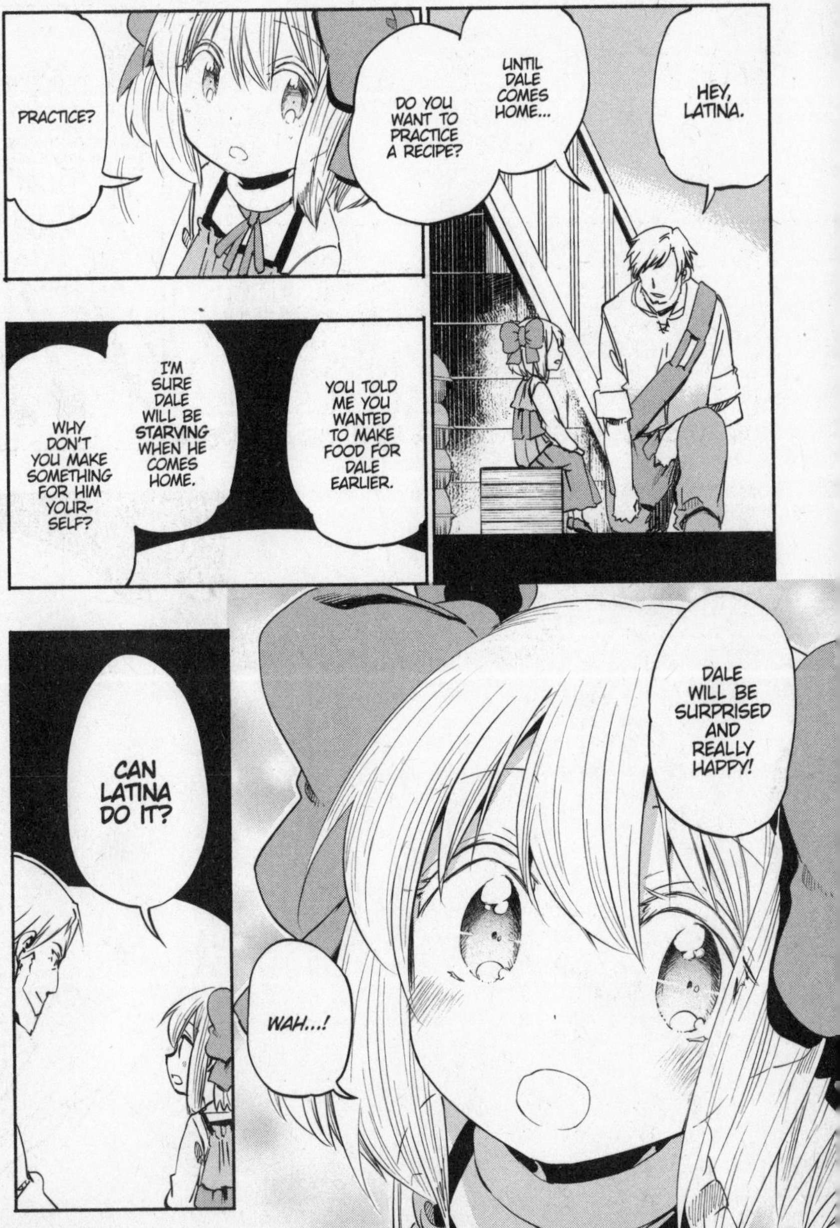
HEY, LATINA.
UNTIL DALE COMES HOME...
DO YOU WANT TO PRACTICE A RECIPE?
PRACTICE?
YOU TOLD ME YOU WANTED TO MAKE FOOD FOR DALE EARLIER.
I'M SURE DALE WILL BE STARVING WHEN HE COMES HOME.
WHY DON'T YOU MAKE SOMETHING FOR HIM YOUR-SELF?
DALE WILL BE SURPRISED AND REALLY HAPPY!
WAH...!
CAN LATINA DO IT?

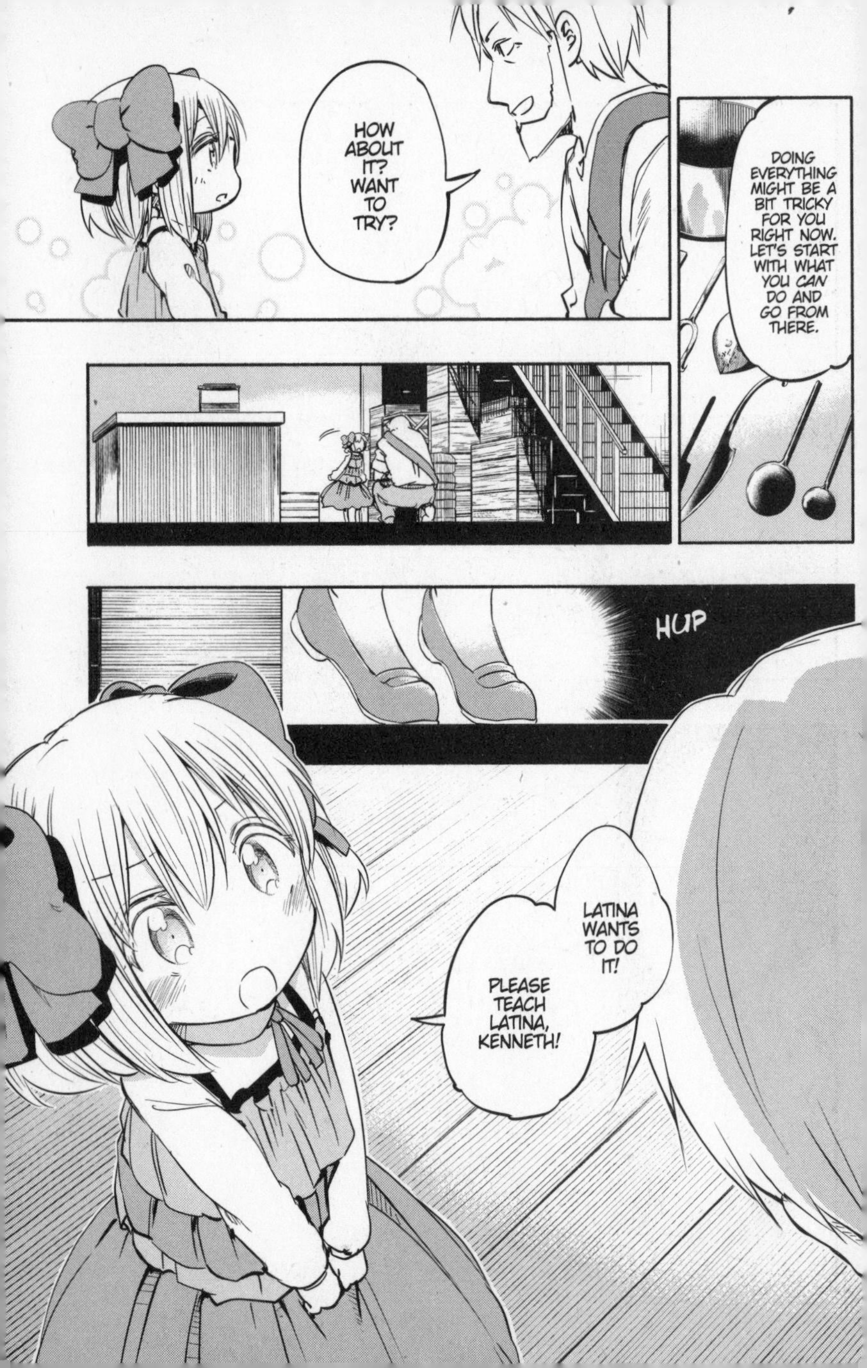
HOW ABOUT IT? WANT TO TRY?
DOING EVERYTHING MIGHT BE A BIT TRICKY FOR YOU RIGHT NOW. LET'S START WITH WHAT YOU *CAN* DO AND GO FROM THERE.
HUP
LATINA WANTS TO DO IT!
PLEASE TEACH LATINA, KENNETH!

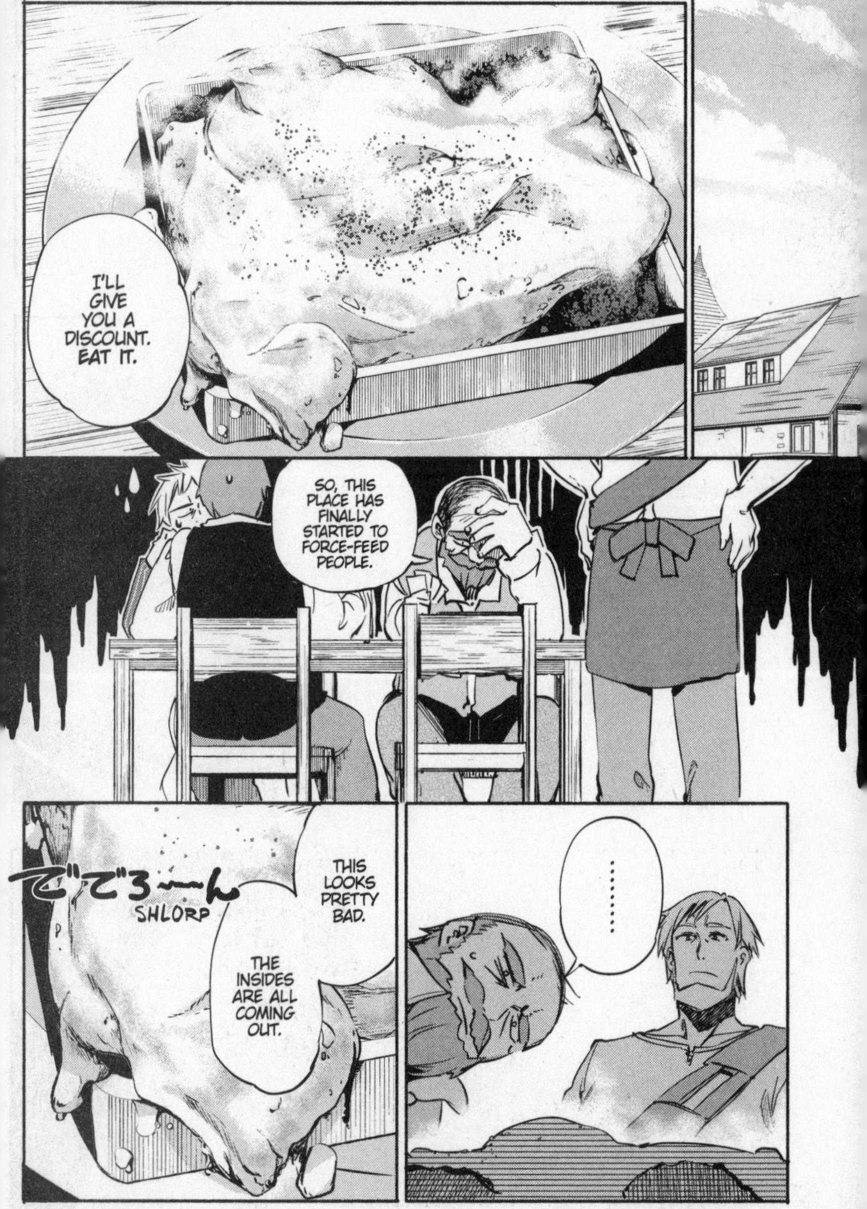
I'LL GIVE YOU A DISCOUNT. EAT IT.
SO, THIS PLACE HAS FINALLY STARTED TO FORCE-FEED PEOPLE.
......
SHLORP
THIS LOOKS PRETTY BAD.
THE INSIDES ARE ALL COMING OUT.

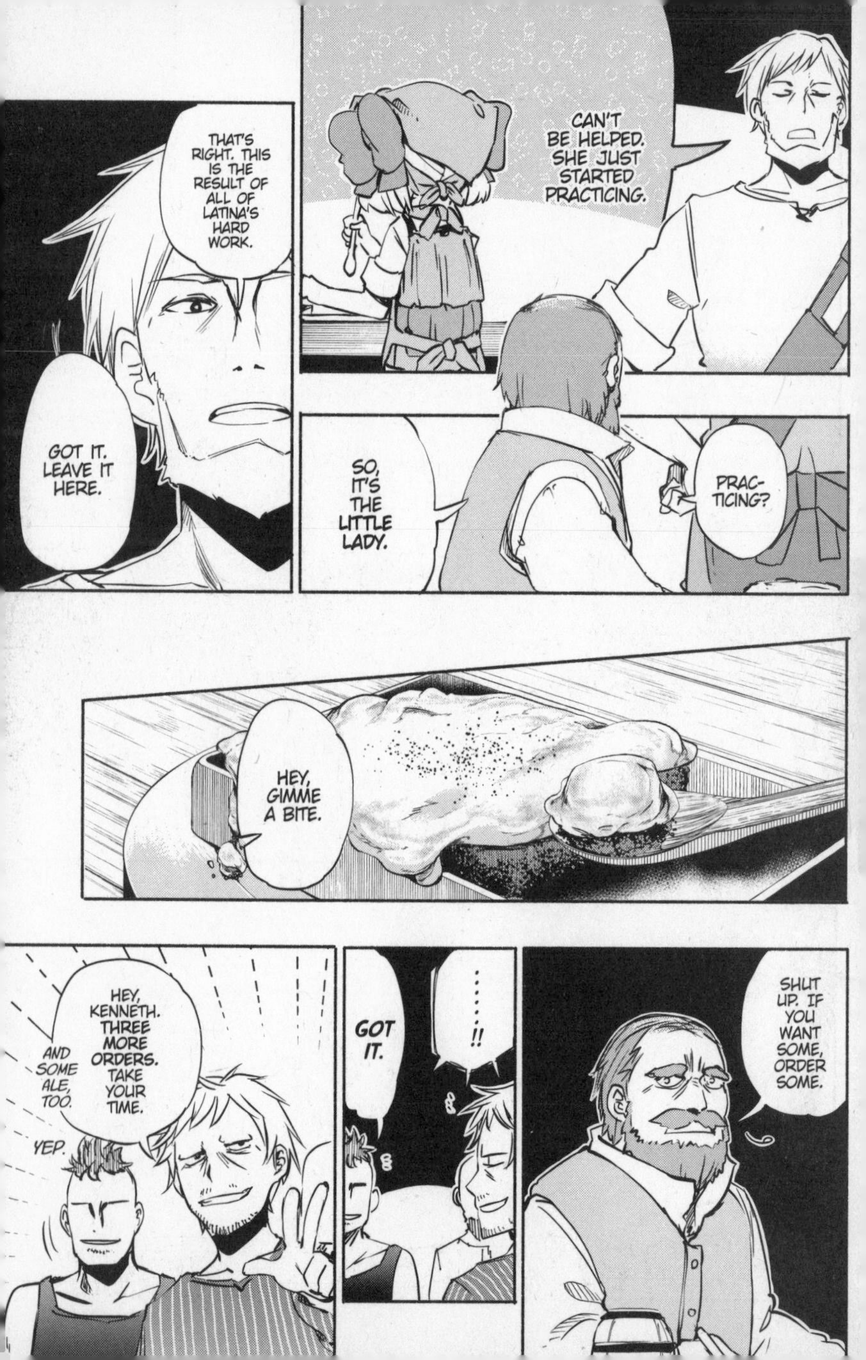
CAN'T BE HELPED. SHE JUST STARTED PRACTICING.
PRAC-TICING?
SO, IT'S THE LITTLE LADY.
THAT'S RIGHT. THIS IS THE RESULT OF ALL OF LATINA'S HARD WORK.
GOT IT. LEAVE IT HERE.
HEY, GIMME A BITE.
SHUT UP. IF YOU WANT SOME, ORDER SOME.
......!!
GOT IT.
HEY, KENNETH. THREE MORE ORDERS. TAKE YOUR TIME.
AND SOME ALE, TOO.
YEP.

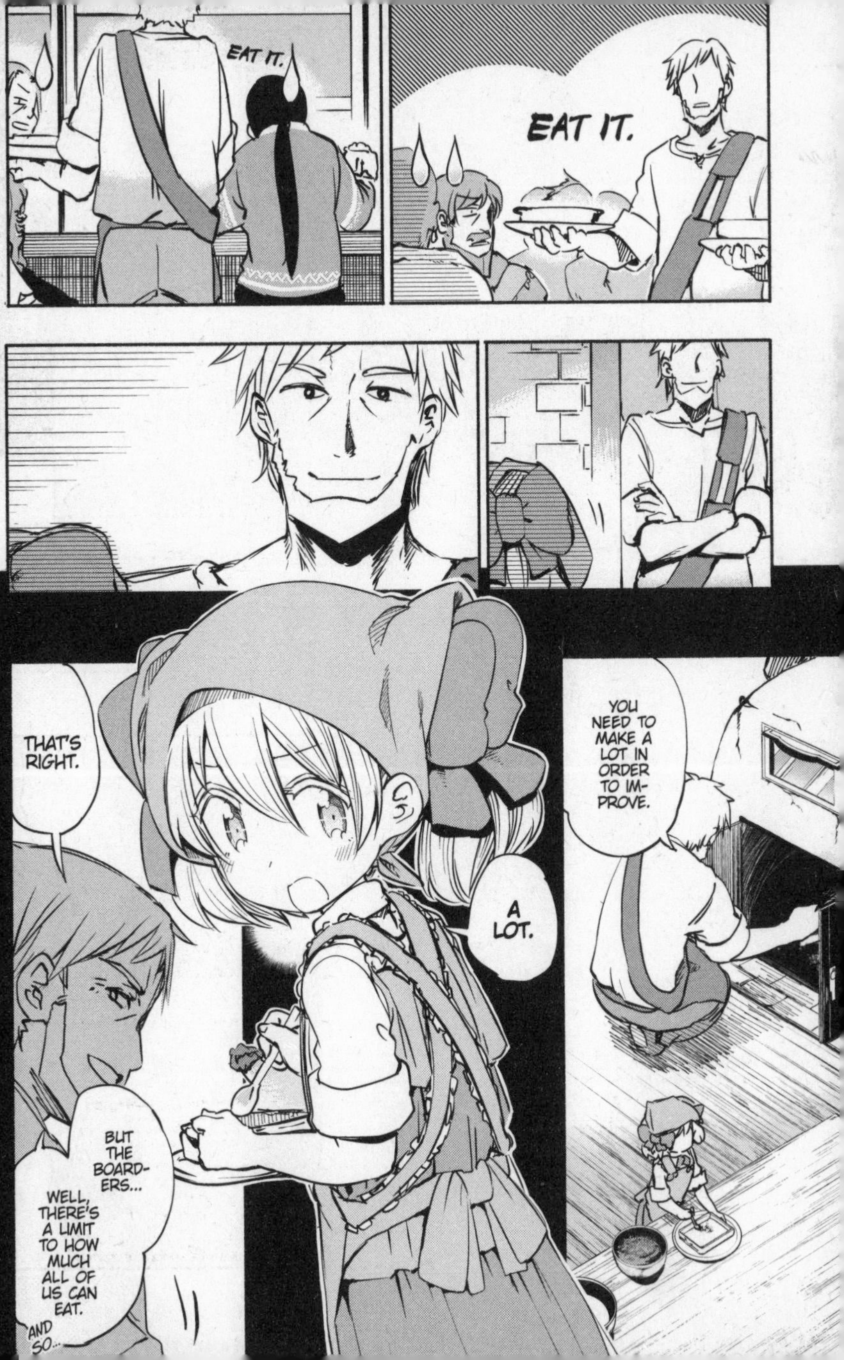
EAT IT.
EAT IT.
YOU NEED TO MAKE A LOT IN ORDER TO IMPROVE.
A LOT.
THAT'S RIGHT.
BUT THE BOARDERS...
WELL, THERE'S A LIMIT TO HOW MUCH ALL OF US CAN EAT.
AND SO...

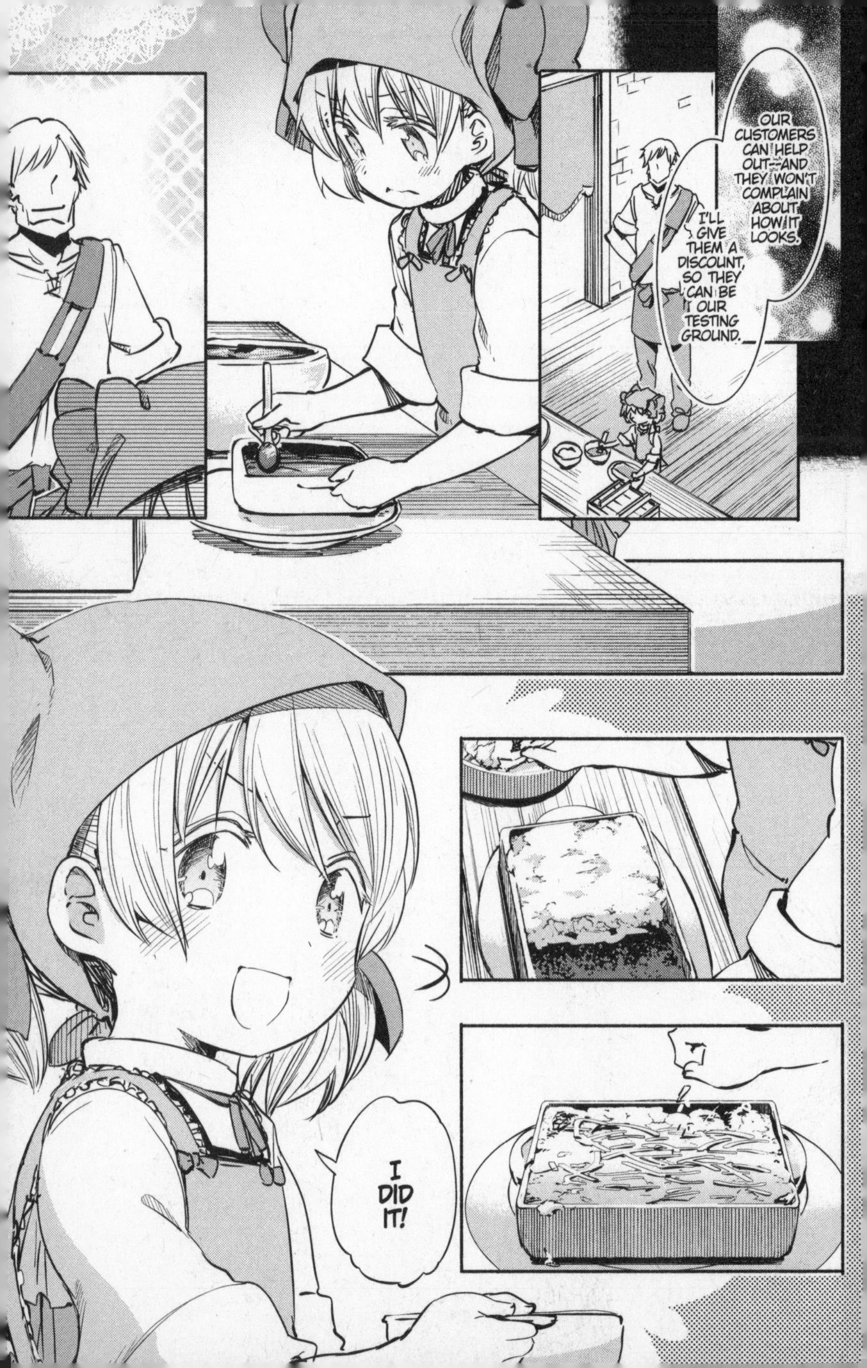
OUR CUSTOMERS CAN HELP OUT--AND THEY WON'T COMPLAIN ABOUT HOW IT LOOKS.
I'LL GIVE THEM A DISCOUNT, SO THEY CAN BE OUR TESTING GROUND.
I DID IT!

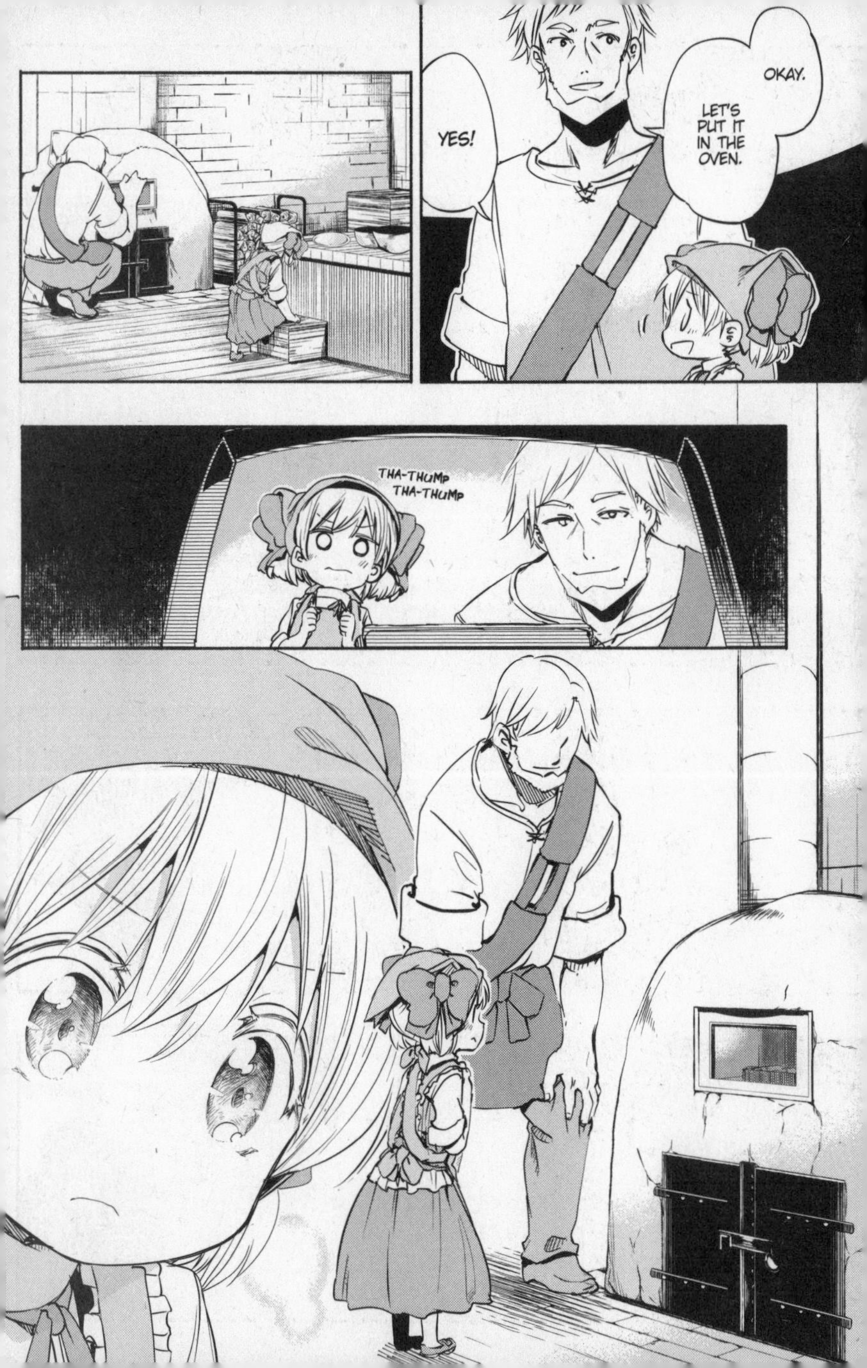
OKAY.
LET'S PUT IT IN THE OVEN.
YES!
THA-THUMP THA-THUMP

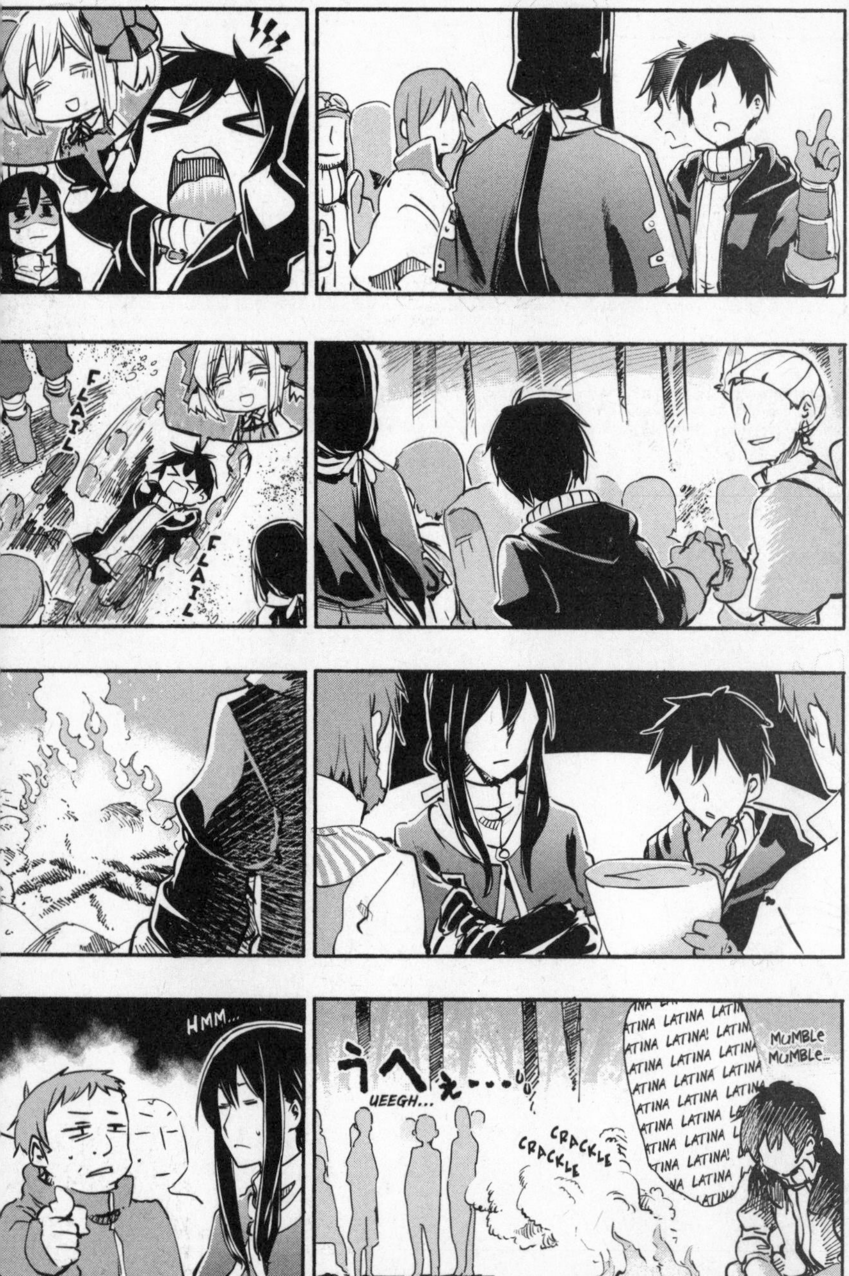
FLAIL
FLAIL
うへぇ……
UEEGH...
CRACKLE
CRACKLE
LATINA LATINA LATINA LATINA LATINA LATINA! LATINA LATINA LATINA LATINA LATINA LATINA LATINA LATINA LATINA LATINA LATINA LATINA LATINA LATINA LATINA! LATINA LATINA LATINA
MUMBLE MUMBLE...
HMM...

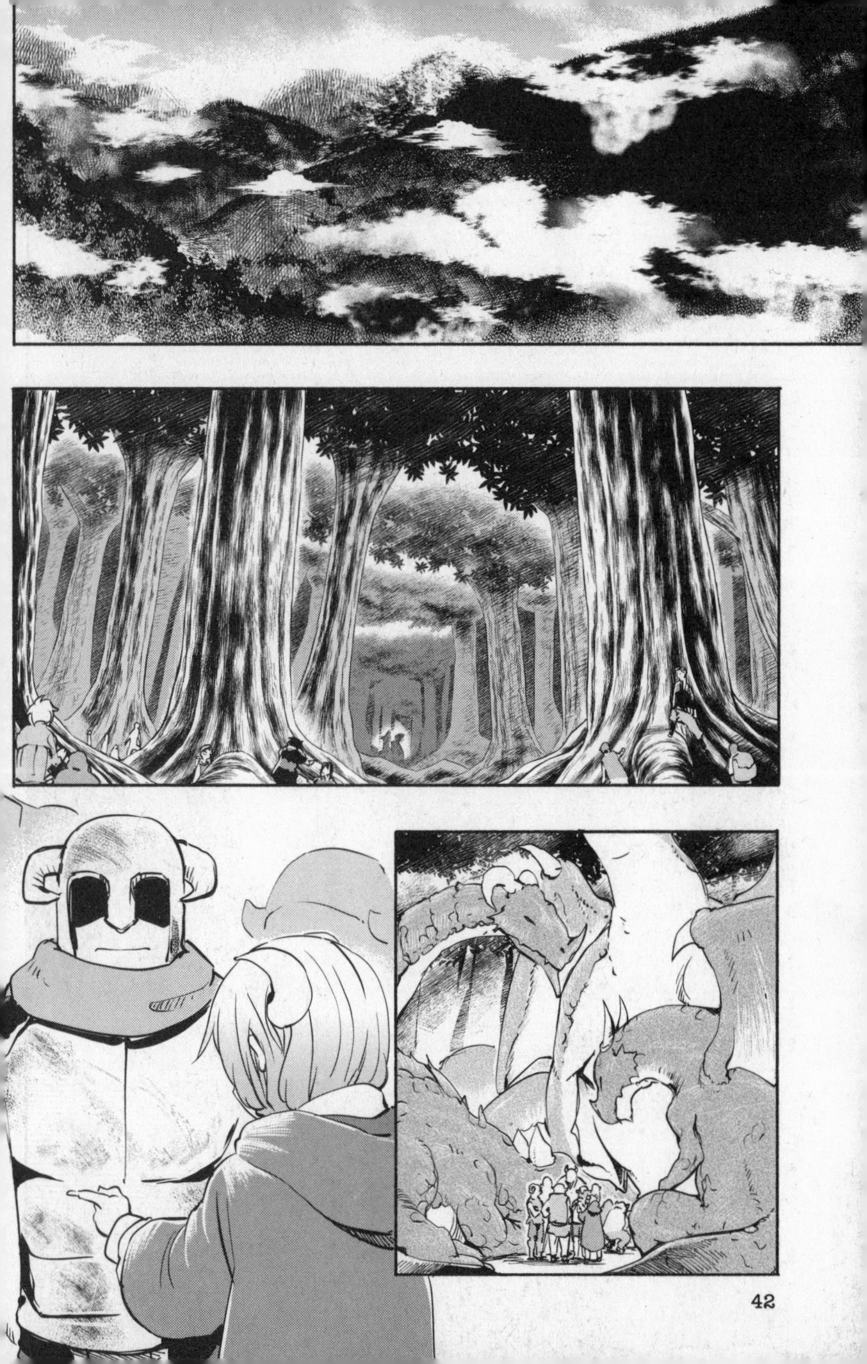

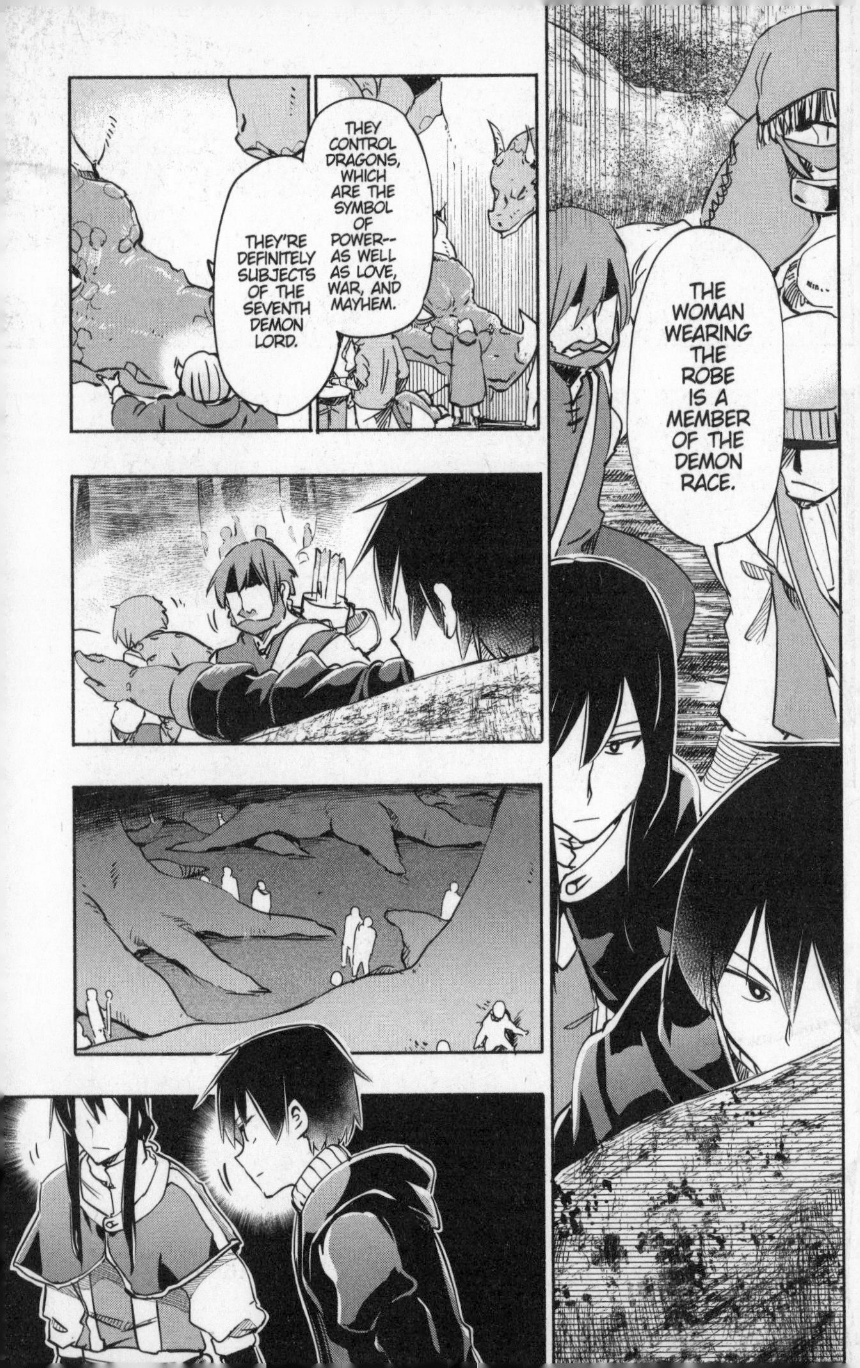
THE WOMAN WEARING THE ROBE IS A MEMBER OF THE DEMON RACE.
THEY CONTROL DRAGONS, WHICH ARE THE SYMBOL OF POWER-- AS WELL AS LOVE, WAR, AND MAYHEM.
THEY'RE DEFINITELY SUBJECTS OF THE SEVENTH DEMON LORD.

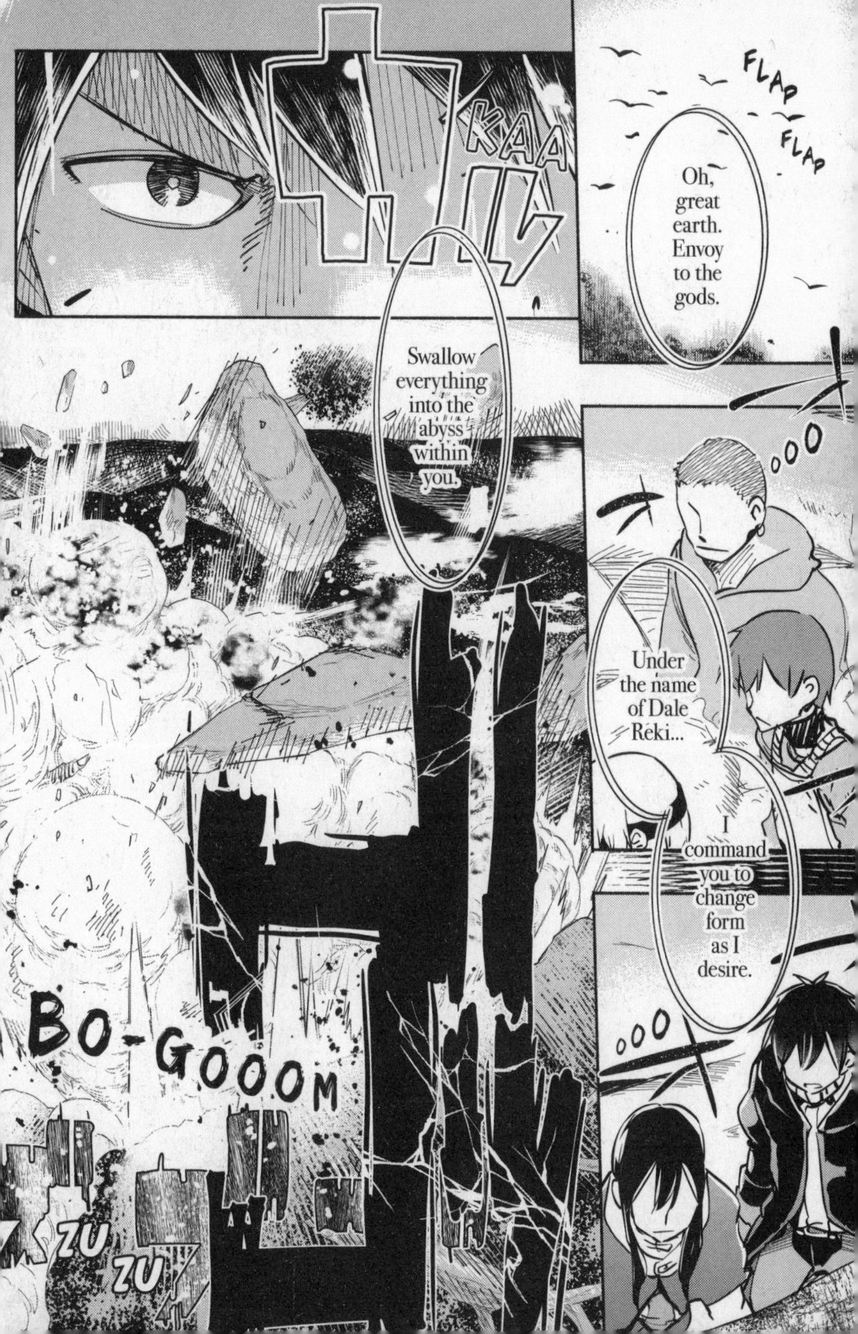
FLAP
FLAP
Oh, great earth. Envoy to the gods.
KAA
OOO
Under the name of Dale Rēki...
I command you to change form as I desire.
OOO
Swallow everything into the abyss within you.
BO-GOOOM
ZU
ZU

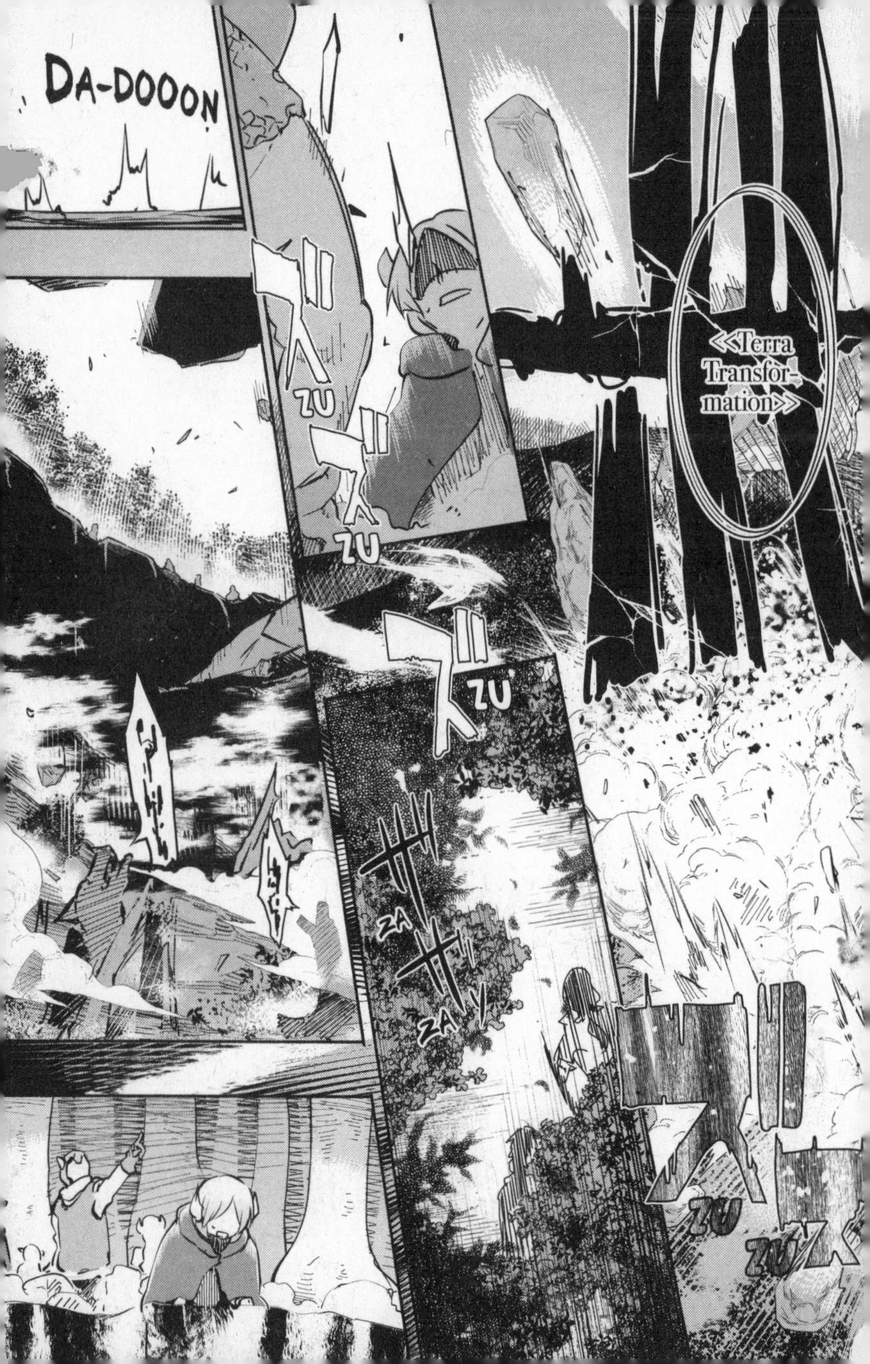

<<Terra Transformation>>
ZU
ZU
DA-DOOON
ZU
ZU
ZU
ZA
ZA

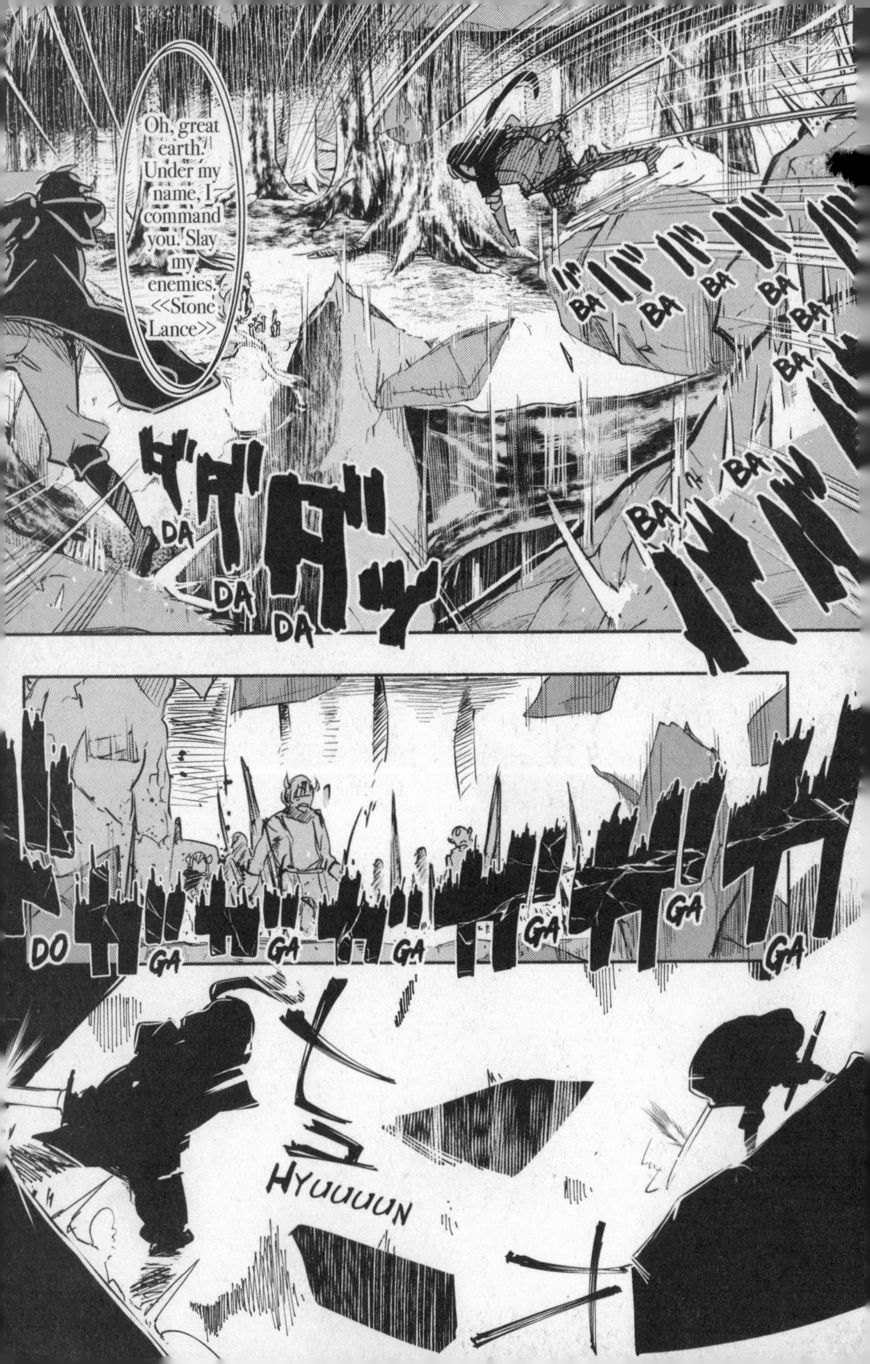
Oh, great earth. Under my name, I command you. Slay my enemies. <<Stone Lance>>
BA BA BA BA BA BA
BA BA
DA DA DA
GA GA GA GA GA GA DO
HYUUUUN

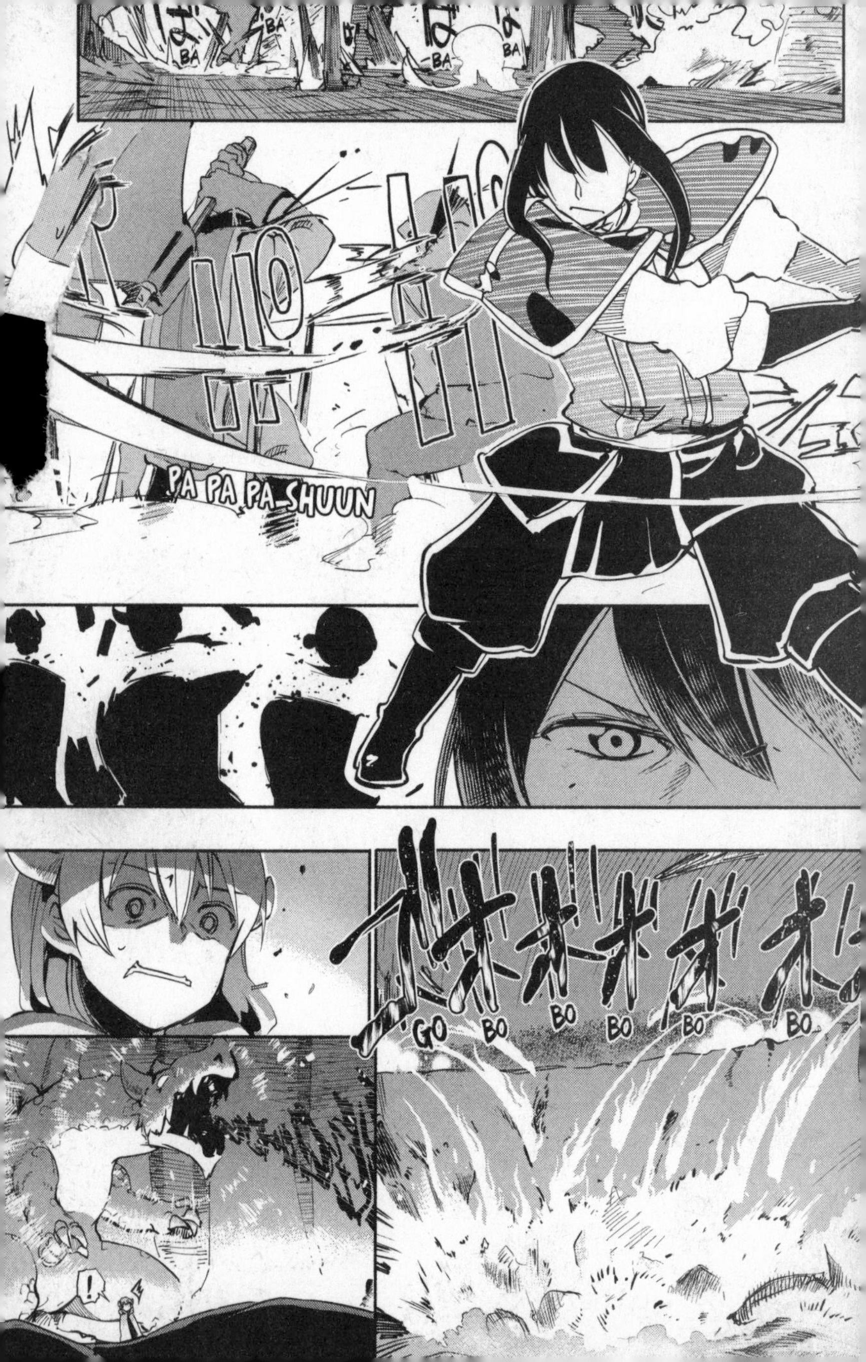
BA
BA
BA
BA
PA PA PA SHUUN
GO BO BO BO BO BO

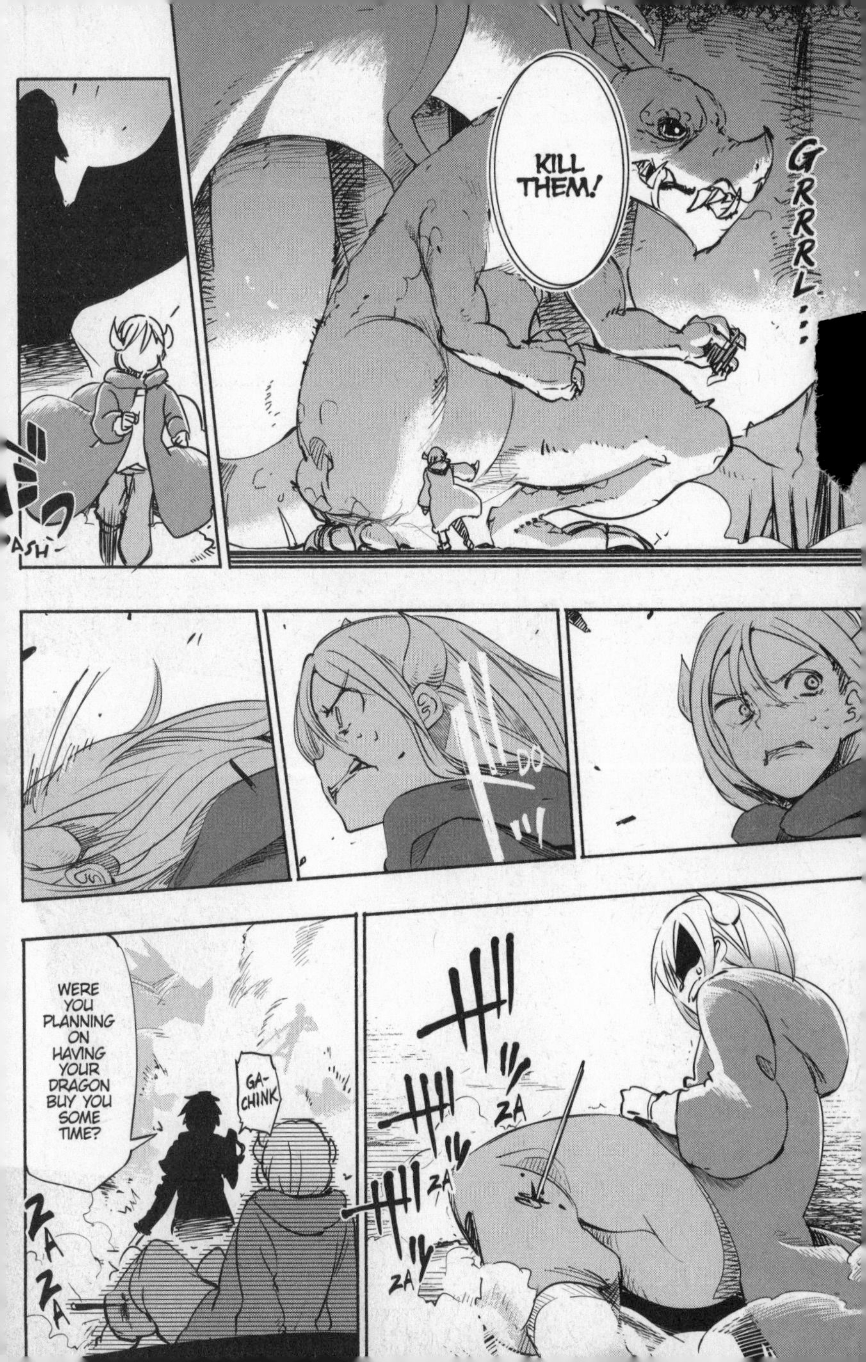
KILL THEM!
GRRRL...
ASH
DO
ZA
ZA
ZA
WERE YOU PLANNING ON HAVING YOUR DRAGON BUY YOU SOME TIME?
GA-CHINK
ZAZAZA

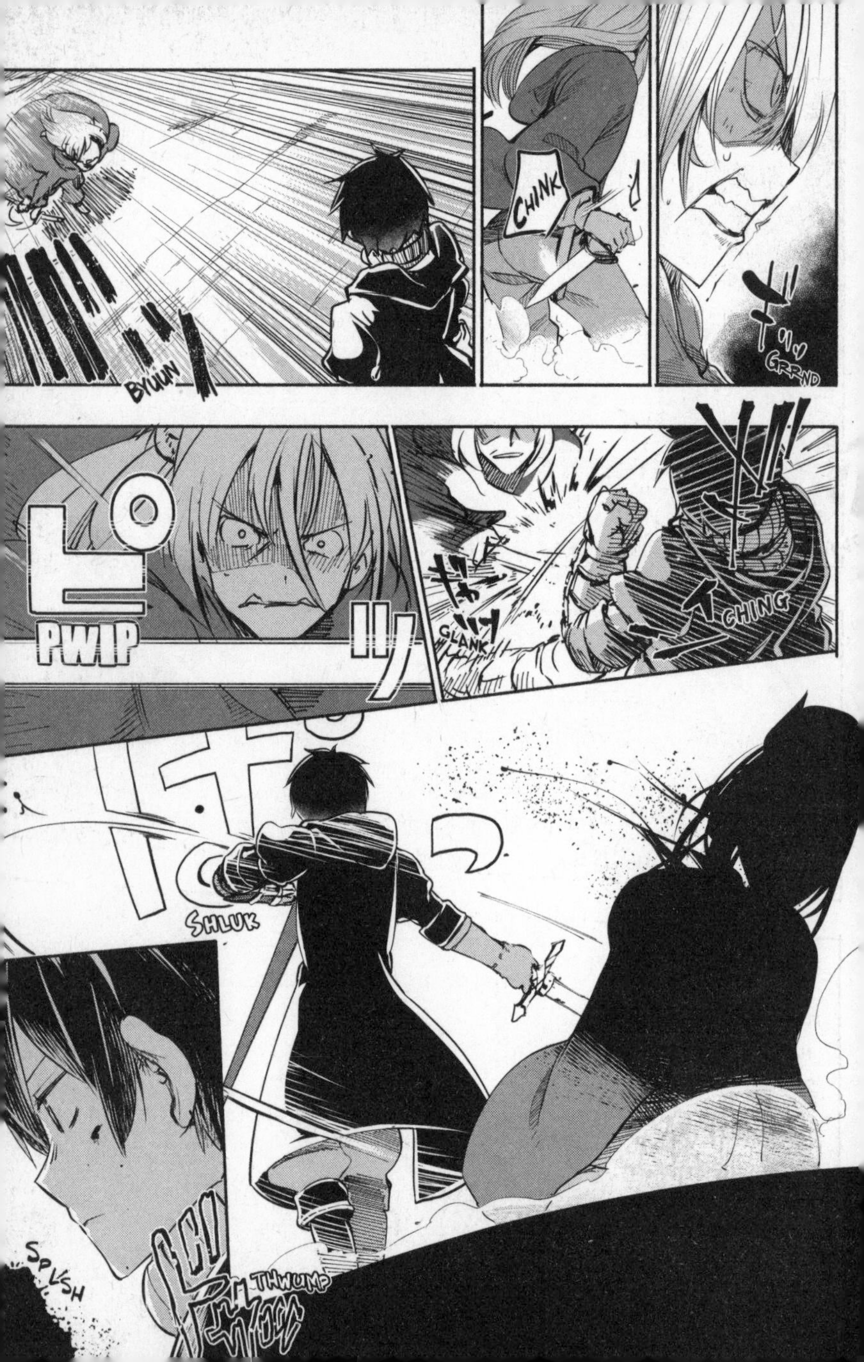
GRRND
CHINK
BYUUN
CHING
GLANK
PWIP
SHLUK
THWUMP
SPLSH

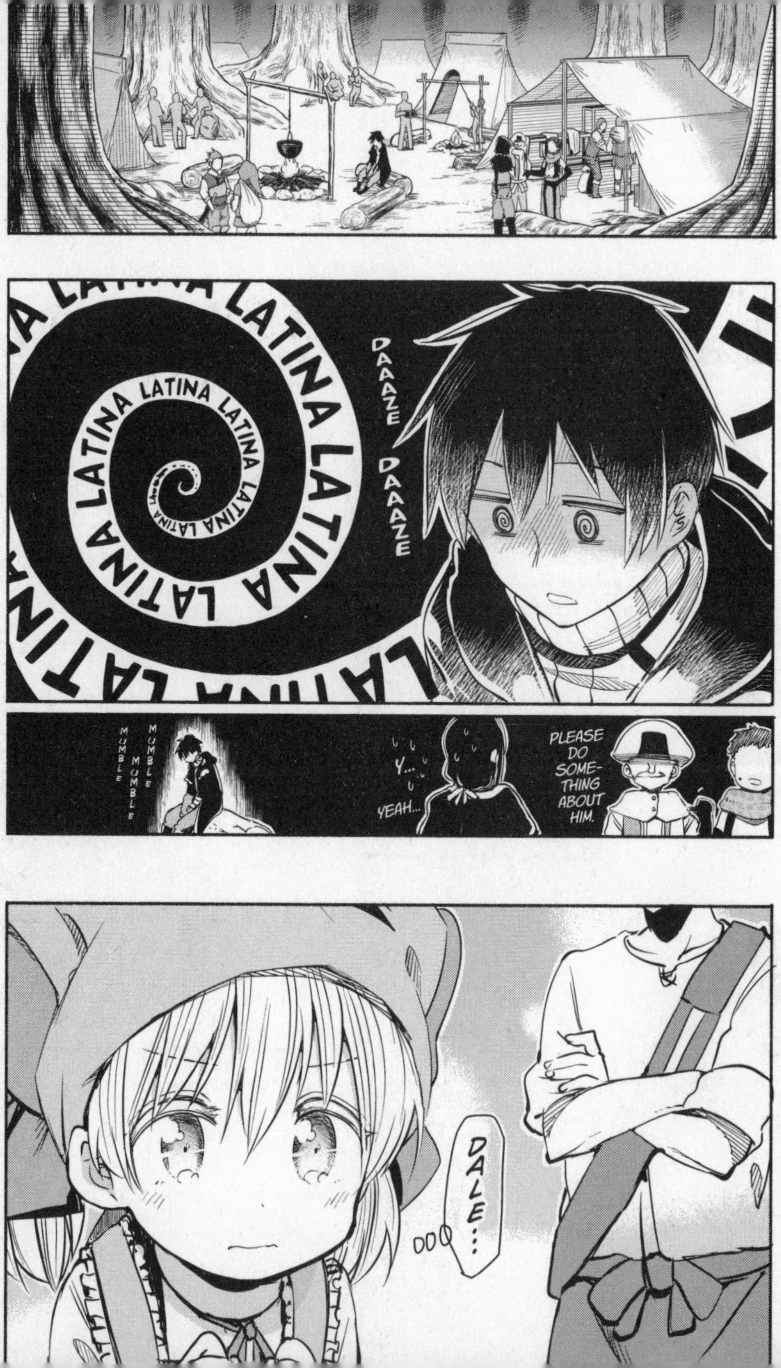

DAAAZE DAAAZE
LATINA LATINA LATINA LATINA LATINA LATINA LATINA LATINA
PLEASE DO SOME-THING ABOUT HIM.
Y... YEAH...
MUMBLE MUMBLE MUMBLE
DALE...
DOO

IF It's
For My
Daughter
I'd Even Defeat
a Demon
Lord

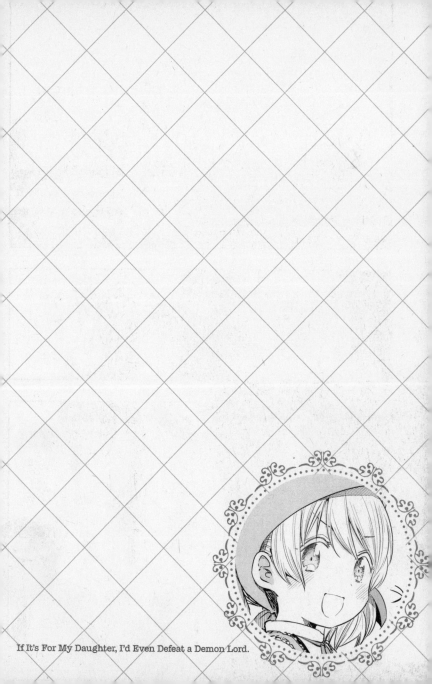

If It's For My Daughter, I'd Even Defeat a Demon Lord.

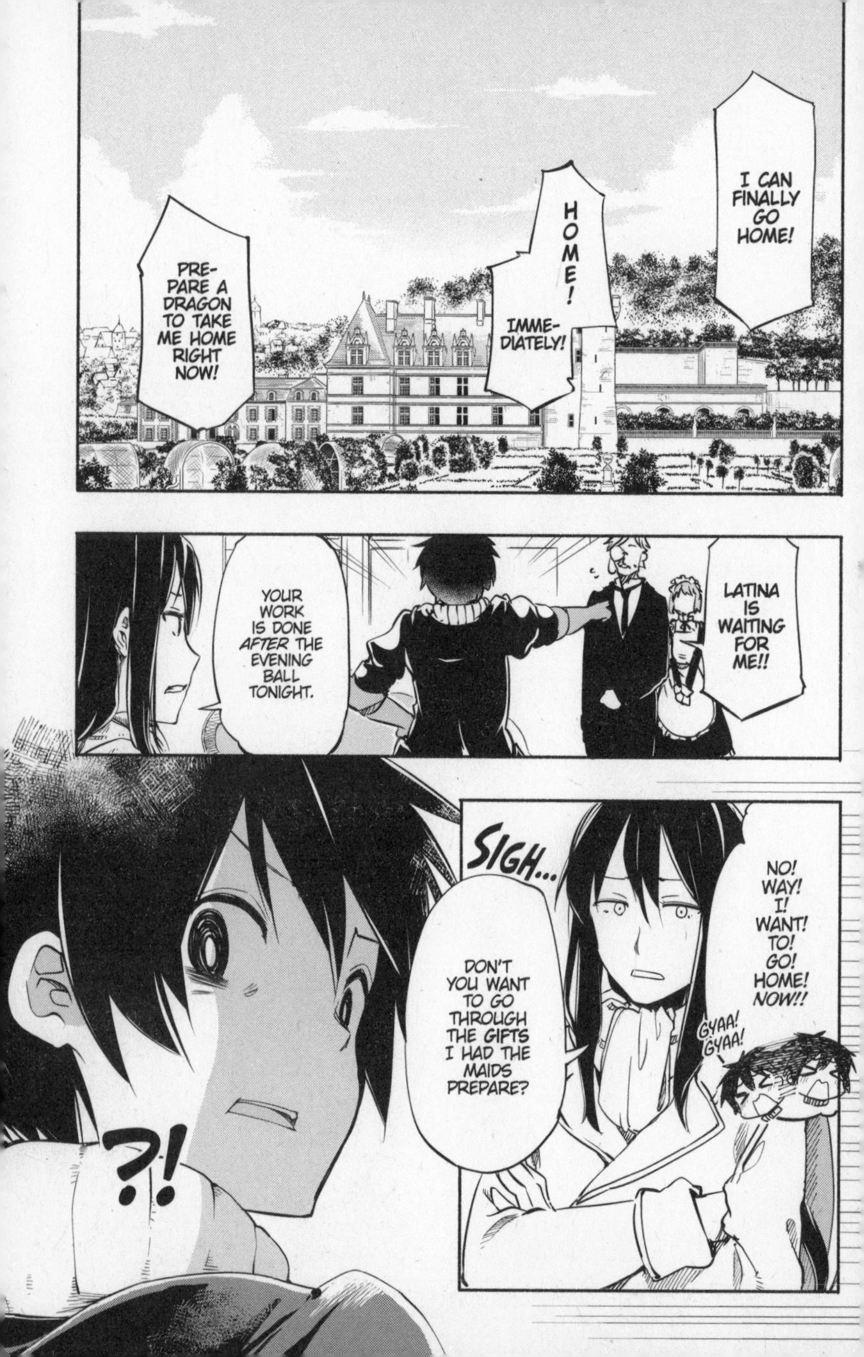
I CAN FINALLY GO HOME!
HOME!
IMMEDIATELY!
PRE-PARE A DRAGON TO TAKE ME HOME RIGHT NOW!
LATINA IS WAITING FOR ME!!
YOUR WORK IS DONE *AFTER* THE EVENING BALL TONIGHT.
NO! WAY! I! WANT! TO! GO! HOME! NOW!!
GYAA! GYAA!
SIGH...
DON'T YOU WANT TO GO THROUGH THE GIFTS I HAD THE MAIDS PREPARE?
?!

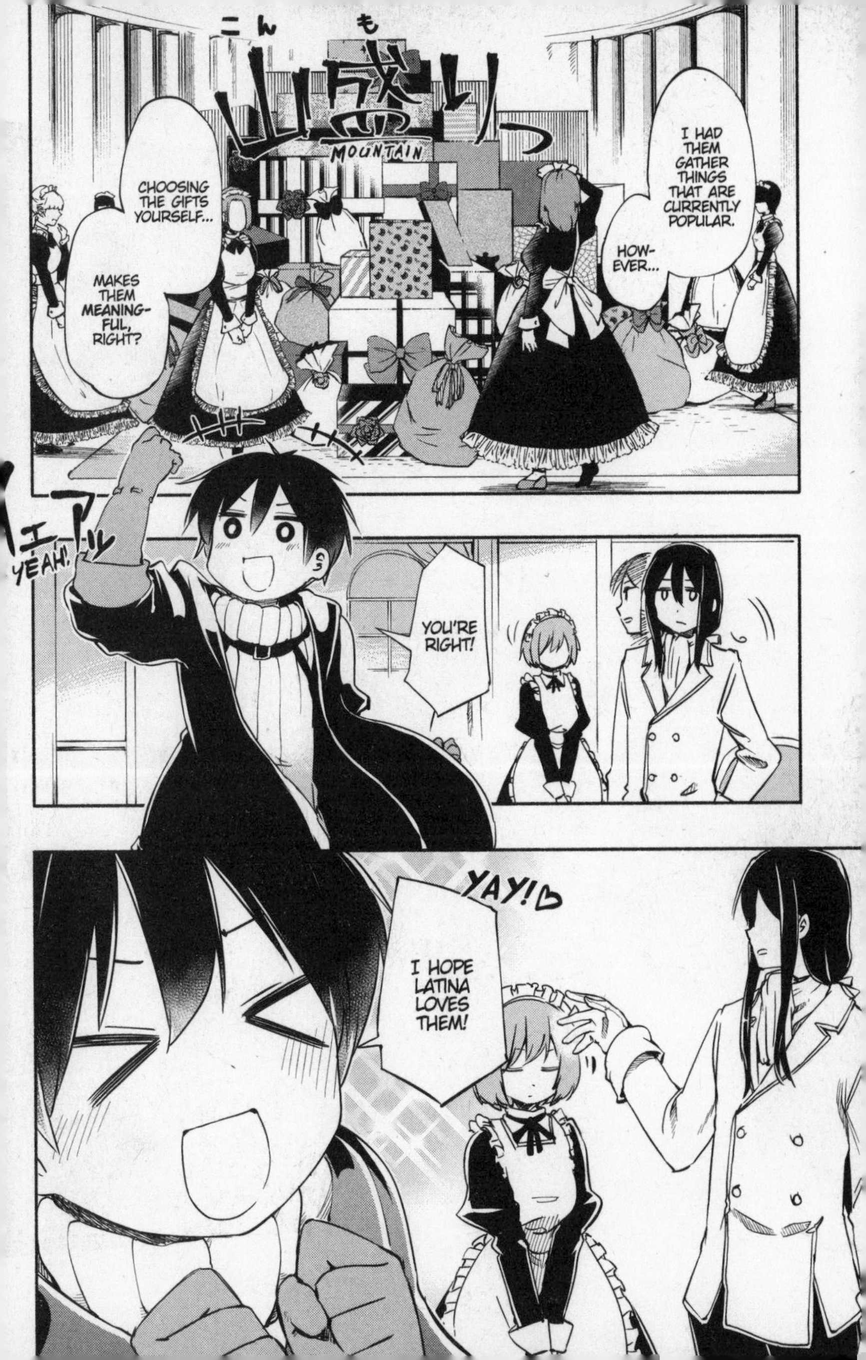
I HAD THEM GATHER THINGS THAT ARE CURRENTLY POPULAR.
HOW-EVER...
山盛りっ
MOUNTAIN
CHOOSING THE GIFTS YOURSELF...
MAKES THEM MEANING-FUL, RIGHT?
YOU'RE RIGHT!
イエアッ
YEAH!
YAY!♡
I HOPE LATINA LOVES THEM!

9. Youth Returns Home

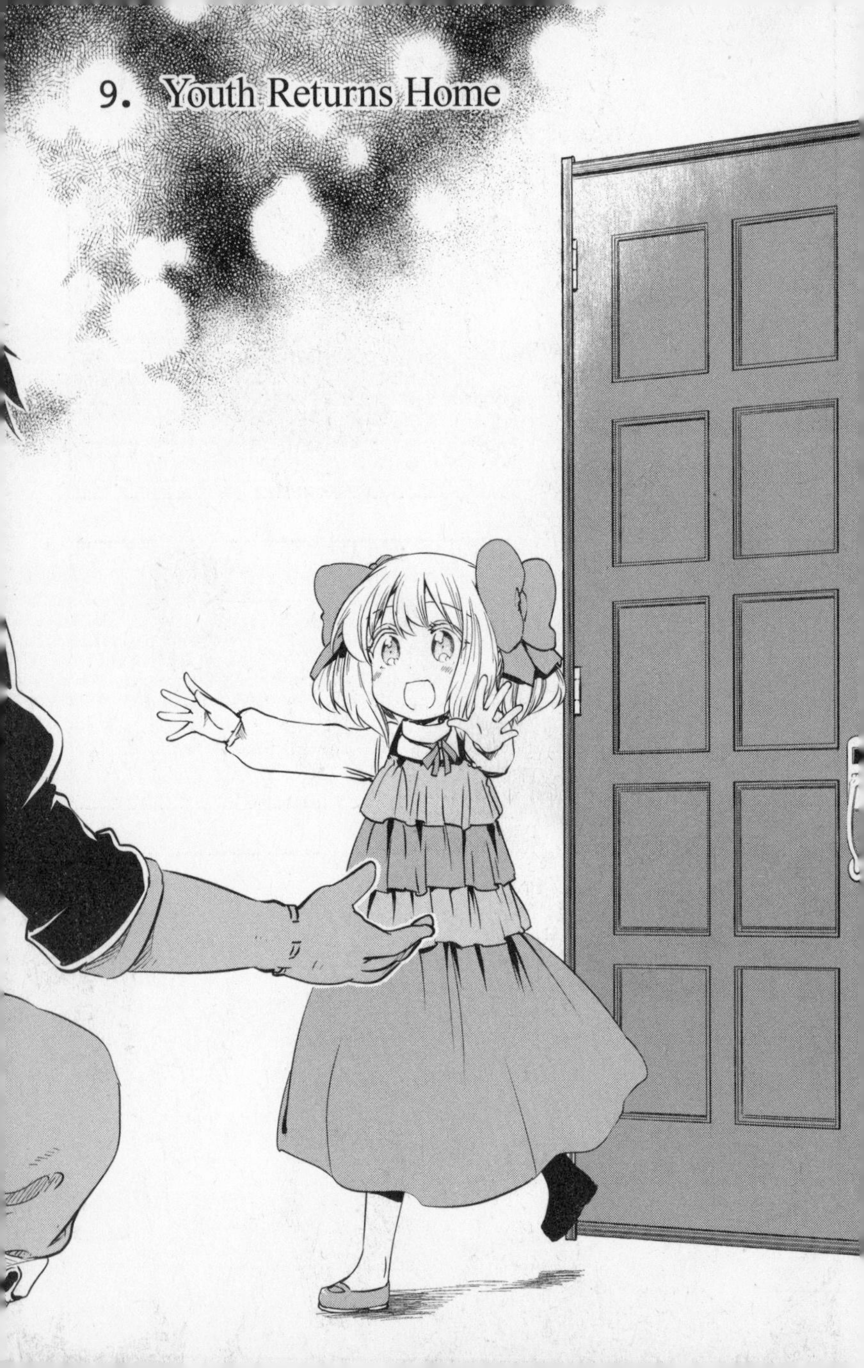

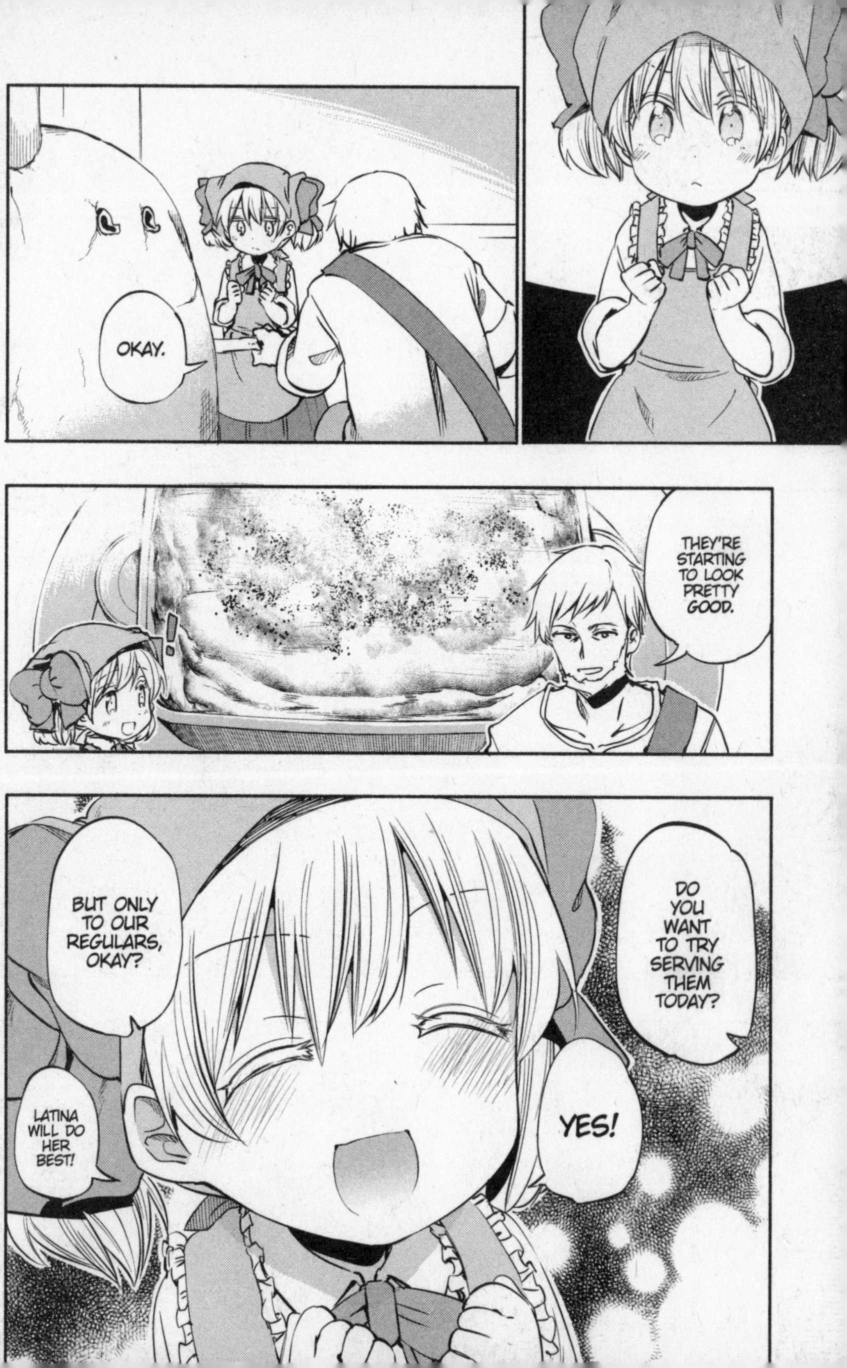
OKAY.
THEY'RE STARTING TO LOOK PRETTY GOOD.
!
DO YOU WANT TO TRY SERVING THEM TODAY?
BUT ONLY TO OUR REGULARS, OKAY?
YES!
LATINA WILL DO HER BEST!

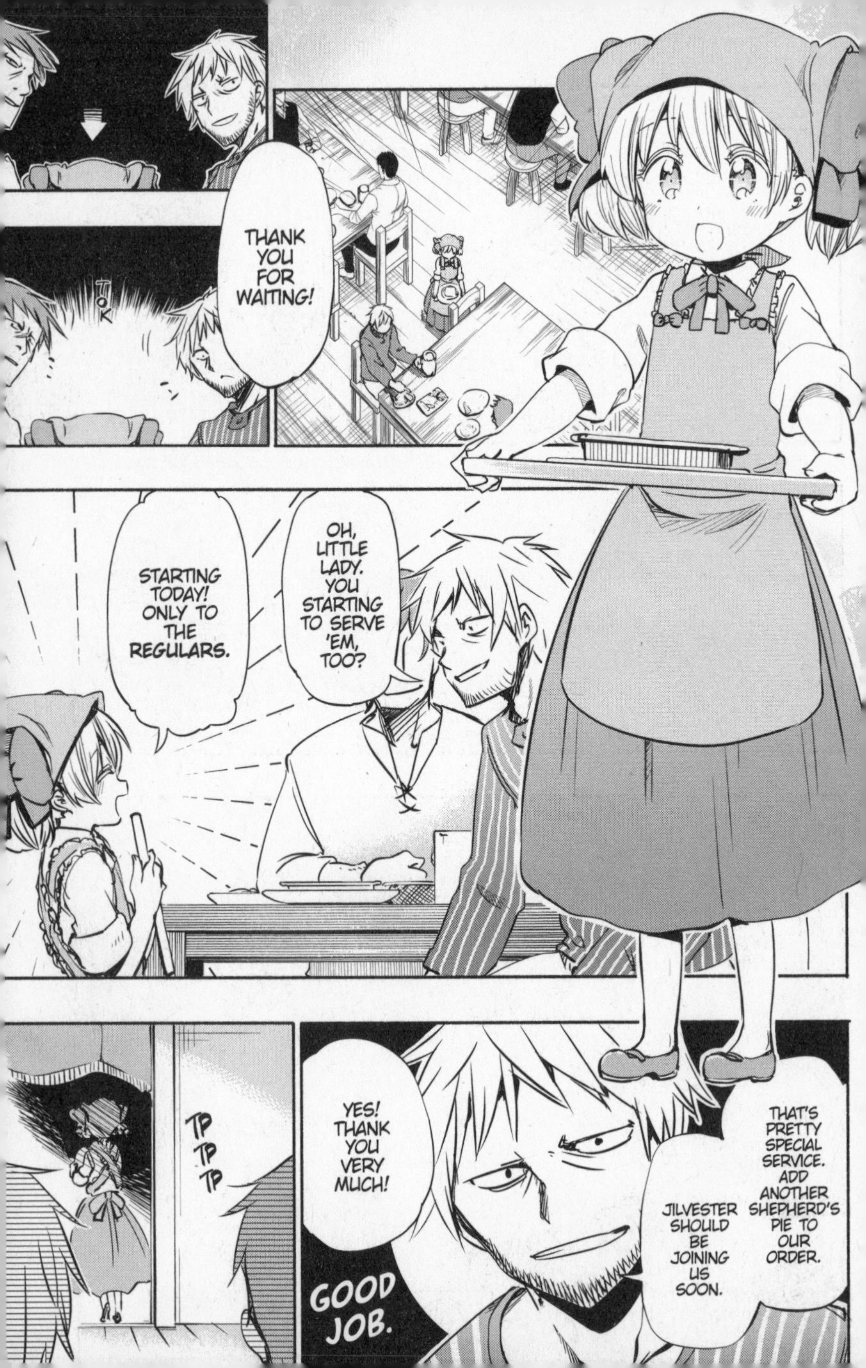
THANK YOU FOR WAITING!
TOK
OH, LITTLE LADY. YOU STARTING TO SERVE 'EM, TOO?
STARTING TODAY! ONLY TO THE REGULARS.
THAT'S PRETTY SPECIAL SERVICE. ADD ANOTHER SHEPHERD'S PIE TO OUR ORDER.
JILVESTER SHOULD BE JOINING US SOON.
YES! THANK YOU VERY MUCH!
GOOD JOB.
TP TP TP

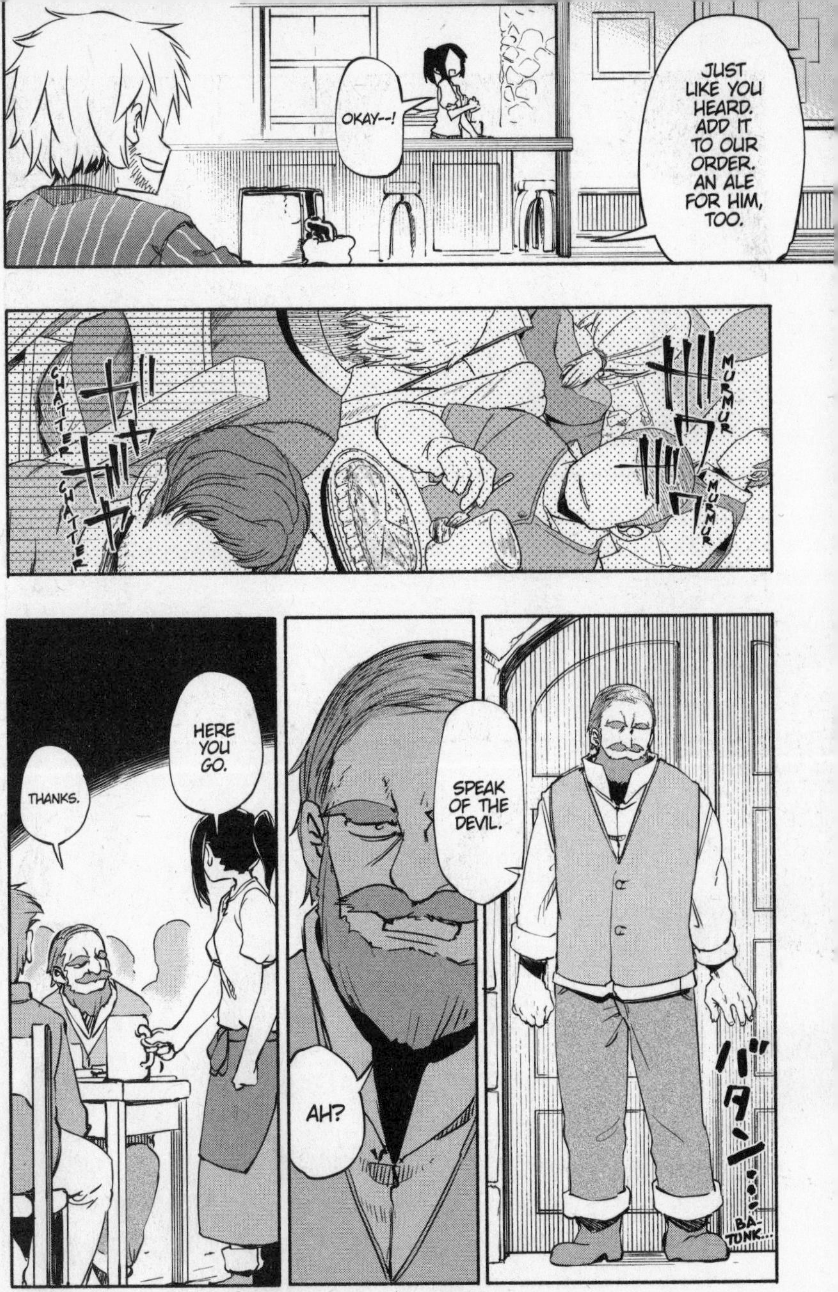
JUST LIKE YOU HEARD. ADD IT TO OUR ORDER. AN ALE FOR HIM, TOO.
OKAY--!
MURMUR
MURMUR
CHATTER
CHATTER
BA-TUNK...
SPEAK OF THE DEVIL.
AH?
HERE YOU GO.
THANKS.

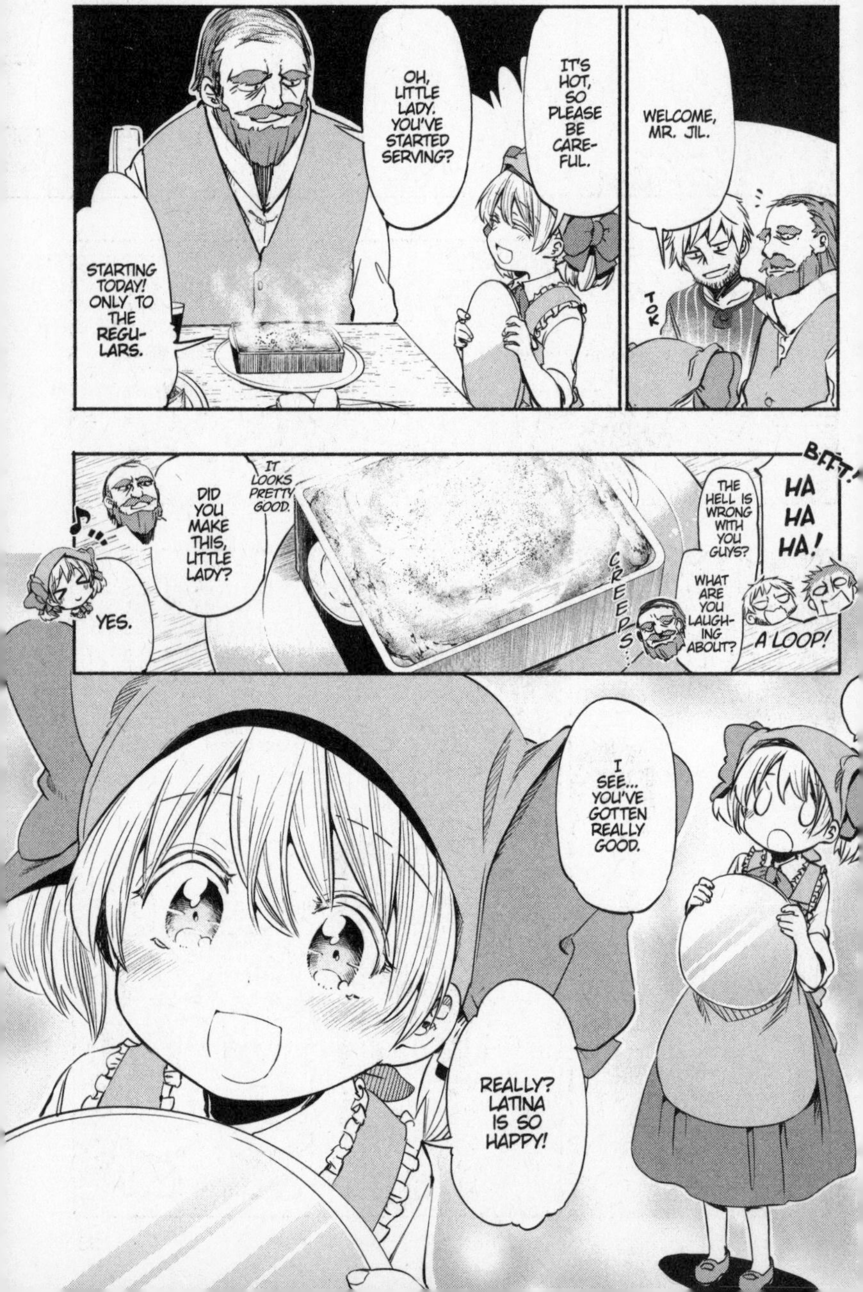
WELCOME, MR. JIL.
TOK
IT'S HOT, SO PLEASE BE CARE-FUL.
OH, LITTLE LADY. YOU'VE STARTED SERVING?
STARTING TODAY! ONLY TO THE REGU-LARS.
B-FFT!
HA HA HA!
THE HELL IS WRONG WITH YOU GUYS?
WHAT ARE YOU LAUGHING ABOUT?
A LOOP!
CREEPS...
IT LOOKS PRETTY GOOD.
DID YOU MAKE THIS, LITTLE LADY?
YES.
I SEE... YOU'VE GOTTEN REALLY GOOD.
REALLY? LATINA IS SO HAPPY!

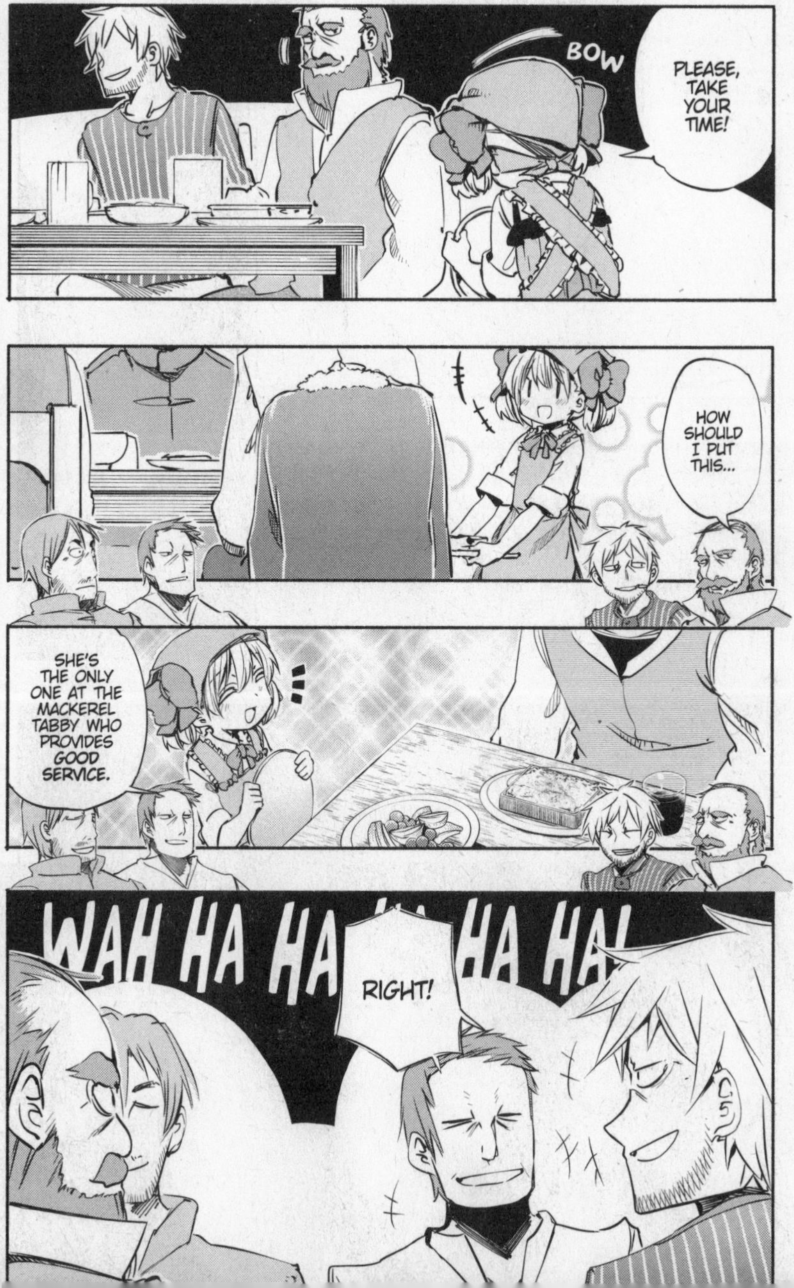
PLEASE, TAKE YOUR TIME!
BOW
HOW SHOULD I PUT THIS...
SHE'S THE ONLY ONE AT THE MACKEREL TABBY WHO PROVIDES GOOD SERVICE.
WAH HA HA HA HA HA!
RIGHT!

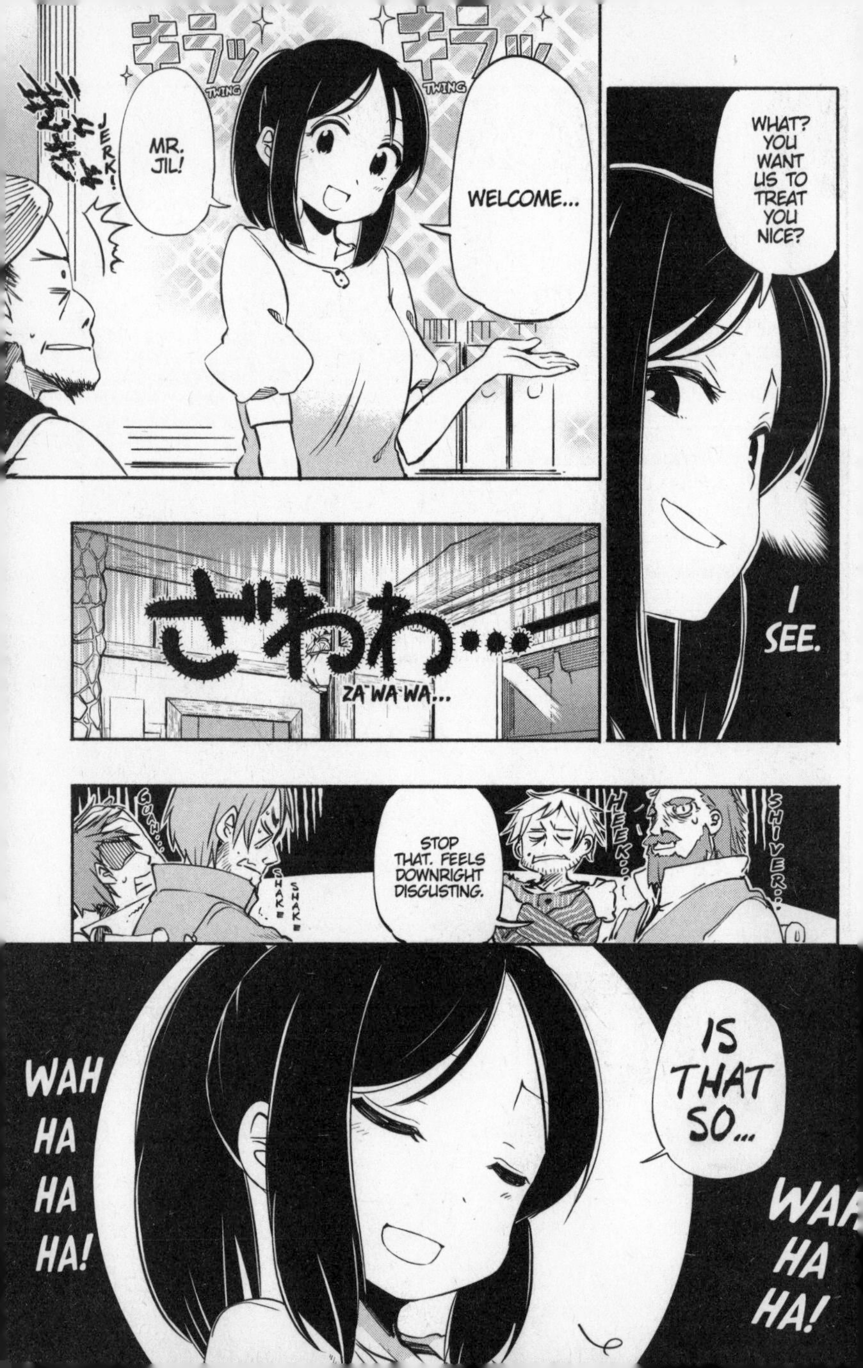
WHAT? YOU WANT US TO TREAT YOU NICE?
I SEE.
TWING
WELCOME...
TWING
MR. JIL!
JERK!
ZA WA WA...
SHIVER...
HEEK...
STOP THAT. FEELS DOWNRIGHT DISGUSTING.
SHAKE SHAKE
GUAH...
IS THAT SO...
HA HA HA!
WAH HA HA HA!

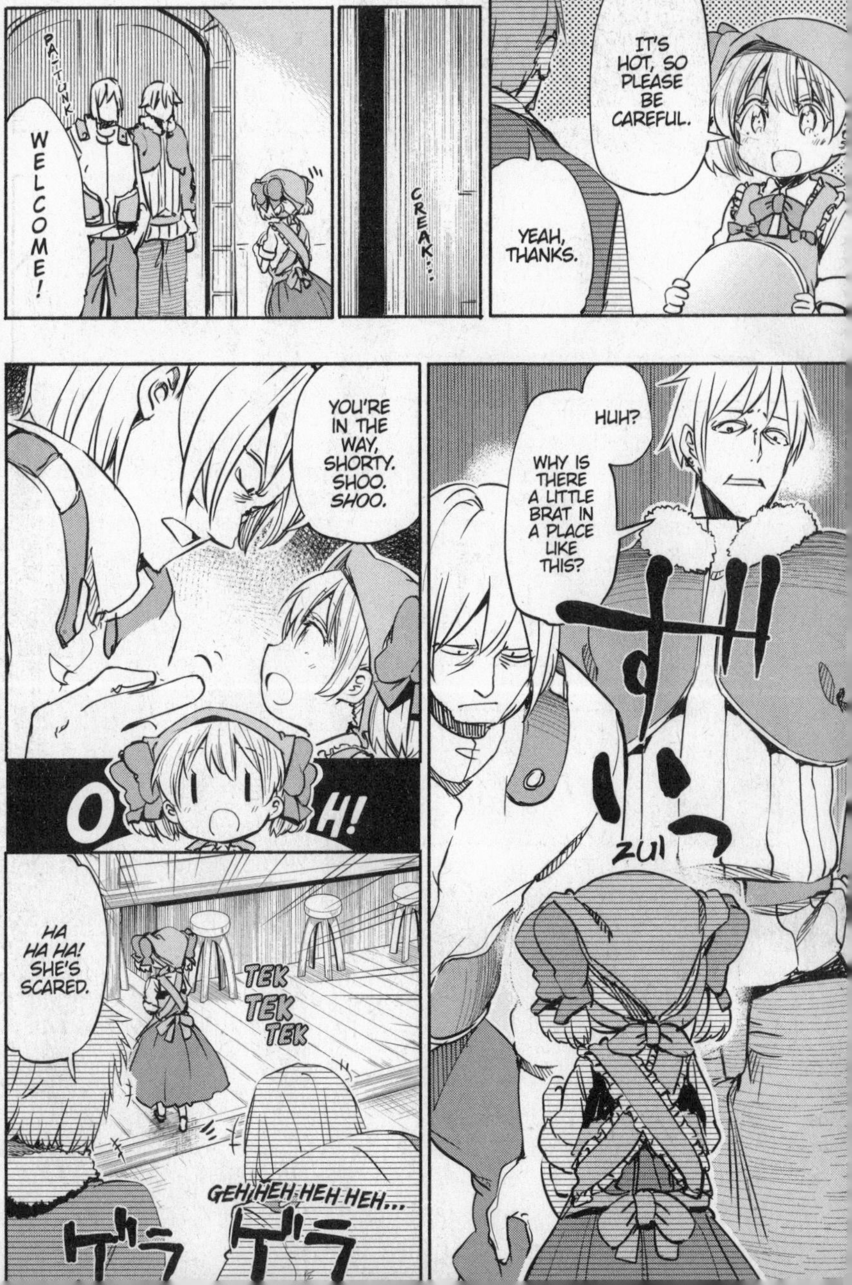
IT'S HOT, SO PLEASE BE CAREFUL.
YEAH, THANKS.
CREAK...
PA-TUNK
WELCOME!
HUH?
WHY IS THERE A LITTLE BRAT IN A PLACE LIKE THIS?
ずいっ
ZUI
YOU'RE IN THE WAY, SHORTY. SHOO. SHOO.
OH!
HA HA HA! SHE'S SCARED.
TEK TEK TEK
GEH HEH HEH HEH...
ゲラ ゲラ

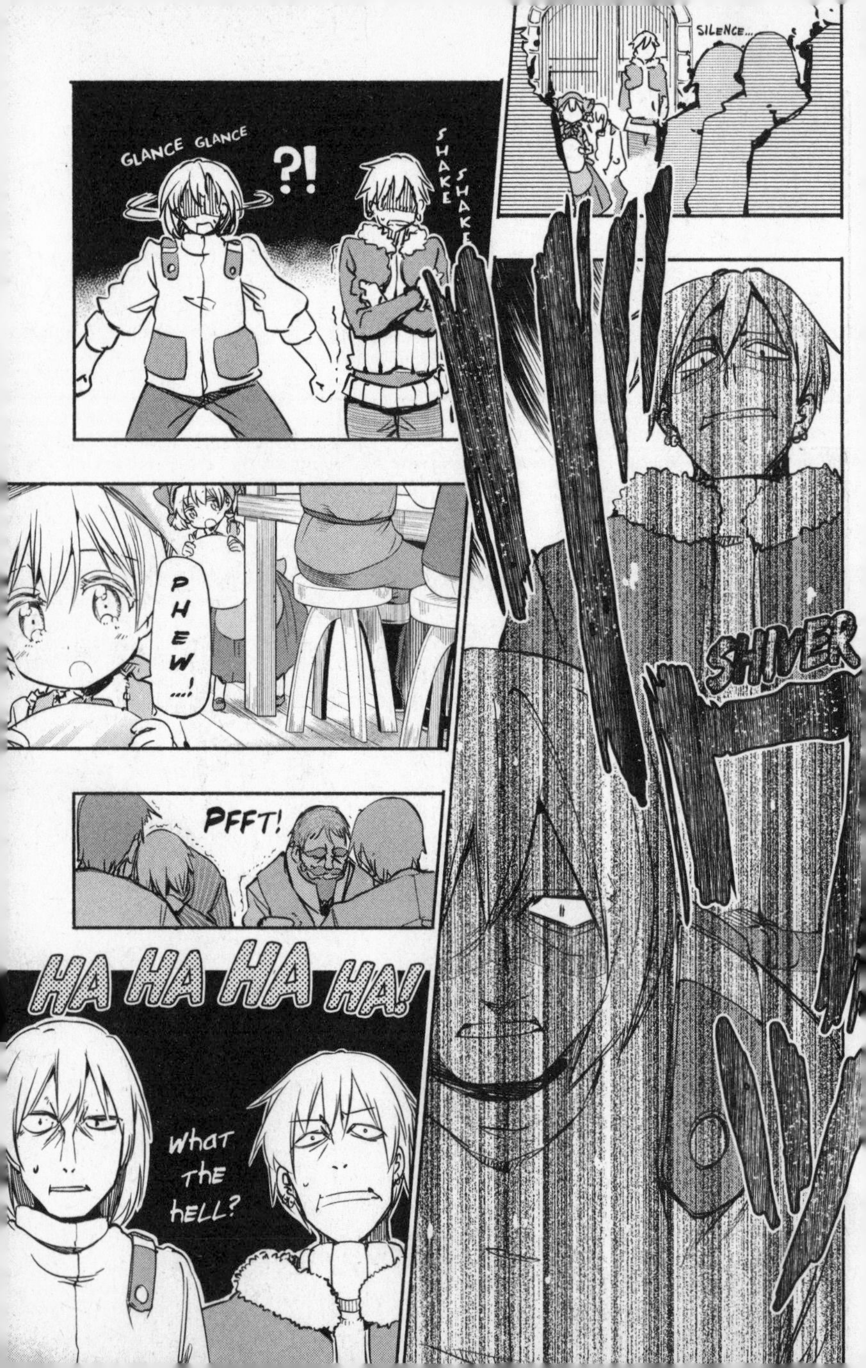
SILENCE...
SHIVER
GLANCE GLANCE
?!
SHAKE SHAKE
PHEW...!
PFFT!
HA HA HA HA HA!
What the hell?

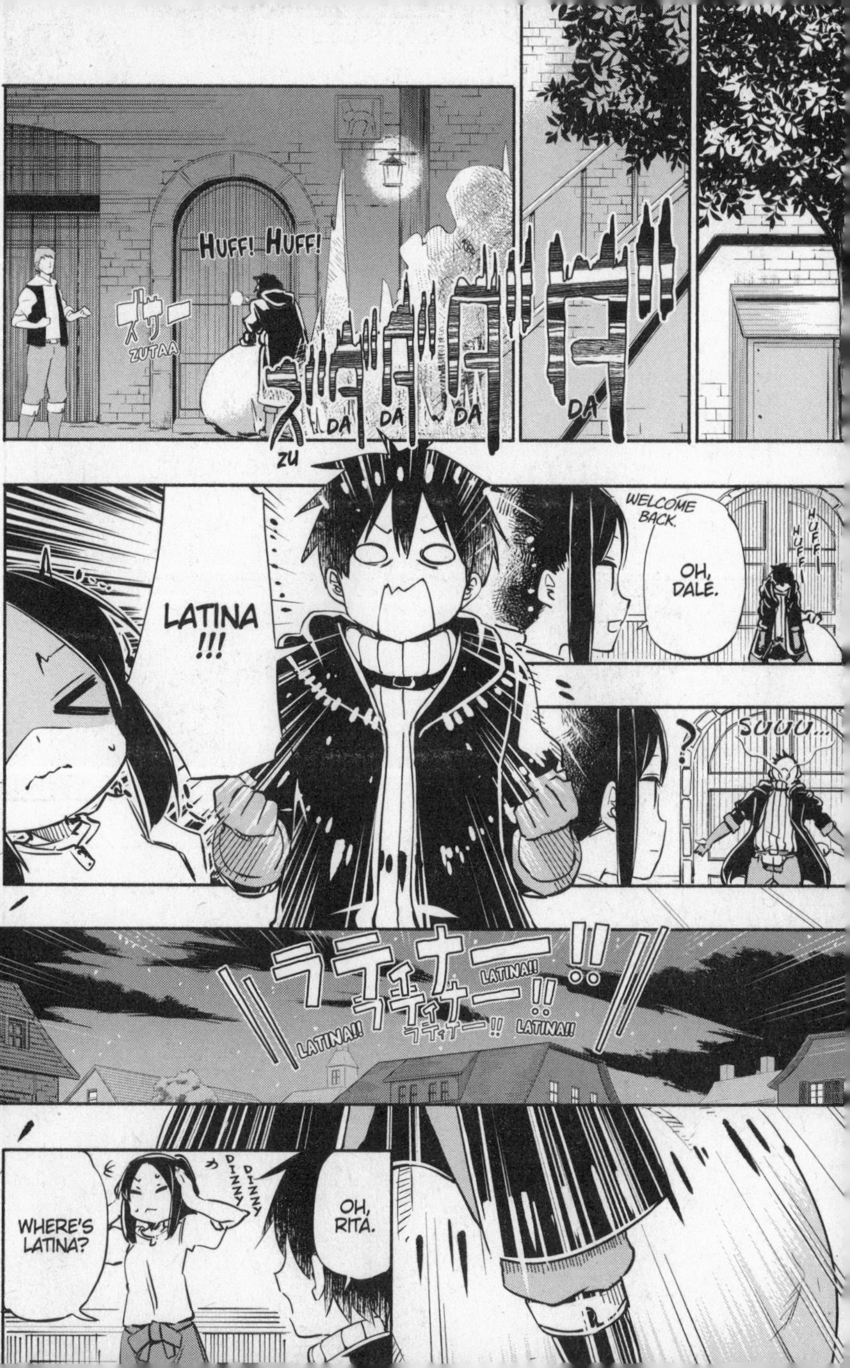
ZU DA DA DA DA
HUFF! HUFF!
ズサー
ZUTAA
OH, DALE.
WELCOME BACK.
HUFF! HUFF!
SUUU...
LATINA!!!
ラティナー!!
LATINA!!
ラティナー!!
LATINA!!
ラティナー!!
LATINA!!
LATINA!!
OH, RITA.
DIZZY DIZZY
WHERE'S LATINA?

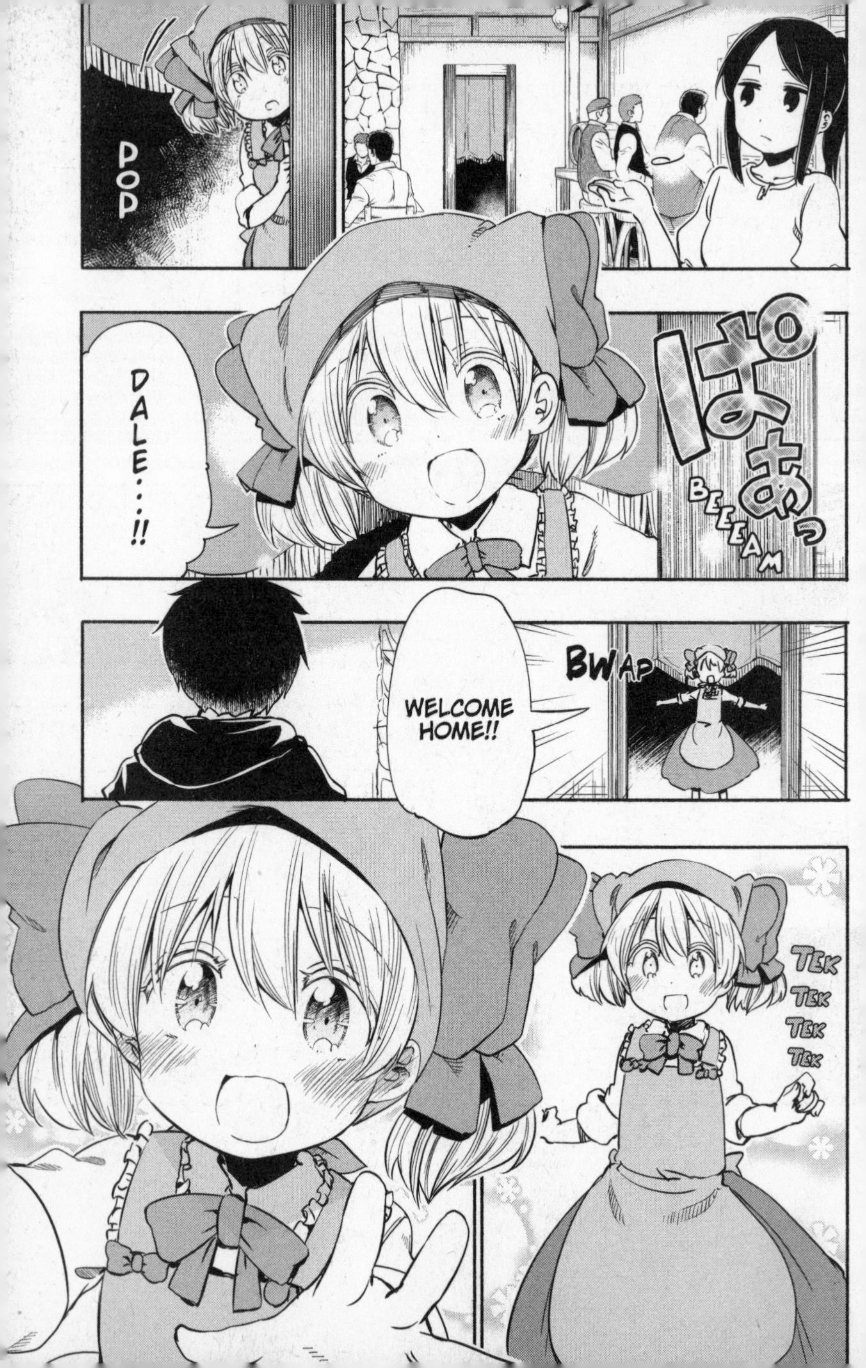
POP
ぱあっ
BEEEAM
DALE...!!
BWAP
WELCOME HOME!!
TEK TEK TEK TEK

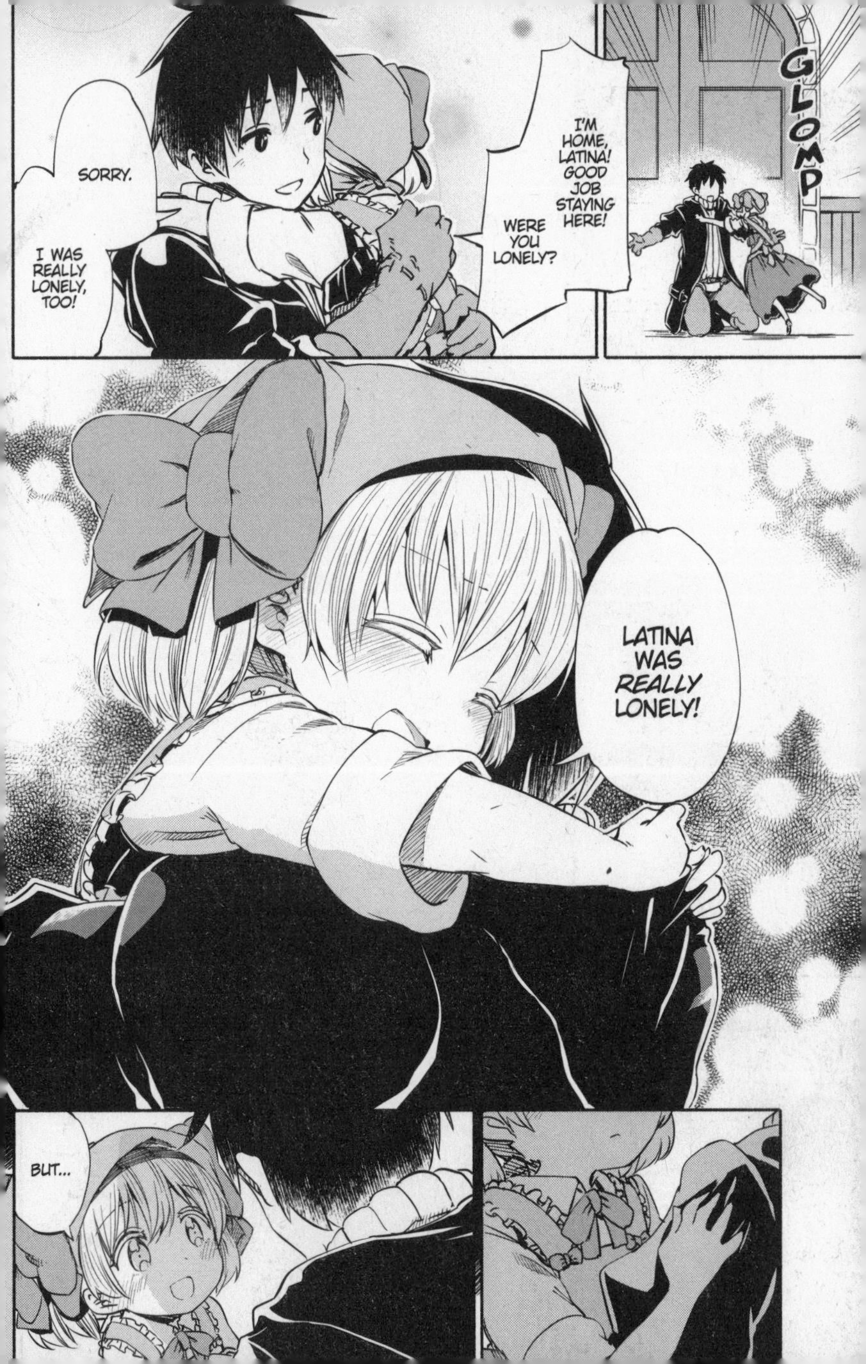
GLOMP
I'M HOME, LATINA! GOOD JOB STAYING HERE!
WERE YOU LONELY?
SORRY.
I WAS REALLY LONELY, TOO!
LATINA WAS *REALLY* LONELY!
BUT...

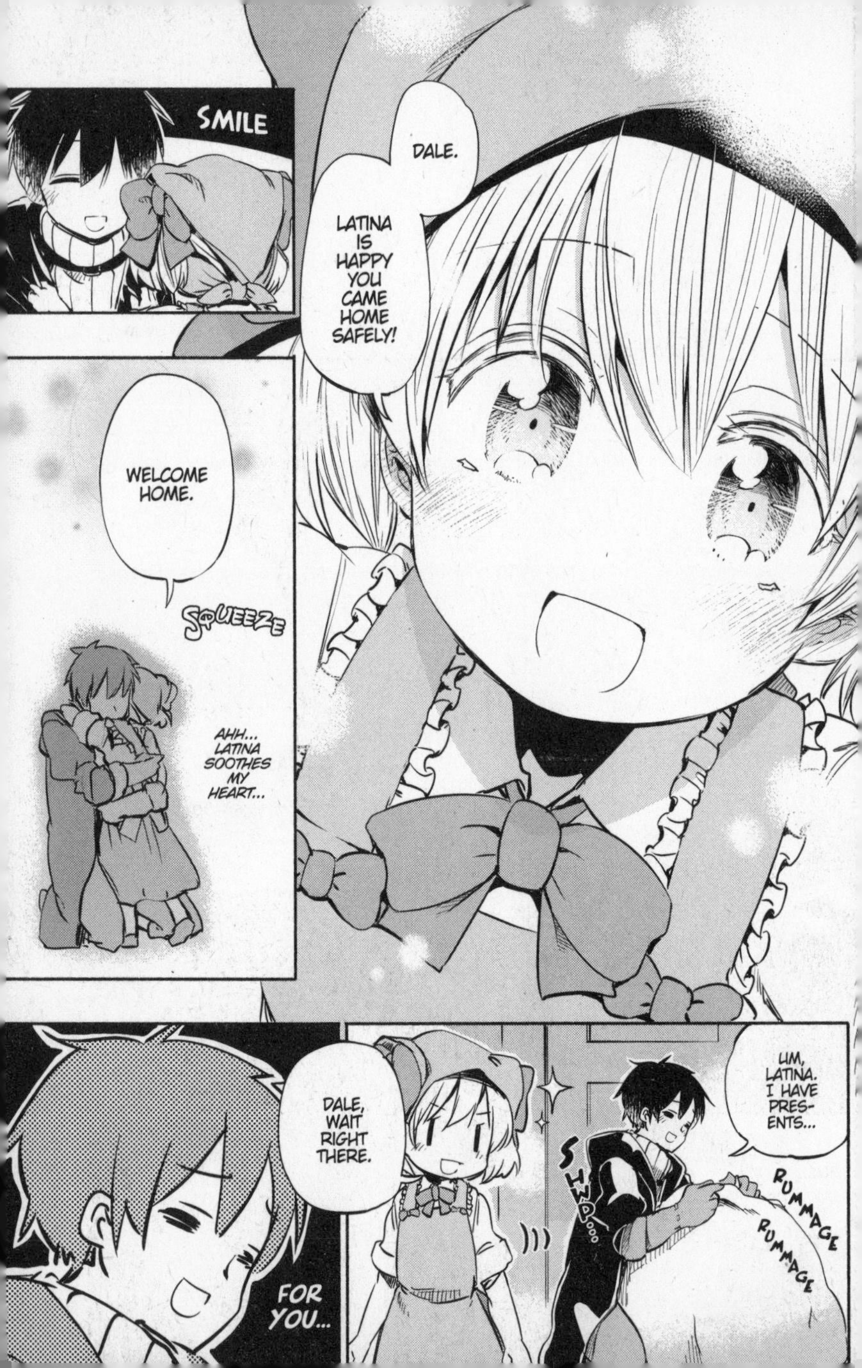
DALE.
LATINA IS HAPPY YOU CAME HOME SAFELY!
SMILE
WELCOME HOME.
SQUEEZE
AHH... LATINA SOOTHES MY HEART...
UM, LATINA. I HAVE PRES- ENTS...
RUMMAGE
RUMMAGE
SHWOOO
DALE, WAIT RIGHT THERE.
FOR YOU...

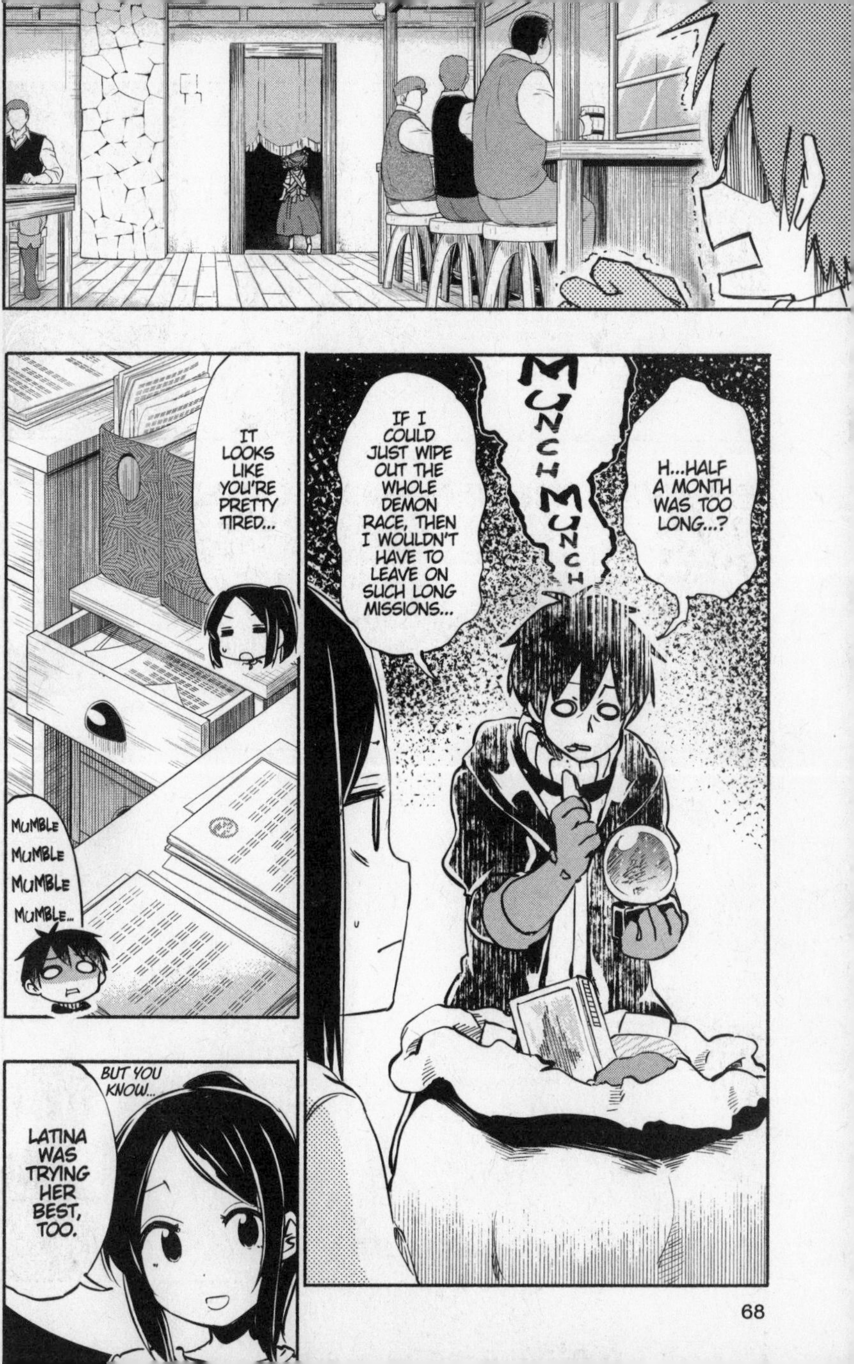
H...HALF A MONTH WAS TOO LONG...?
MUNCH MUNCH MUNCH MUNCH
IF I COULD JUST WIPE OUT THE WHOLE DEMON RACE, THEN I WOULDN'T HAVE TO LEAVE ON SUCH LONG MISSIONS...
IT LOOKS LIKE YOU'RE PRETTY TIRED...
MUMBLE MUMBLE MUMBLE MUMBLE...
BUT YOU KNOW...
LATINA WAS TRYING HER BEST, TOO.

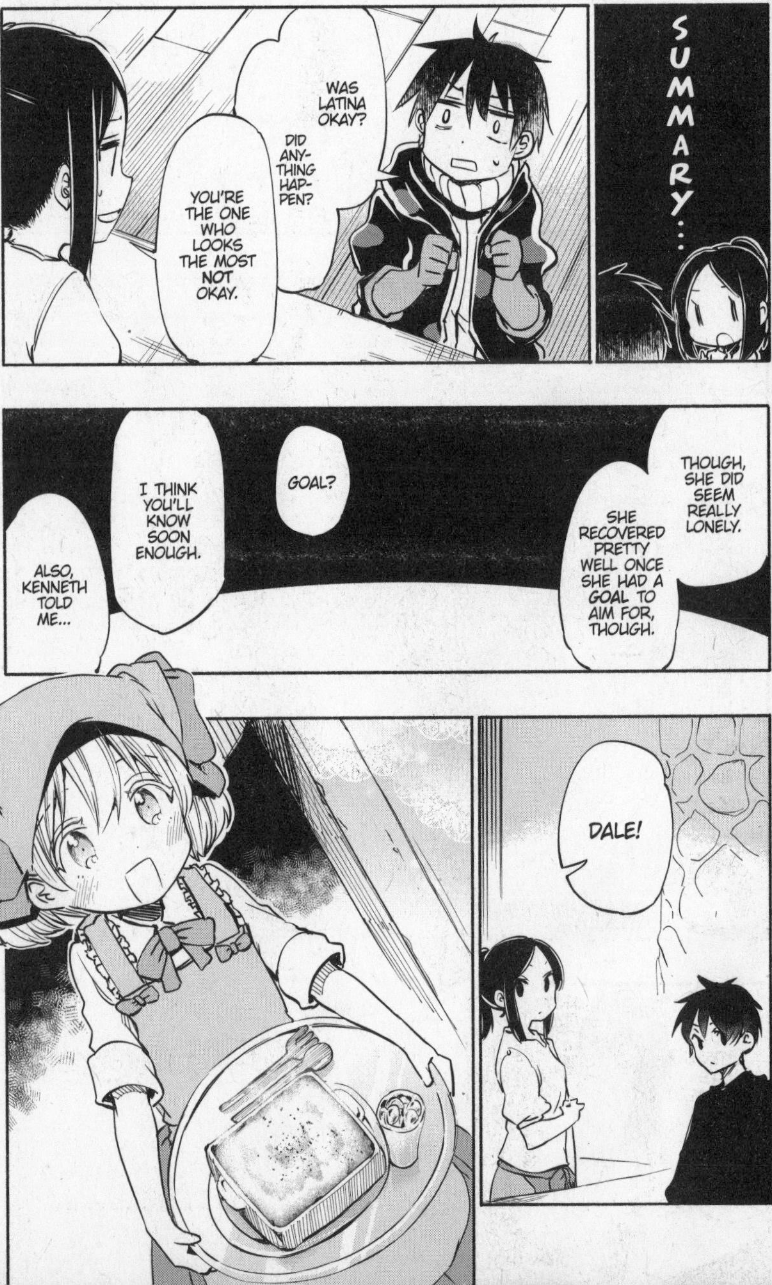
SUMMARY...
WAS LATINA OKAY?
DID ANYTHING HAPPEN?
YOU'RE THE ONE WHO LOOKS THE MOST NOT OKAY.
THOUGH, SHE DID SEEM REALLY LONELY.
SHE RECOVERED PRETTY WELL ONCE SHE HAD A GOAL TO AIM FOR, THOUGH.
GOAL?
I THINK YOU'LL KNOW SOON ENOUGH.
ALSO, KENNETH TOLD ME...
DALE!

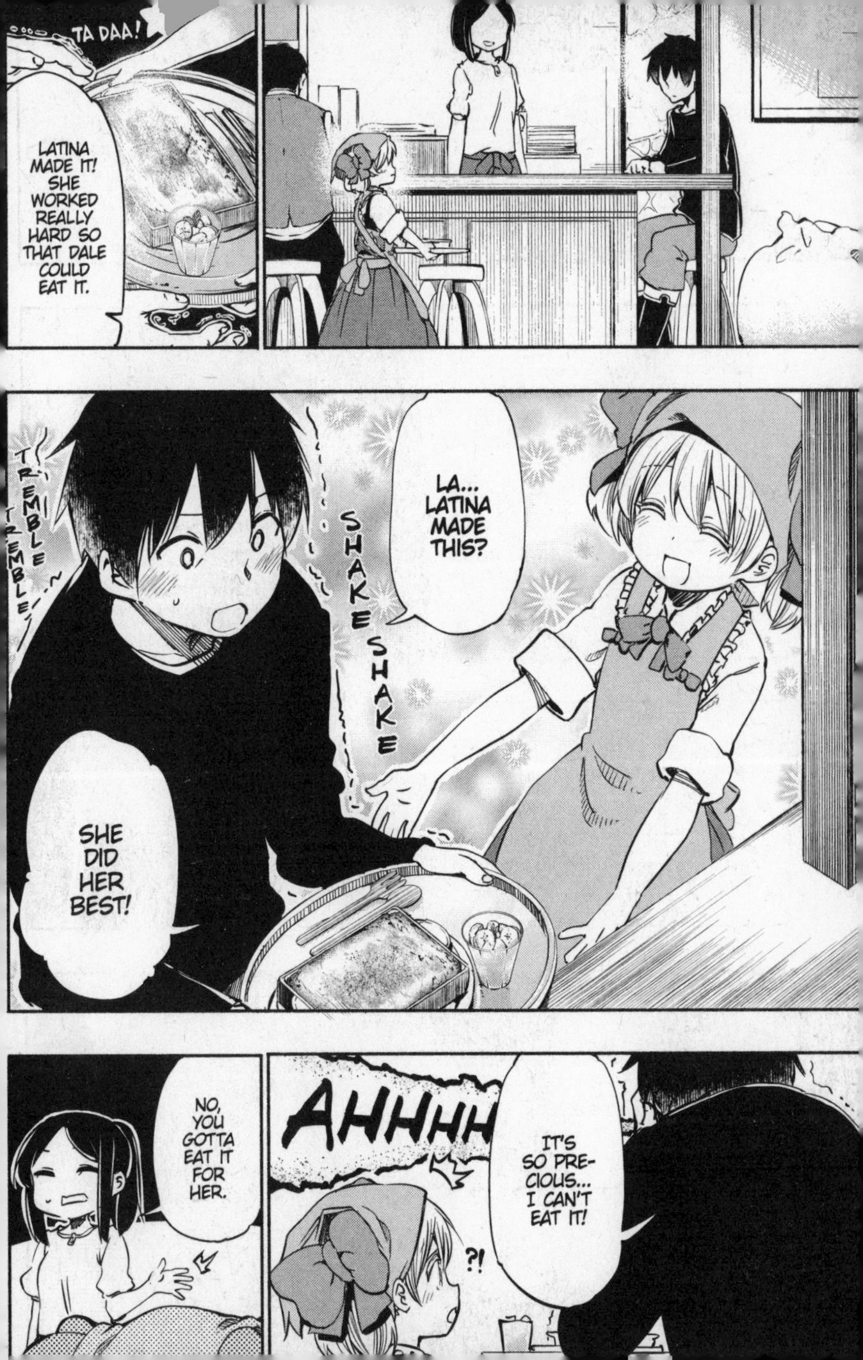
TA DAA!
LATINA MADE IT! SHE WORKED REALLY HARD SO THAT DALE COULD EAT IT.
LA... LATINA MADE THIS?
SHAKE SHAKE
TREMBLE TREMBLE
SHE DID HER BEST!
IT'S SO PRECIOUS... I CAN'T EAT IT!
AHHHH
?!
NO, YOU GOTTA EAT IT FOR HER.

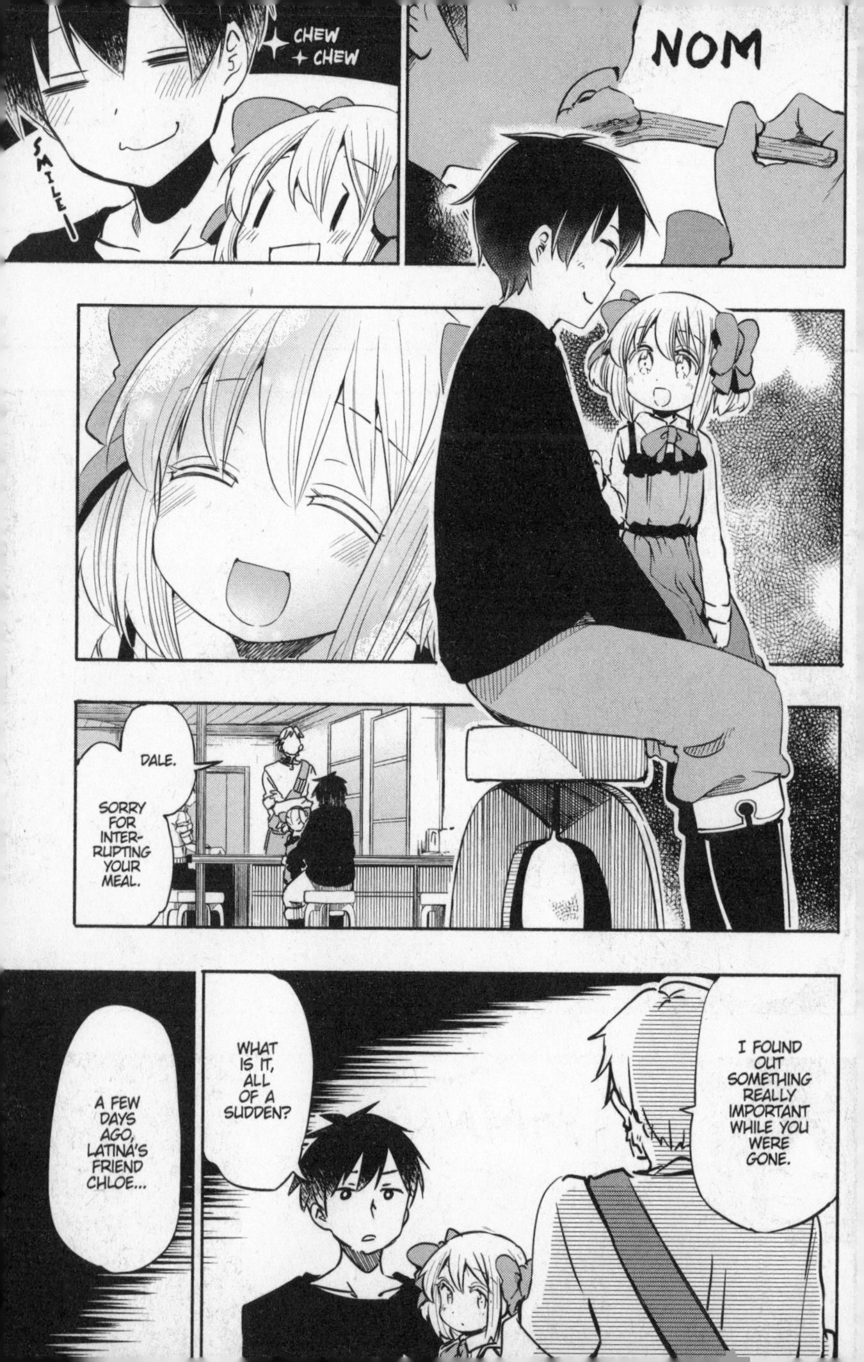
NOM
CHEW
CHEW
SMILE
DALE.
SORRY FOR INTERRUPTING YOUR MEAL.
I FOUND OUT SOMETHING REALLY IMPORTANT WHILE YOU WERE GONE.
WHAT IS IT, ALL OF A SUDDEN?
A FEW DAYS AGO, LATINA'S FRIEND CHLOE...

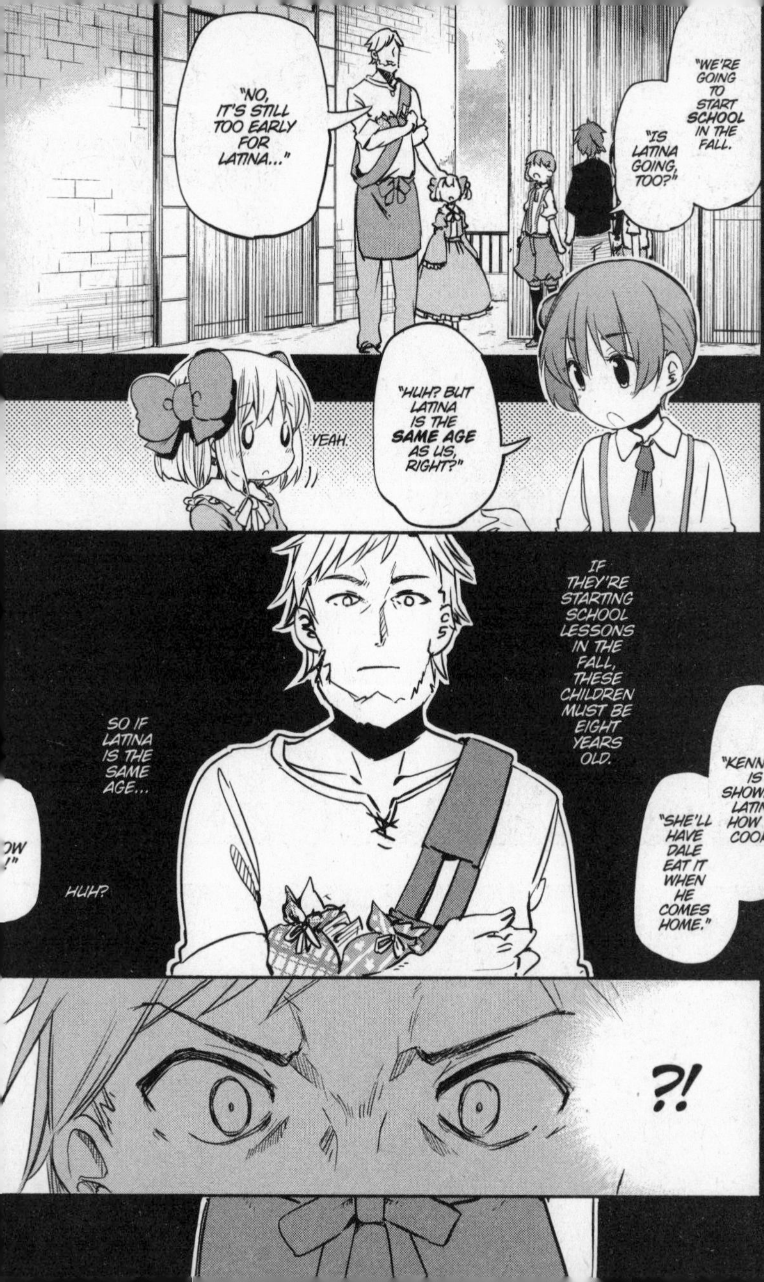
"WE'RE GOING TO START SCHOOL IN THE FALL.
"IS LATINA GOING, TOO?"
"NO, IT'S STILL TOO EARLY FOR LATINA..."
"HUH? BUT LATINA IS THE SAME AGE AS US, RIGHT?"
YEAH.
"KENNETH IS SHOWING LATINA HOW TO COOK."
"SHE'LL HAVE DALE EAT IT WHEN HE COMES HOME."
IF THEY'RE STARTING SCHOOL LESSONS IN THE FALL, THESE CHILDREN MUST BE EIGHT YEARS OLD.
SO IF LATINA IS THE SAME AGE...
HUH?
?!

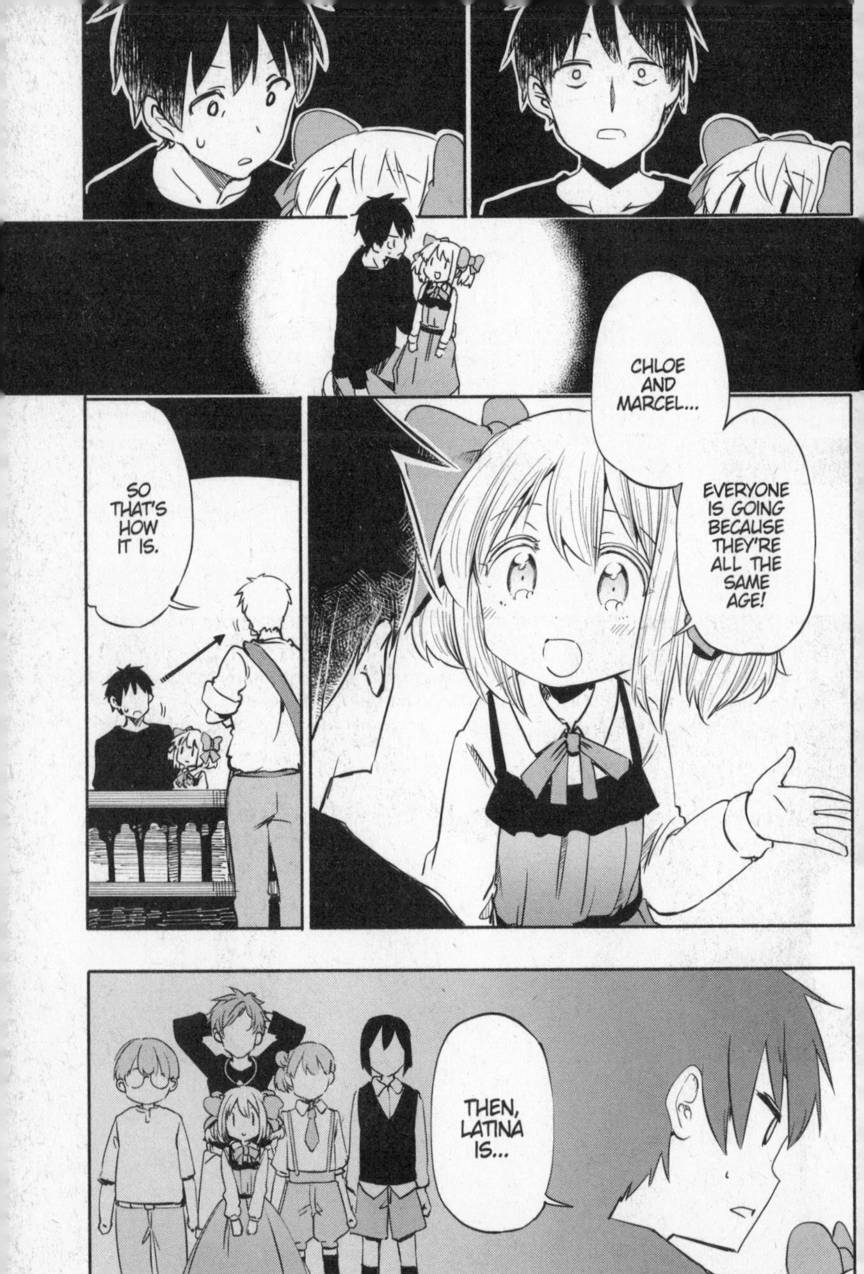
CHLOE AND MARCEL...
EVERYONE IS GOING BECAUSE THEY'RE ALL THE SAME AGE!
SO THAT'S HOW IT IS.
THEN, LATINA IS...

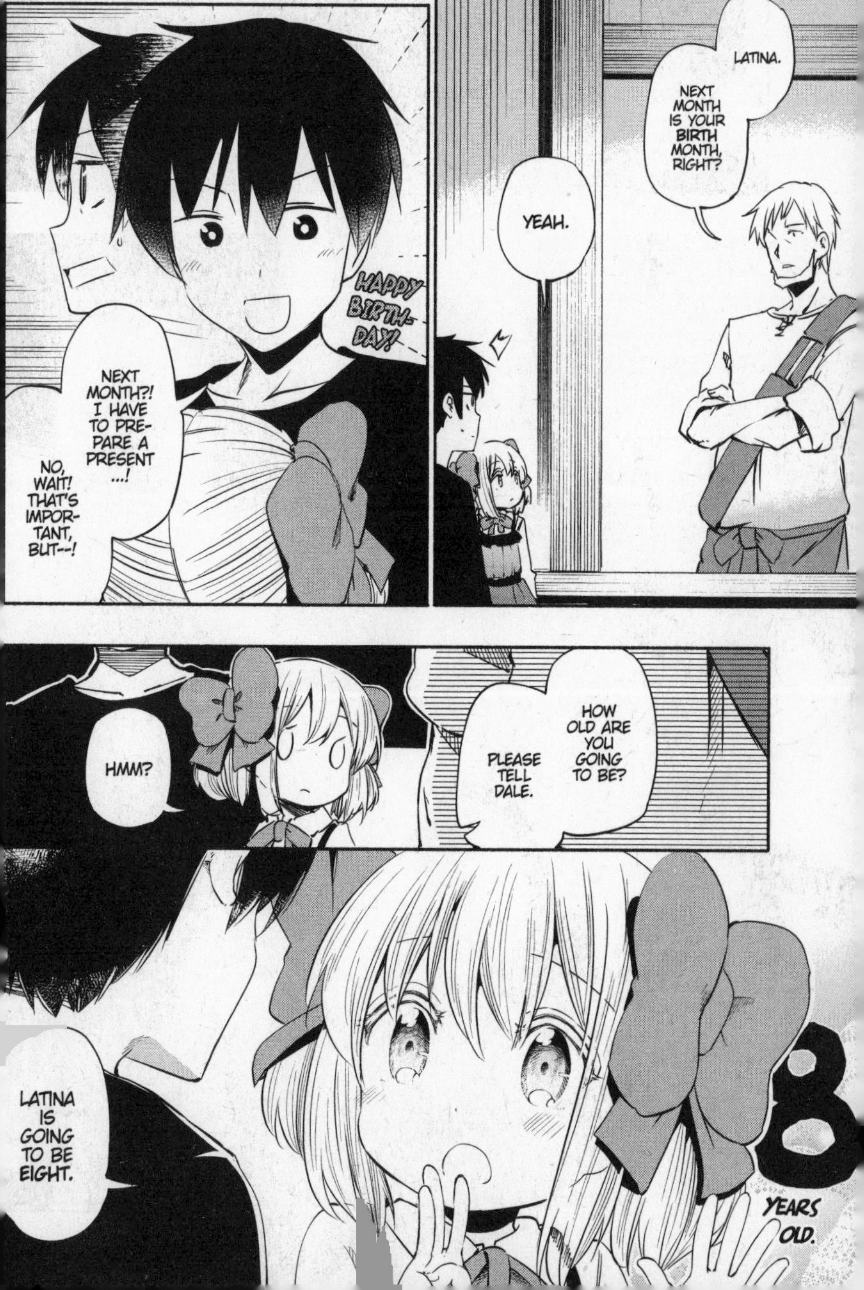
LATINA.
NEXT MONTH IS YOUR BIRTH MONTH, RIGHT?
YEAH.
HAPPY BIRTH-DAY!
NEXT MONTH?! I HAVE TO PRE-PARE A PRESENT ...!
NO, WAIT! THAT'S IMPOR-TANT, BUT--!
HOW OLD ARE YOU GOING TO BE?
PLEASE TELL DALE.
HMM?
LATINA IS GOING TO BE EIGHT.
8
YEARS OLD.

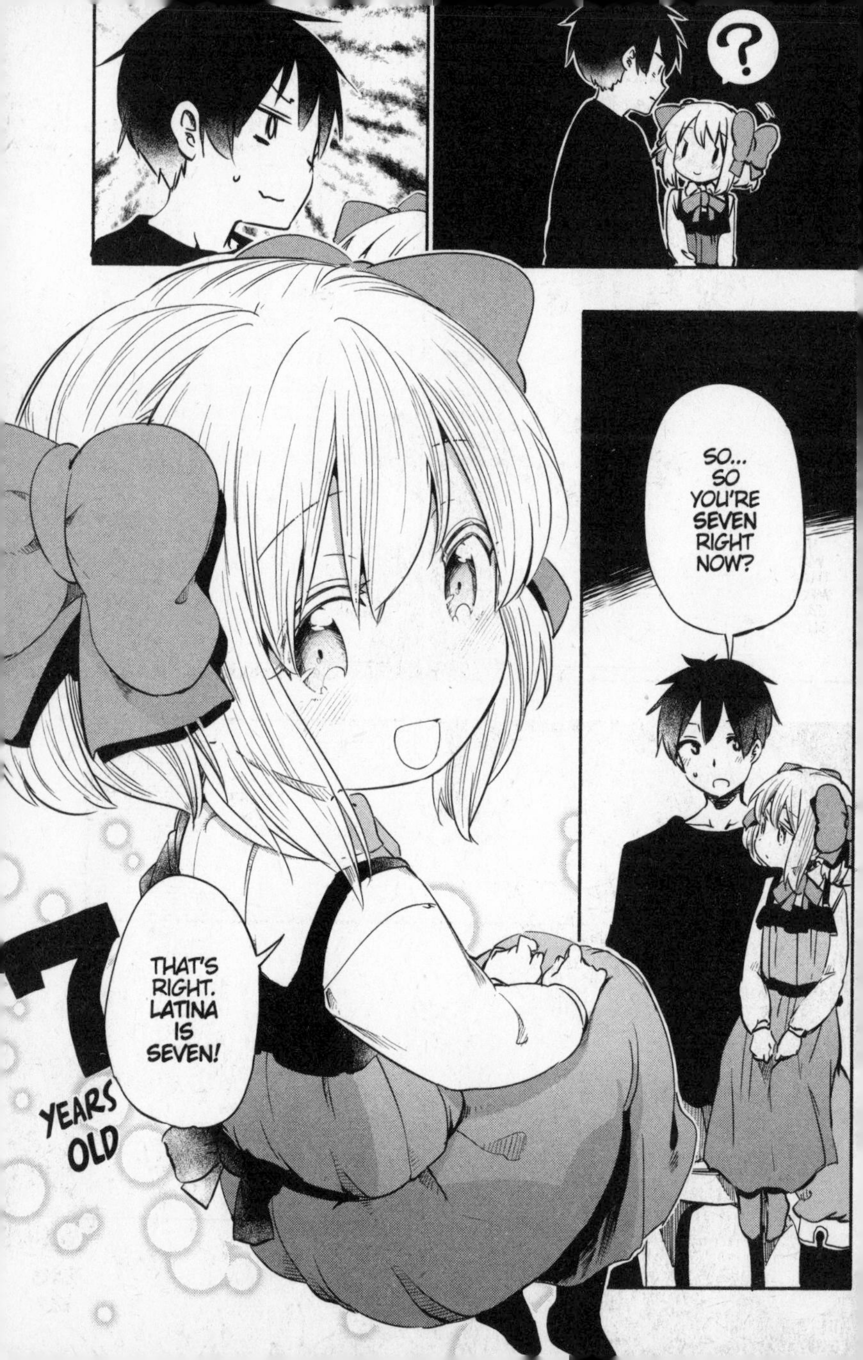
?
SO... SO YOU'RE SEVEN RIGHT NOW?
THAT'S RIGHT. LATINA IS SEVEN!
7 YEARS OLD

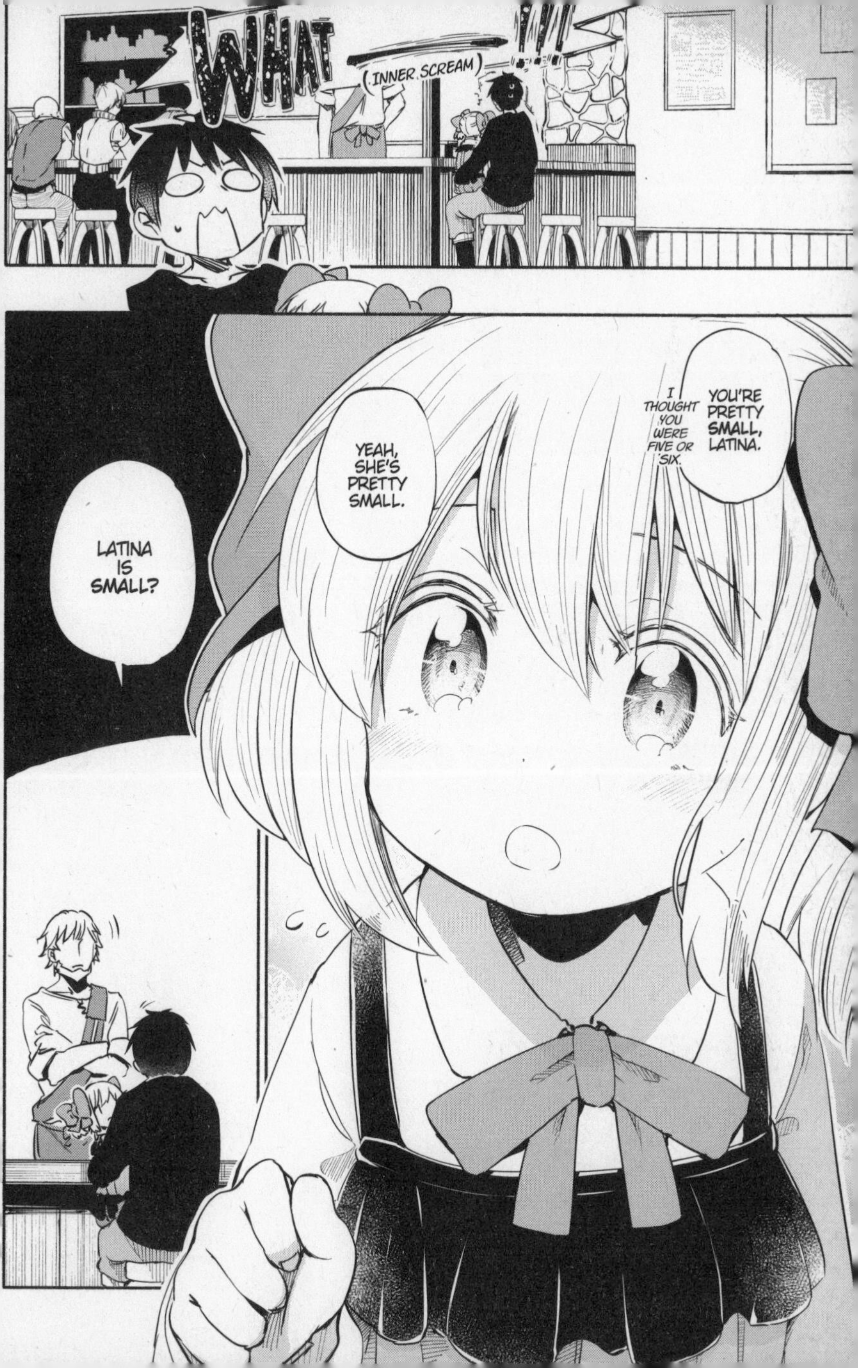
WHAT!!!
(INNER SCREAM)
YOU'RE PRETTY SMALL, LATINA.
I THOUGHT YOU WERE FIVE OR SIX.
YEAH, SHE'S PRETTY SMALL.
LATINA IS SMALL?

IF It's
For My
Daughter,
I'd Even Defeat
a Demon
Lord

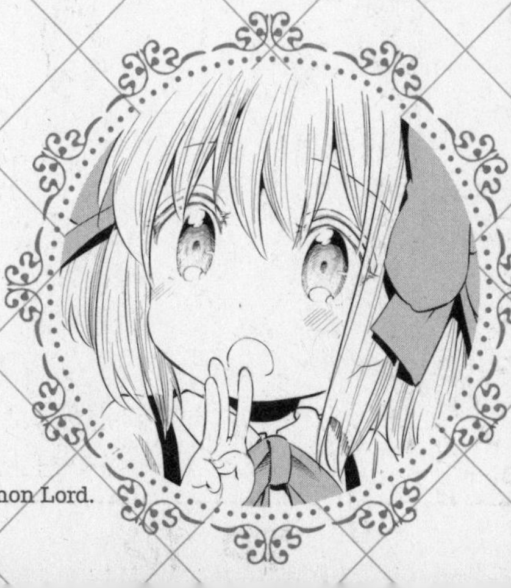

If It's For My Daughter, I'd Even Defeat a Demon Lord.

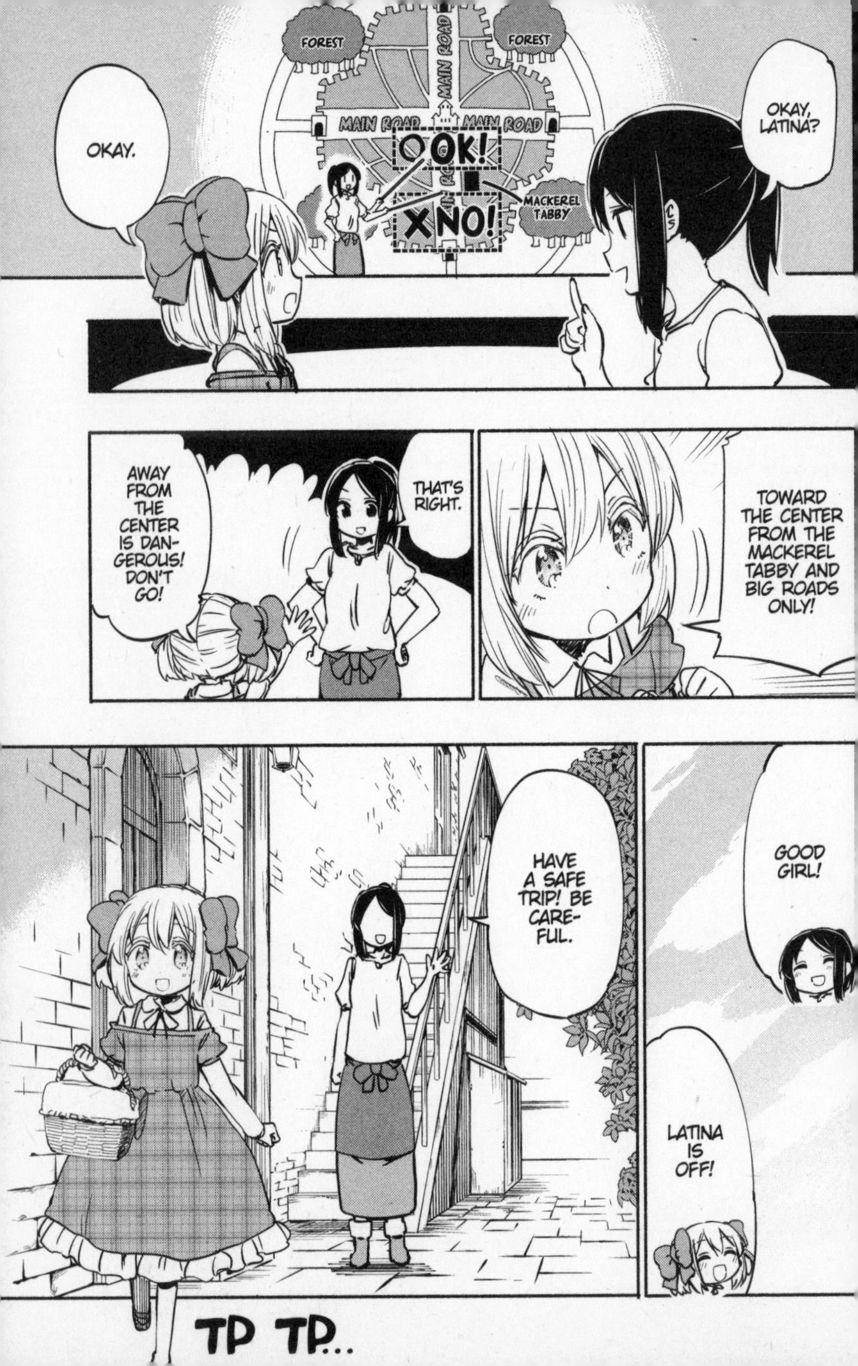
OKAY, LATINA?
FOREST
FOREST
MAIN ROAD
MAIN ROAD
MAIN ROAD
○OK!
MACKEREL TABBY
×NO!
OKAY.
TOWARD THE CENTER FROM THE MACKEREL TABBY AND BIG ROADS ONLY!
THAT'S RIGHT.
AWAY FROM THE CENTER IS DANGEROUS! DON'T GO!
GOOD GIRL!
LATINA IS OFF!
HAVE A SAFE TRIP! BE CAREFUL.
TP TP...

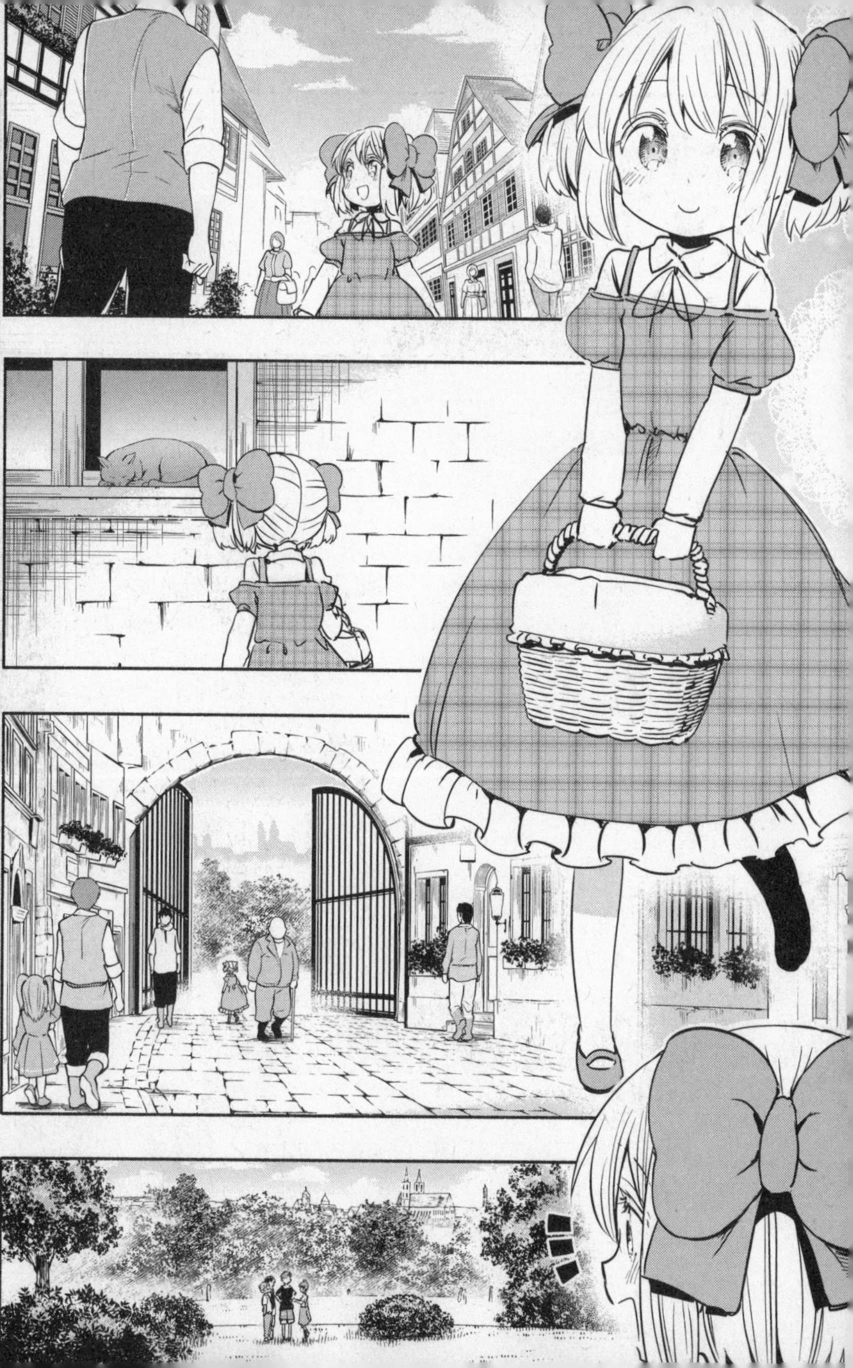

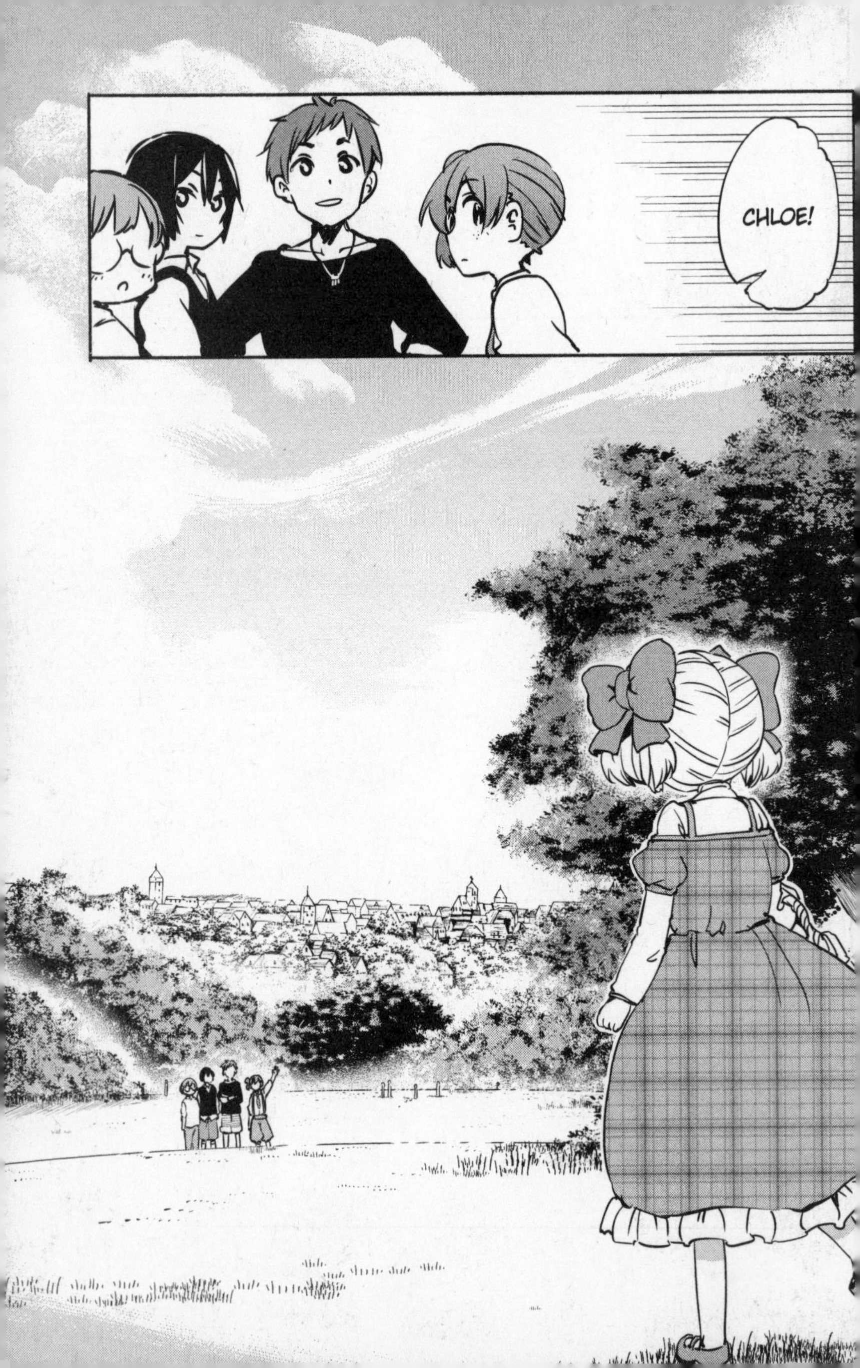
CHLOE!

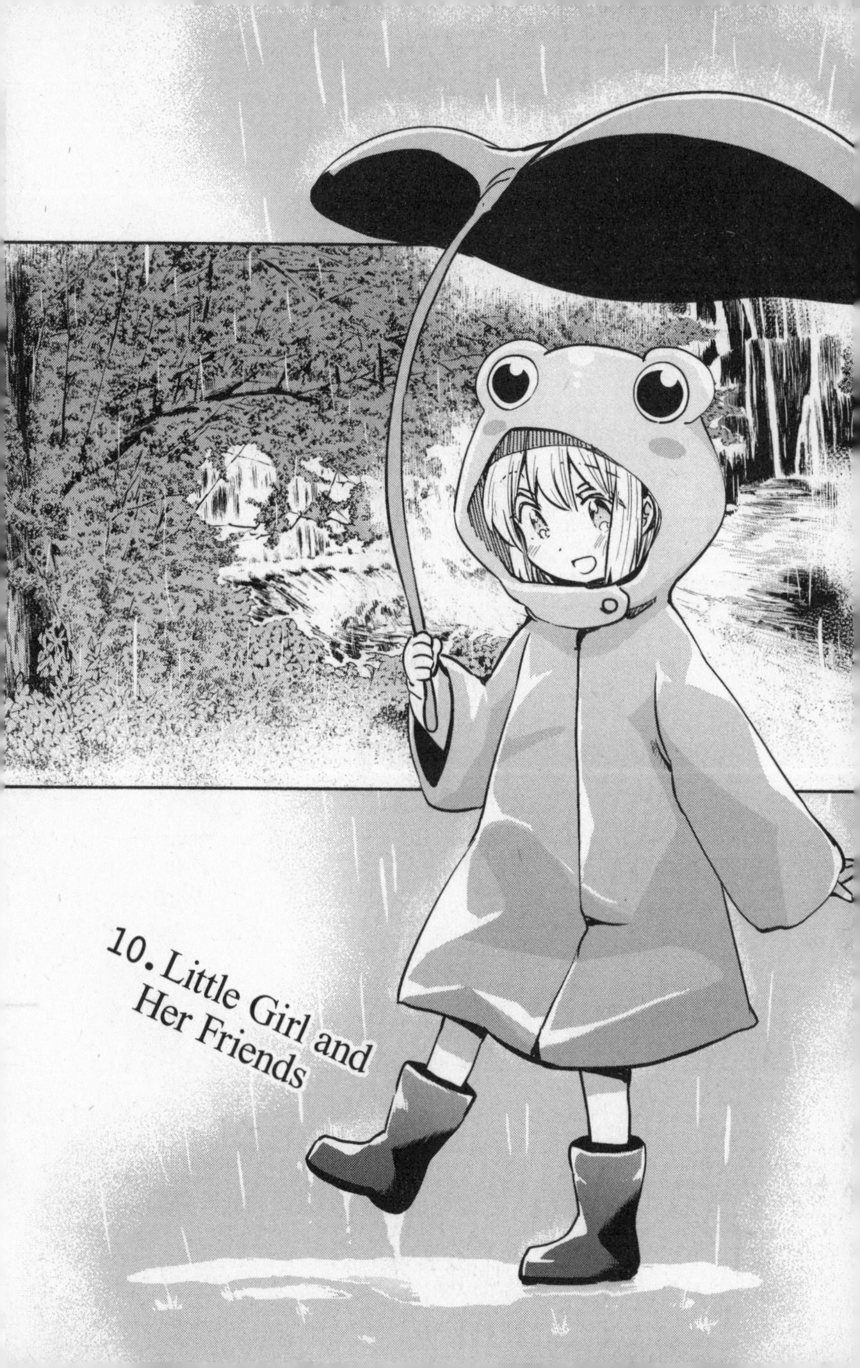
10. Little Girl and Her Friends

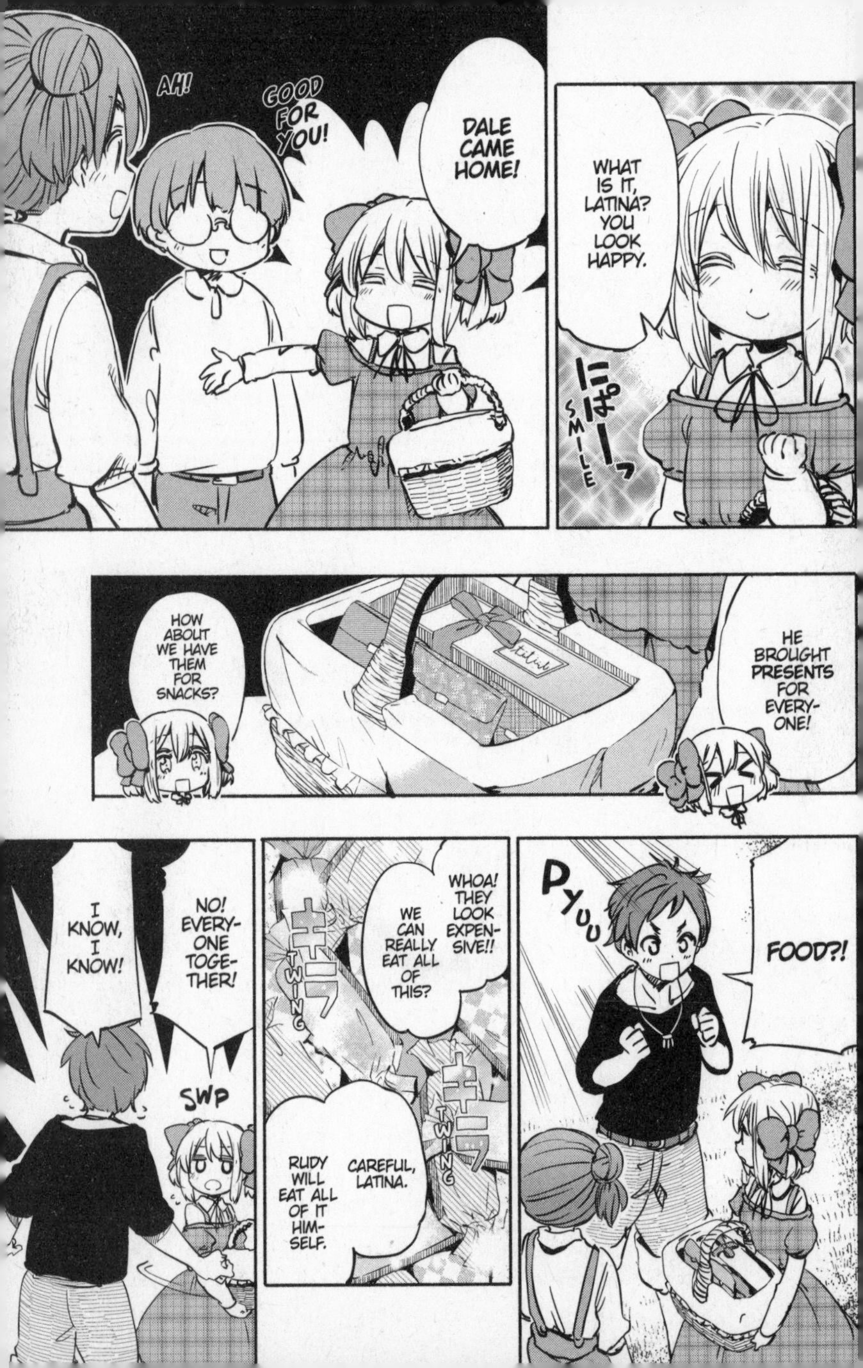
WHAT IS IT, LATINA? YOU LOOK HAPPY.
にぱーっ
SMILE
DALE CAME HOME!
GOOD FOR YOU!
AH!
HE BROUGHT PRESENTS FOR EVERY-ONE!
HOW ABOUT WE HAVE THEM FOR SNACKS?
FOOD?!
PYUU
WHOA! THEY LOOK EXPEN-SIVE!!
WE CAN REALLY EAT ALL OF THIS?
キラー
TWING
CAREFUL, LATINA.
RUDY WILL EAT ALL OF IT HIM-SELF.
キラ
TWING
NO! EVERY-ONE TOGE-THER!
I KNOW, I KNOW!
SWP

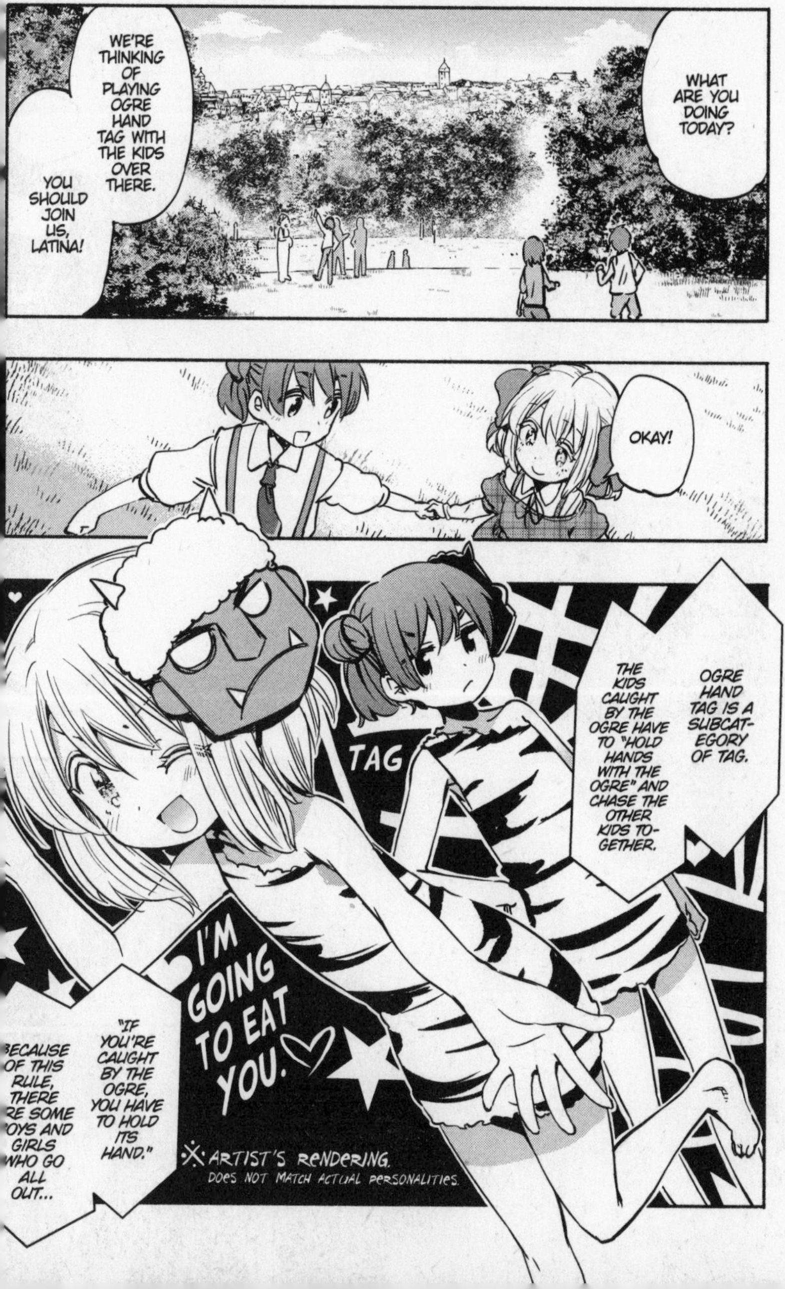
WHAT ARE YOU DOING TODAY?
WE'RE THINKING OF PLAYING OGRE HAND TAG WITH THE KIDS OVER THERE.
YOU SHOULD JOIN US, LATINA!
OKAY!
OGRE HAND TAG IS A SUBCATEGORY OF TAG.
THE KIDS CAUGHT BY THE OGRE HAVE TO "HOLD HANDS WITH THE OGRE" AND CHASE THE OTHER KIDS TOGETHER.
TAG
I'M GOING TO EAT YOU.
"IF YOU'RE CAUGHT BY THE OGRE, YOU HAVE TO HOLD ITS HAND."
BECAUSE OF THIS RULE, THERE ARE SOME BOYS AND GIRLS WHO GO ALL OUT...
※ARTIST'S RENDERING. DOES NOT MATCH ACTUAL PERSONALITIES.

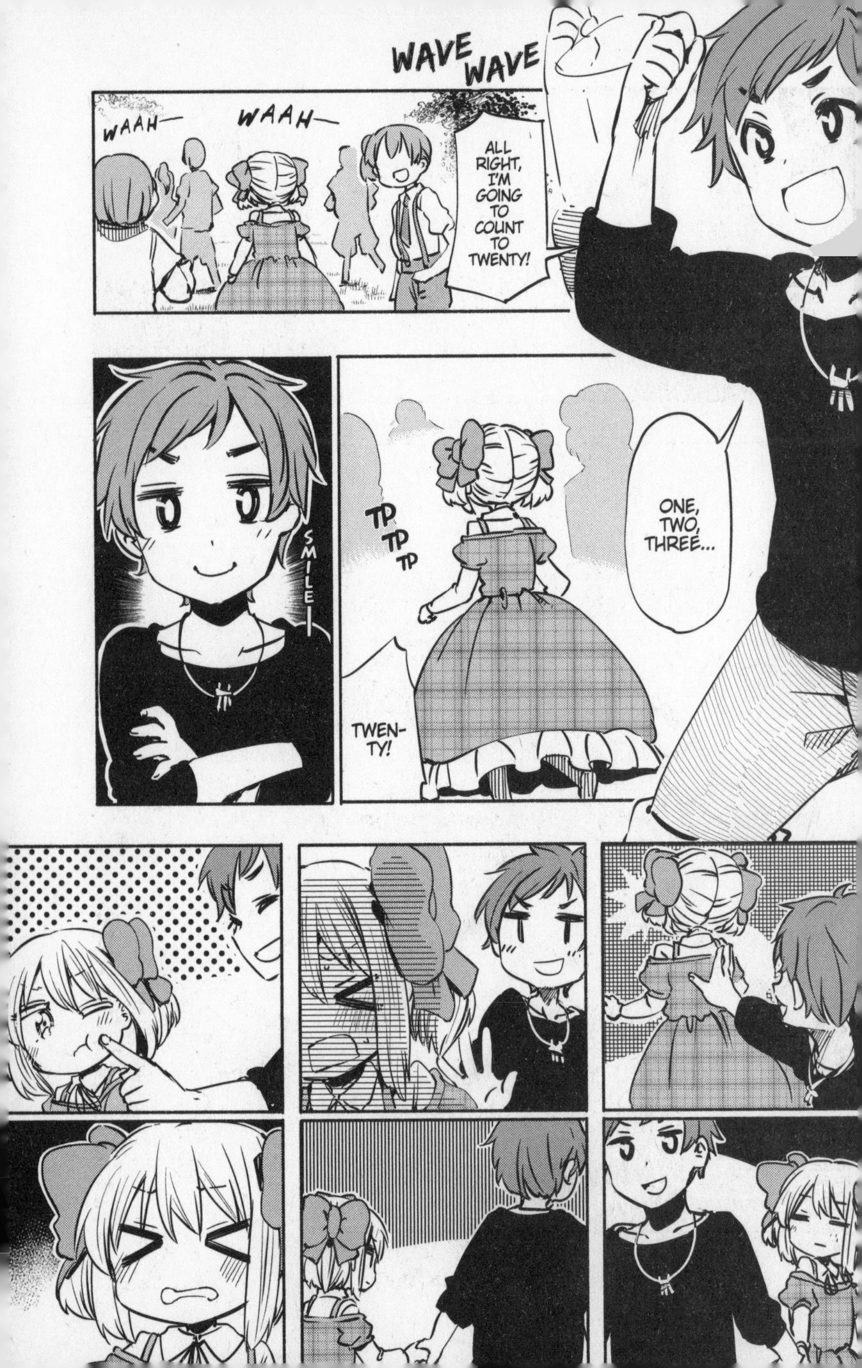
WAVE WAVE
ALL RIGHT, I'M GOING TO COUNT TO TWENTY!
WAAH—
WAAH—
ONE, TWO, THREE...
TP TP TP
TWEN-TY!
SMILE

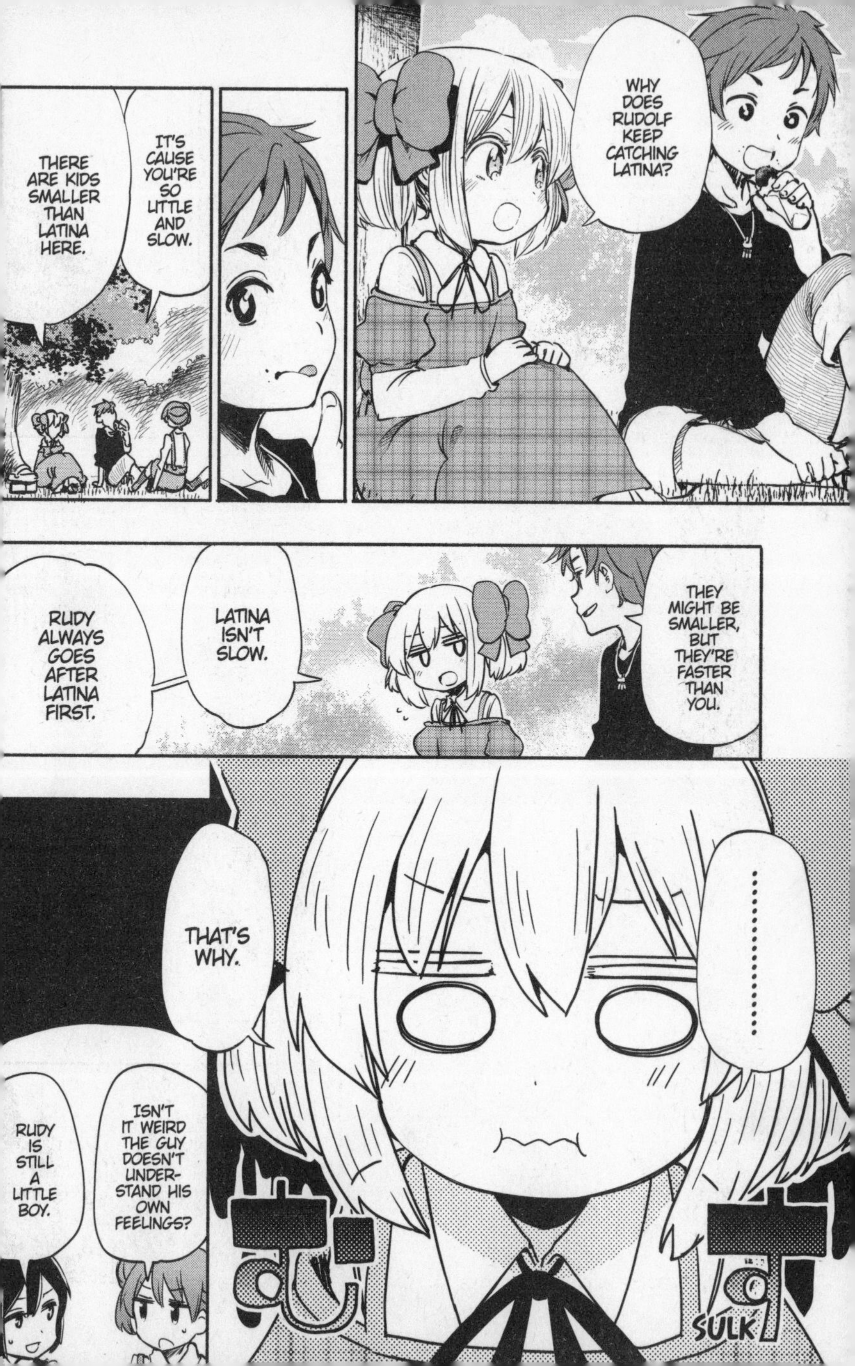
WHY DOES RUDOLF KEEP CATCHING LATINA?
IT'S CAUSE YOU'RE SO LITTLE AND SLOW.
THERE ARE KIDS SMALLER THAN LATINA HERE.
THEY MIGHT BE SMALLER, BUT THEY'RE FASTER THAN YOU.
LATINA ISN'T SLOW.
RUDY ALWAYS GOES AFTER LATINA FIRST.
......
SULK
THAT'S WHY.
ISN'T IT WEIRD THE GUY DOESN'T UNDERSTAND HIS OWN FEELINGS?
RUDY IS STILL A LITTLE BOY.

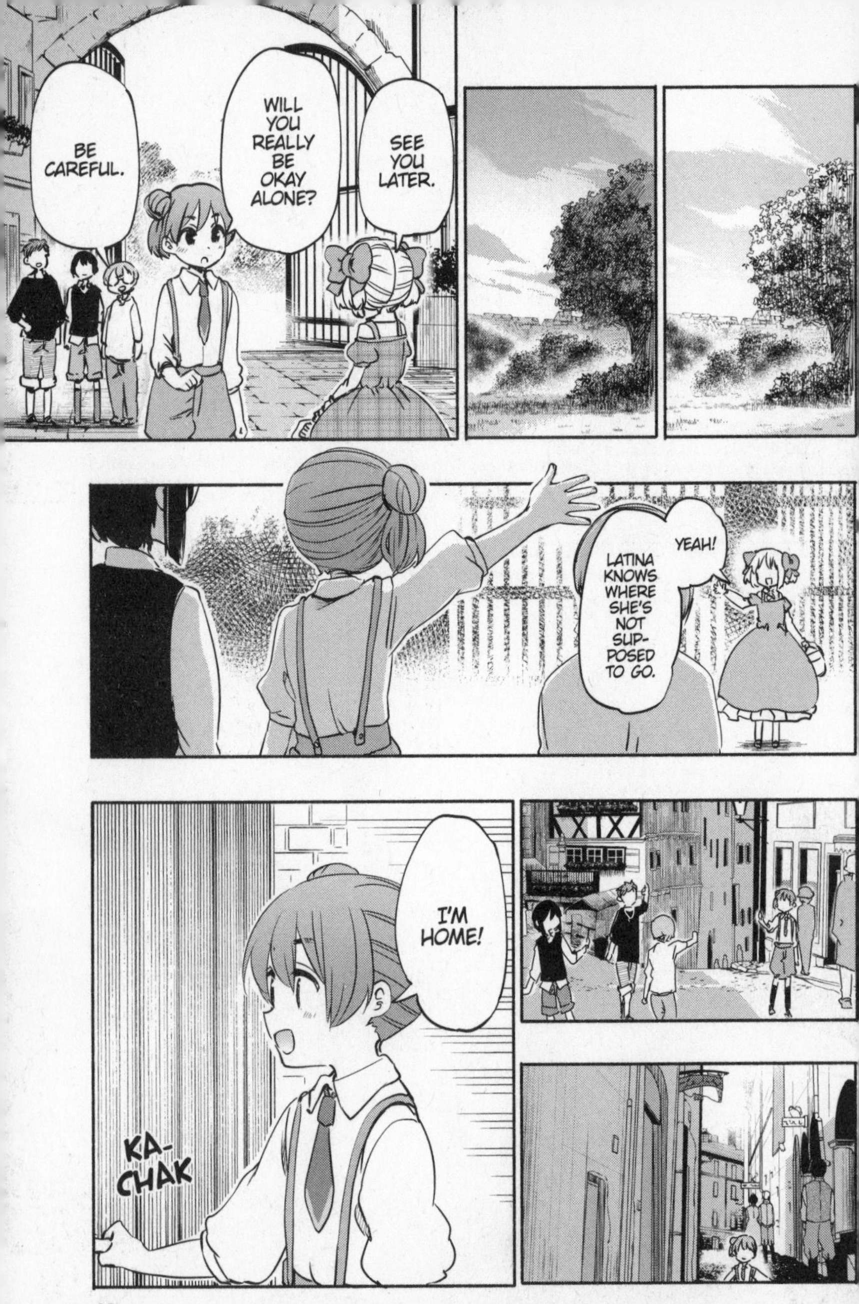
SEE YOU LATER.
WILL YOU REALLY BE OKAY ALONE?
BE CAREFUL.
YEAH!
LATINA KNOWS WHERE SHE'S NOT SUP-POSED TO GO.
I'M HOME!
KA-CHAK

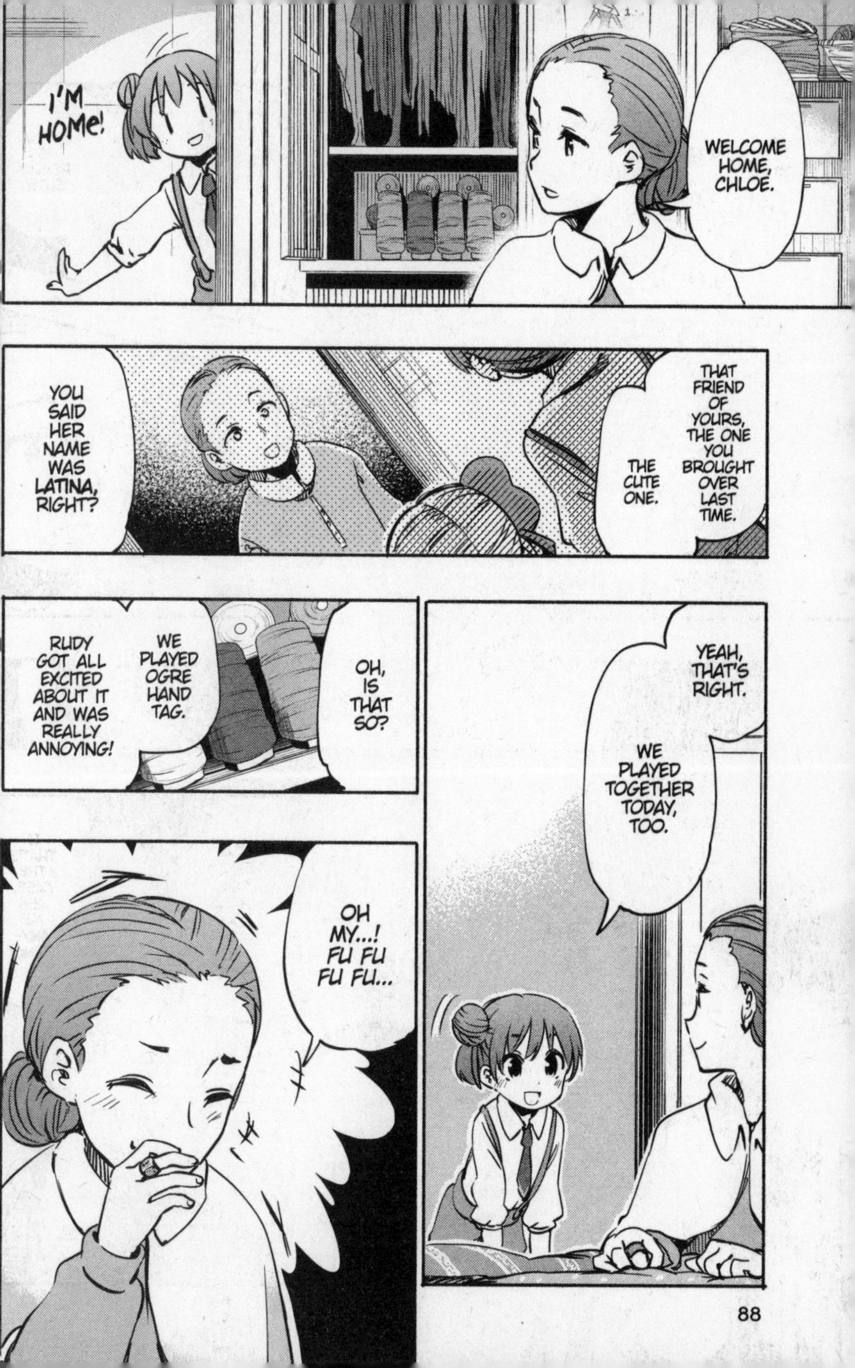

I'M HOME!
WELCOME HOME, CHLOE.
THAT FRIEND OF YOURS, THE ONE YOU BROUGHT OVER LAST TIME.
THE CUTE ONE.
YOU SAID HER NAME WAS LATINA, RIGHT?
YEAH, THAT'S RIGHT.
WE PLAYED TOGETHER TODAY, TOO.
OH, IS THAT SO?
WE PLAYED OGRE HAND TAG.
RUDY GOT ALL EXCITED ABOUT IT AND WAS REALLY ANNOYING!
OH MY...! FU FU FU FU...

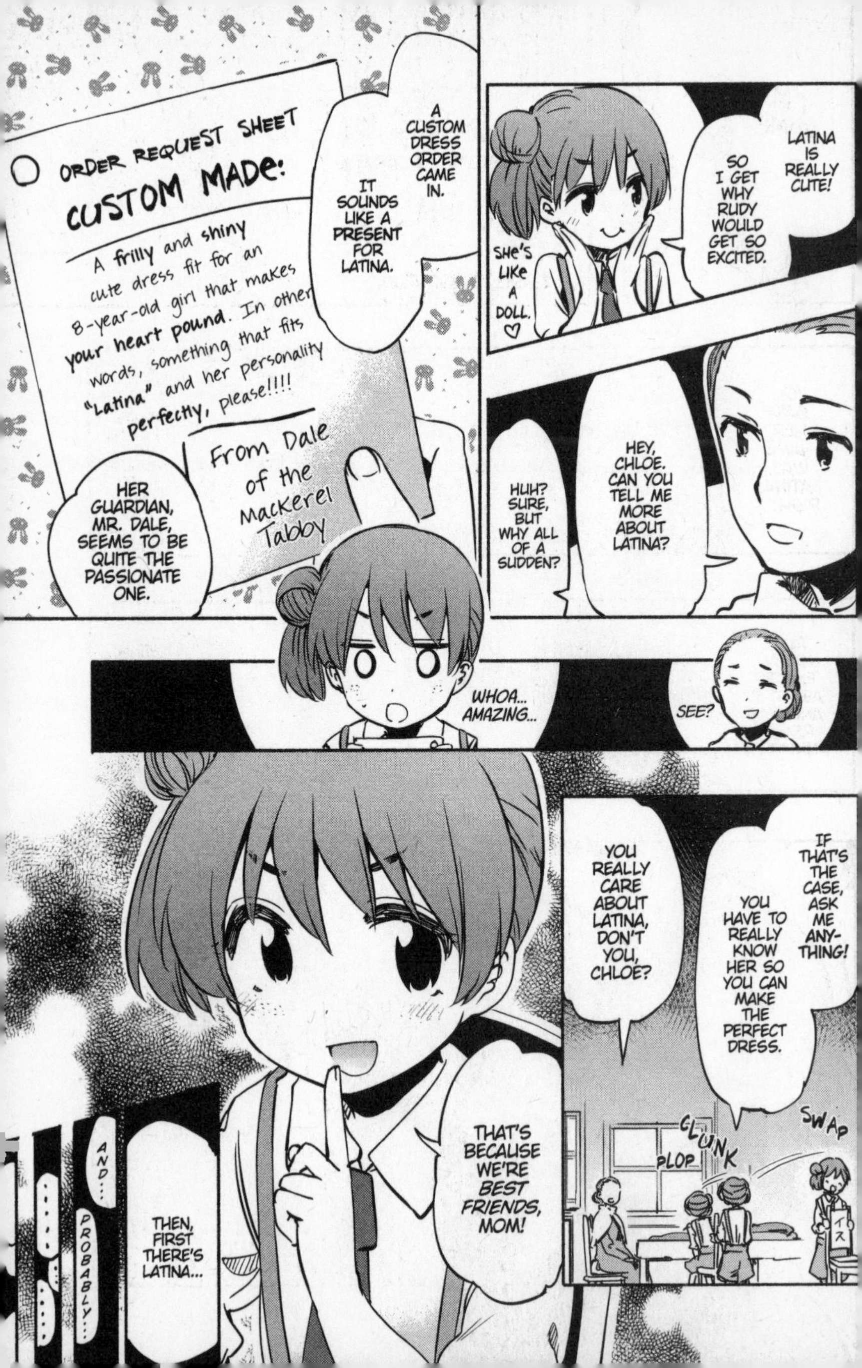
LATINA IS REALLY CUTE!
SO I GET WHY RUDY WOULD GET SO EXCITED.
SHE'S LIKE A DOLL. ♡
HEY, CHLOE. CAN YOU TELL ME MORE ABOUT LATINA?
HUH? SURE, BUT WHY ALL OF A SUDDEN?
A CUSTOM DRESS ORDER CAME IN.
IT SOUNDS LIKE A PRESENT FOR LATINA.
ORDER REQUEST SHEET
CUSTOM MADE:
A frilly and shiny cute dress fit for an 8-year-old girl that makes your heart pound. In other words, something that fits "Latina" and her personality perfectly, please!!!!
From Dale of the Mackerel Tabby
HER GUARDIAN, MR. DALE, SEEMS TO BE QUITE THE PASSIONATE ONE.
SEE?
WHOA... AMAZING...
IF THAT'S THE CASE, ASK ME ANYTHING!
YOU HAVE TO REALLY KNOW HER SO YOU CAN MAKE THE PERFECT DRESS.
YOU REALLY CARE ABOUT LATINA, DON'T YOU, CHLOE?
SWAP
CLUNK
PLOP
THAT'S BECAUSE WE'RE BEST FRIENDS, MOM!
THEN, FIRST THERE'S LATINA...
AND... PROBABLY...
......

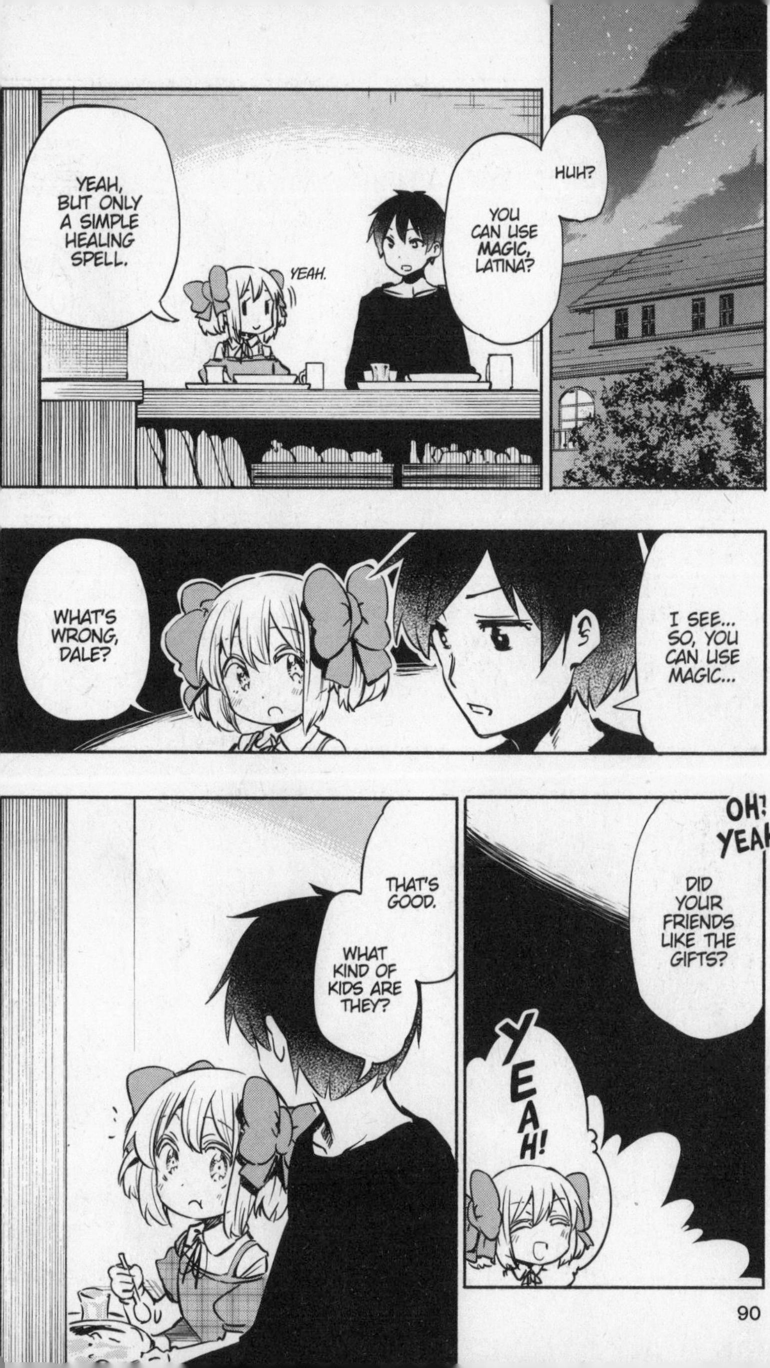
HUH?
YOU CAN USE MAGIC, LATINA?
YEAH.
YEAH, BUT ONLY A SIMPLE HEALING SPELL.
I SEE... SO, YOU CAN USE MAGIC...
WHAT'S WRONG, DALE?
OH! YEAH!
DID YOUR FRIENDS LIKE THE GIFTS?
YEAH!
THAT'S GOOD.
WHAT KIND OF KIDS ARE THEY?

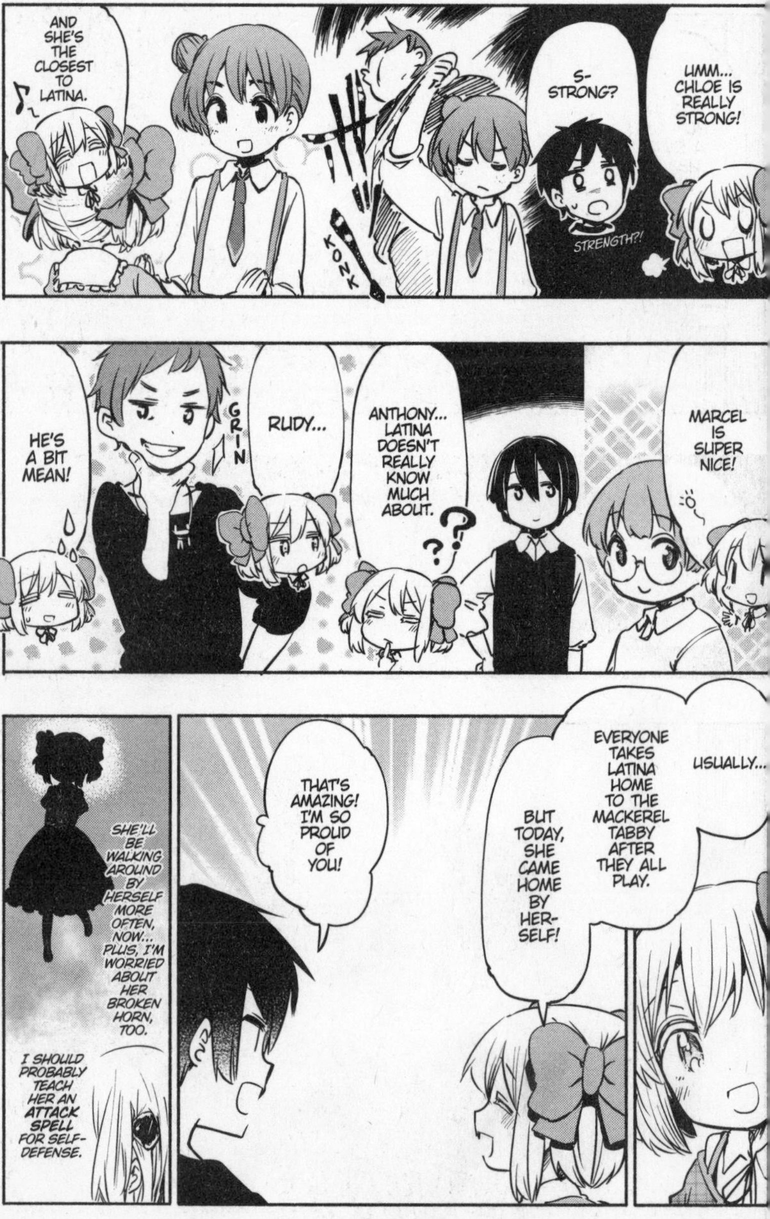
UMM... CHLOE IS REALLY STRONG!
S-STRONG?
STRENGTH?!
KONK
AND SHE'S THE CLOSEST TO LATINA.
MARCEL IS SUPER NICE!
ANTHONY... LATINA DOESN'T REALLY KNOW MUCH ABOUT.
RUDY...
GRIN
HE'S A BIT MEAN!
USUALLY...
EVERYONE TAKES LATINA HOME TO THE MACKEREL TABBY AFTER THEY ALL PLAY.
BUT TODAY, SHE CAME HOME BY HERSELF!
THAT'S AMAZING! I'M SO PROUD OF YOU!
SHE'LL BE WALKING AROUND BY HERSELF MORE OFTEN, NOW... PLUS, I'M WORRIED ABOUT HER BROKEN HORN, TOO.
I SHOULD PROBABLY TEACH HER AN ATTACK SPELL FOR SELF-DEFENSE.

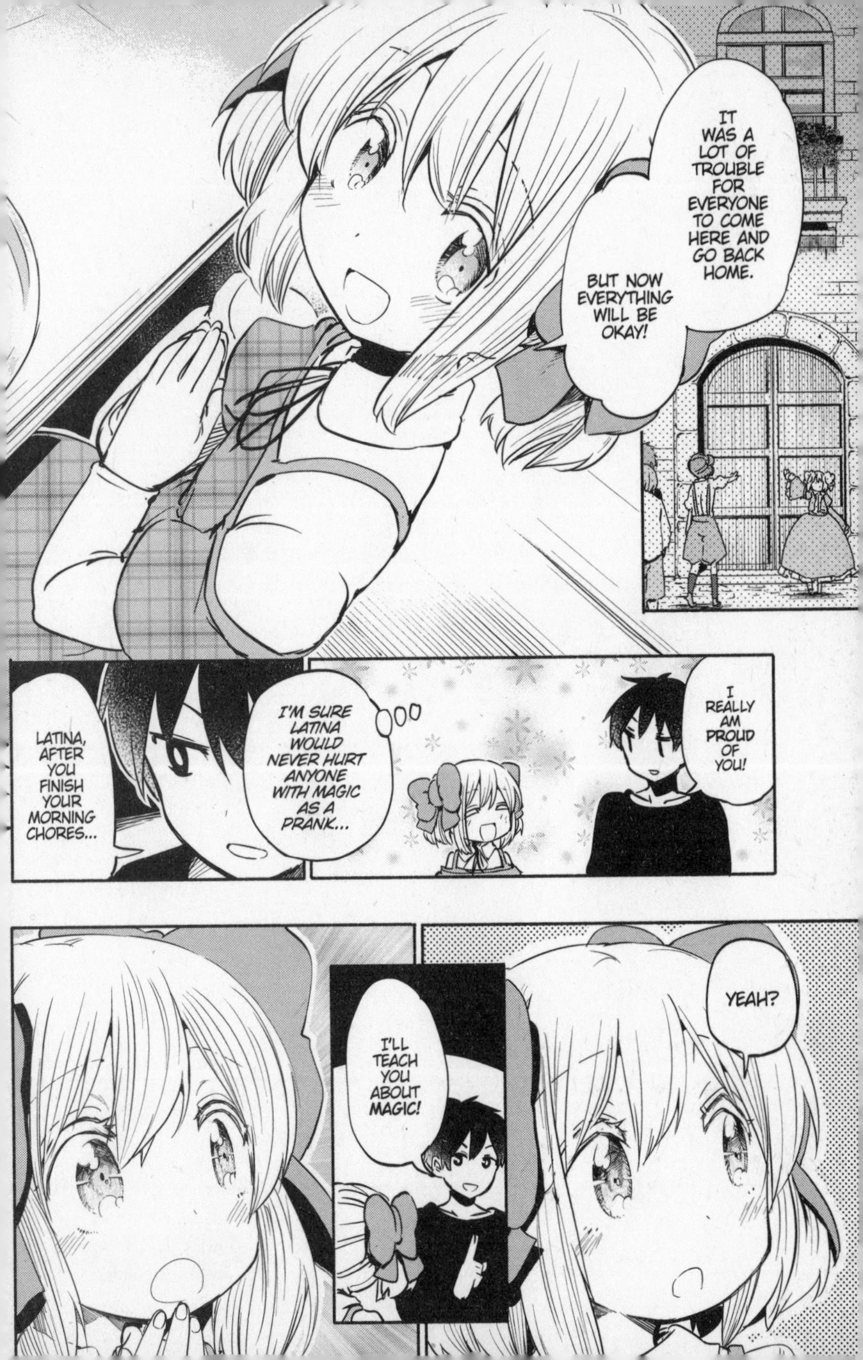
IT WAS A LOT OF TROUBLE FOR EVERYONE TO COME HERE AND GO BACK HOME.
BUT NOW EVERYTHING WILL BE OKAY!
I REALLY AM PROUD OF YOU!
I'M SURE LATINA WOULD NEVER HURT ANYONE WITH MAGIC AS A PRANK...
LATINA, AFTER YOU FINISH YOUR MORNING CHORES...
YEAH?
I'LL TEACH YOU ABOUT MAGIC!

IF It's
For My
Daughter
I'd Even DeFeat
a Demon
Lord

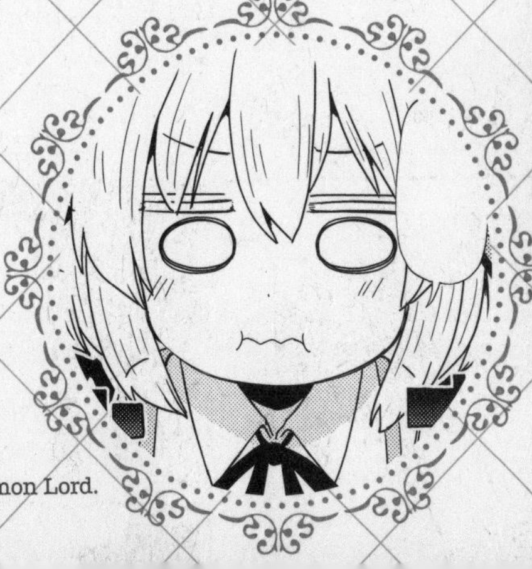

If It's For My Daughter, I'd Even Defeat a Demon Lord.

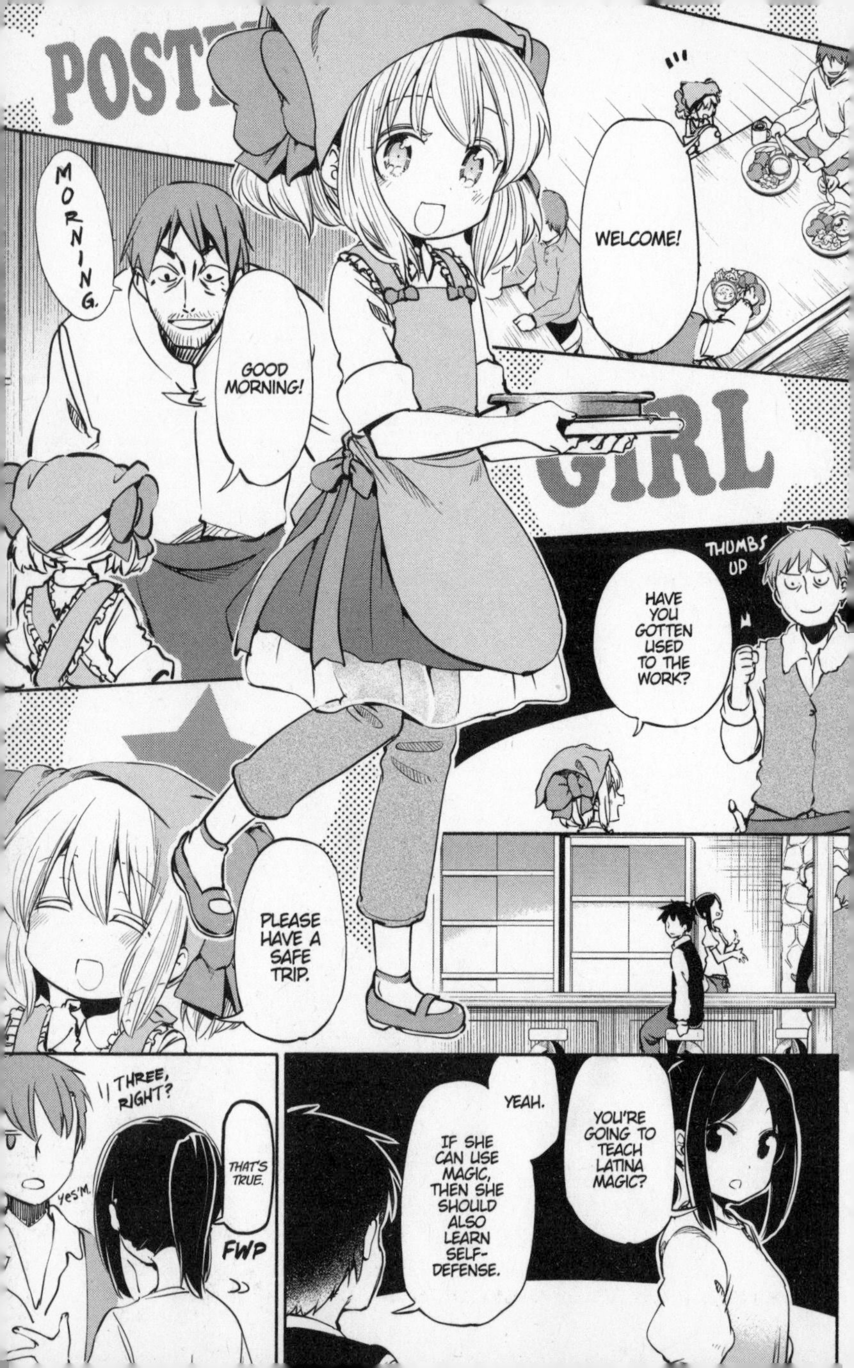

POST
WELCOME!
MORNING.
GOOD MORNING!
GIRL
THUMBS UP
HAVE YOU GOTTEN USED TO THE WORK?
PLEASE HAVE A SAFE TRIP.
YOU'RE GOING TO TEACH LATINA MAGIC?
YEAH.
IF SHE CAN USE MAGIC, THEN SHE SHOULD ALSO LEARN SELF-DEFENSE.
THREE, RIGHT?
THAT'S TRUE.
YES'M.
FWP

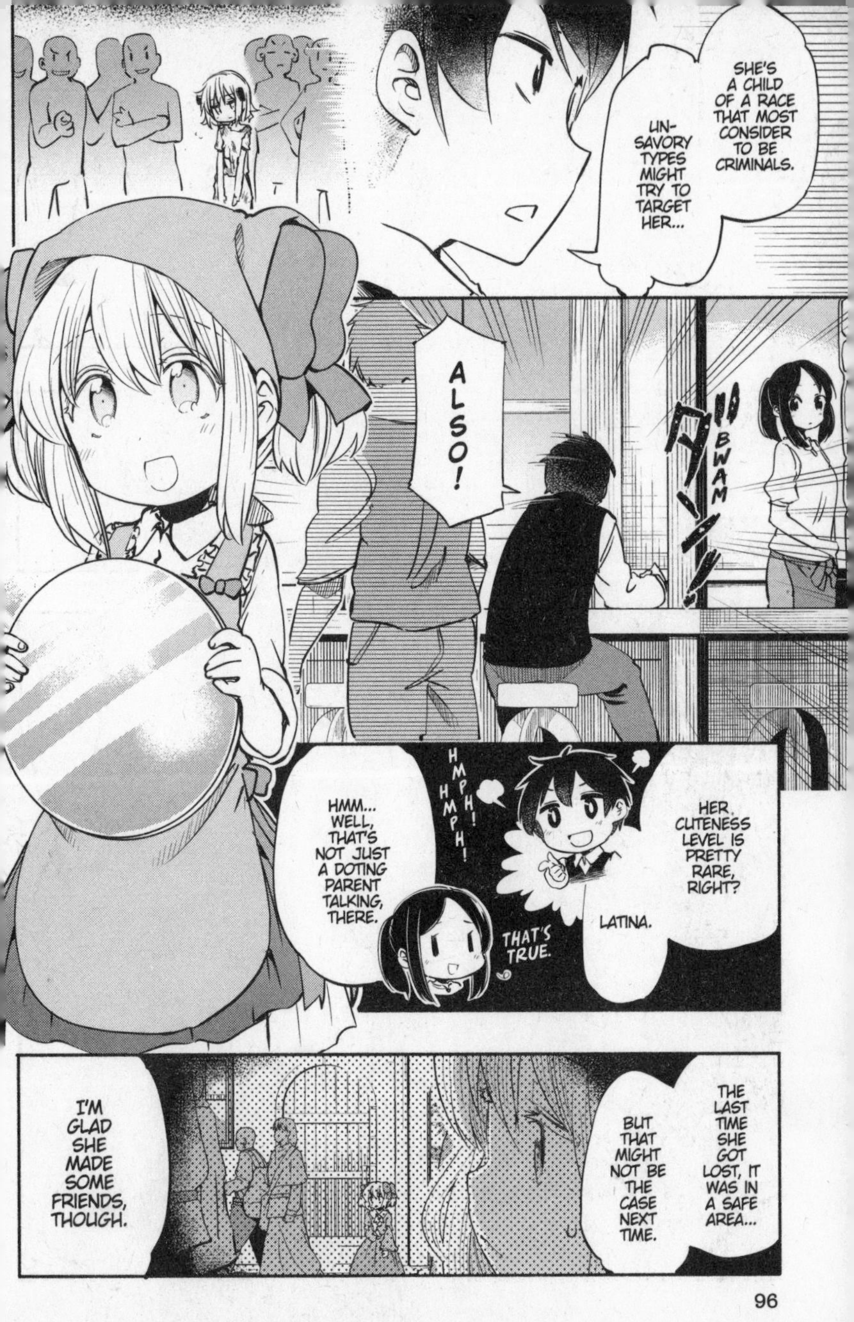
SHE'S A CHILD OF A RACE THAT MOST CONSIDER TO BE CRIMINALS.
UN-SAVORY TYPES MIGHT TRY TO TARGET HER...
BWAM
ALSO!
HER CUTENESS LEVEL IS PRETTY RARE, RIGHT?
HMPH HMPH!
LATINA.
HMM... WELL, THAT'S NOT JUST A DOTING PARENT TALKING, THERE.
THAT'S TRUE.
THE LAST TIME SHE GOT LOST, IT WAS IN A SAFE AREA...
BUT THAT MIGHT NOT BE THE CASE NEXT TIME.
I'M GLAD SHE MADE SOME FRIENDS, THOUGH.

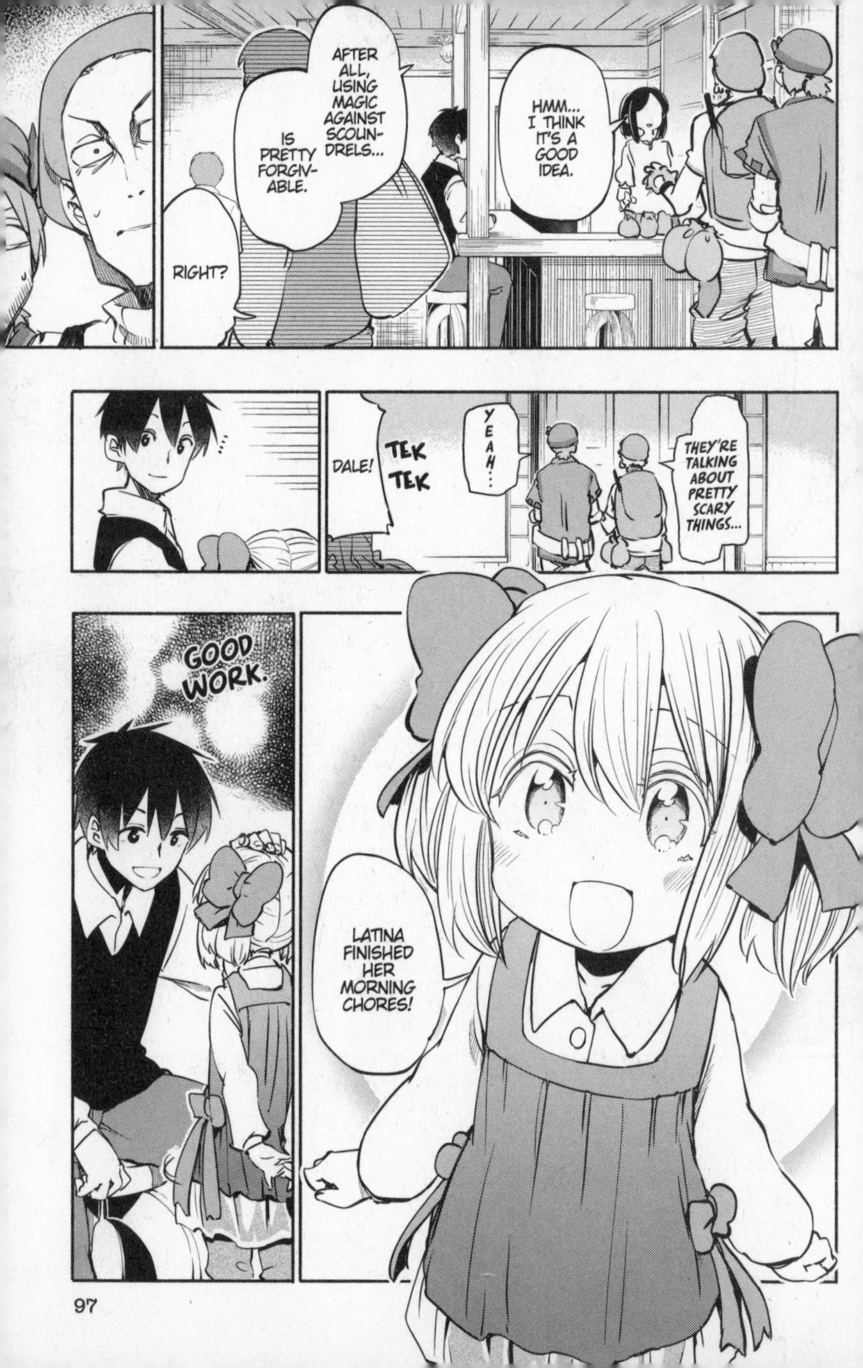

HMM... I THINK IT'S A GOOD IDEA.
AFTER ALL, USING MAGIC AGAINST SCOUN-DRELS...
IS PRETTY FORGIV-ABLE.
RIGHT?
THEY'RE TALKING ABOUT PRETTY SCARY THINGS...
YEAH...
TEK TEK
DALE!
LATINA FINISHED HER MORNING CHORES!
GOOD WORK.

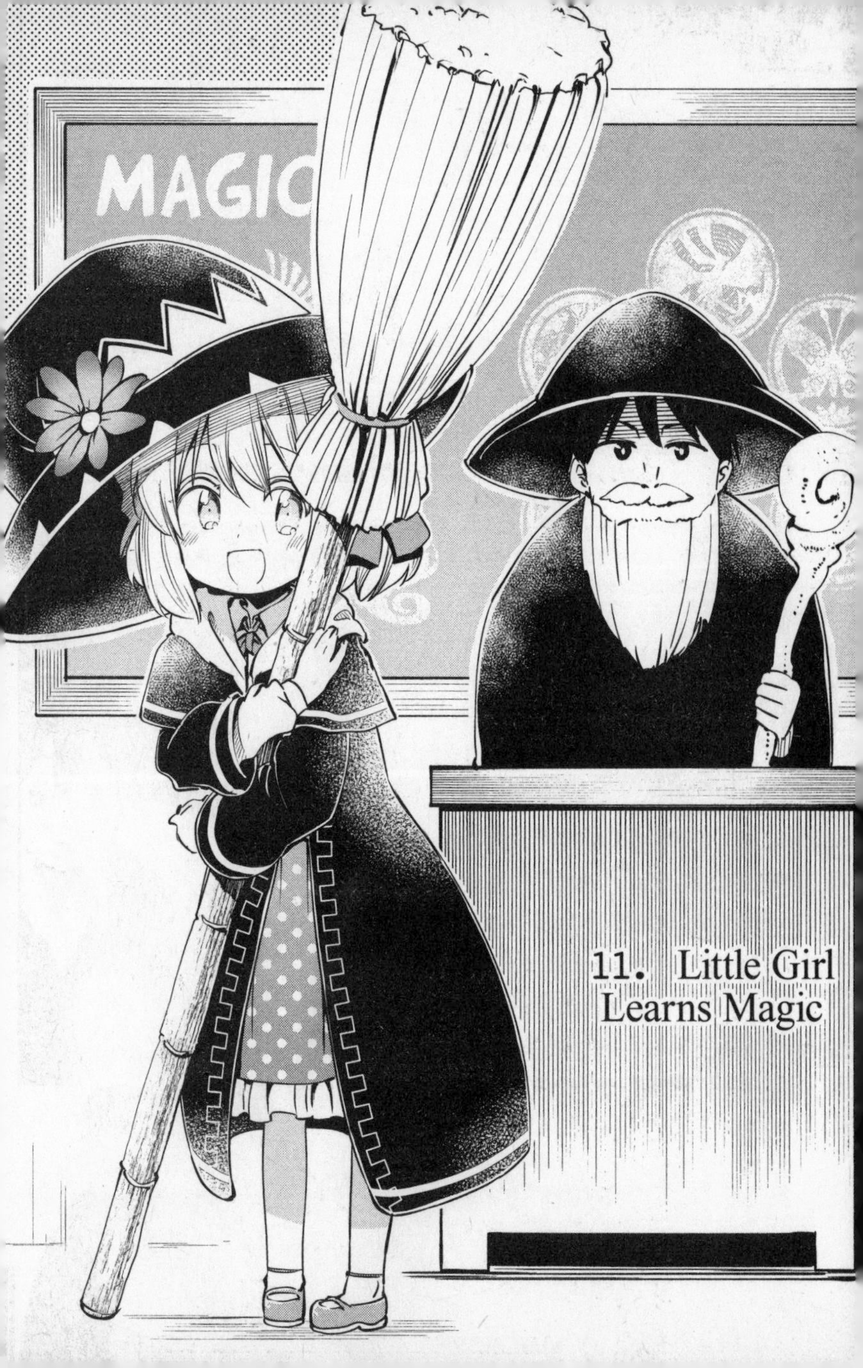
MAGIC
11. Little Girl Learns Magic

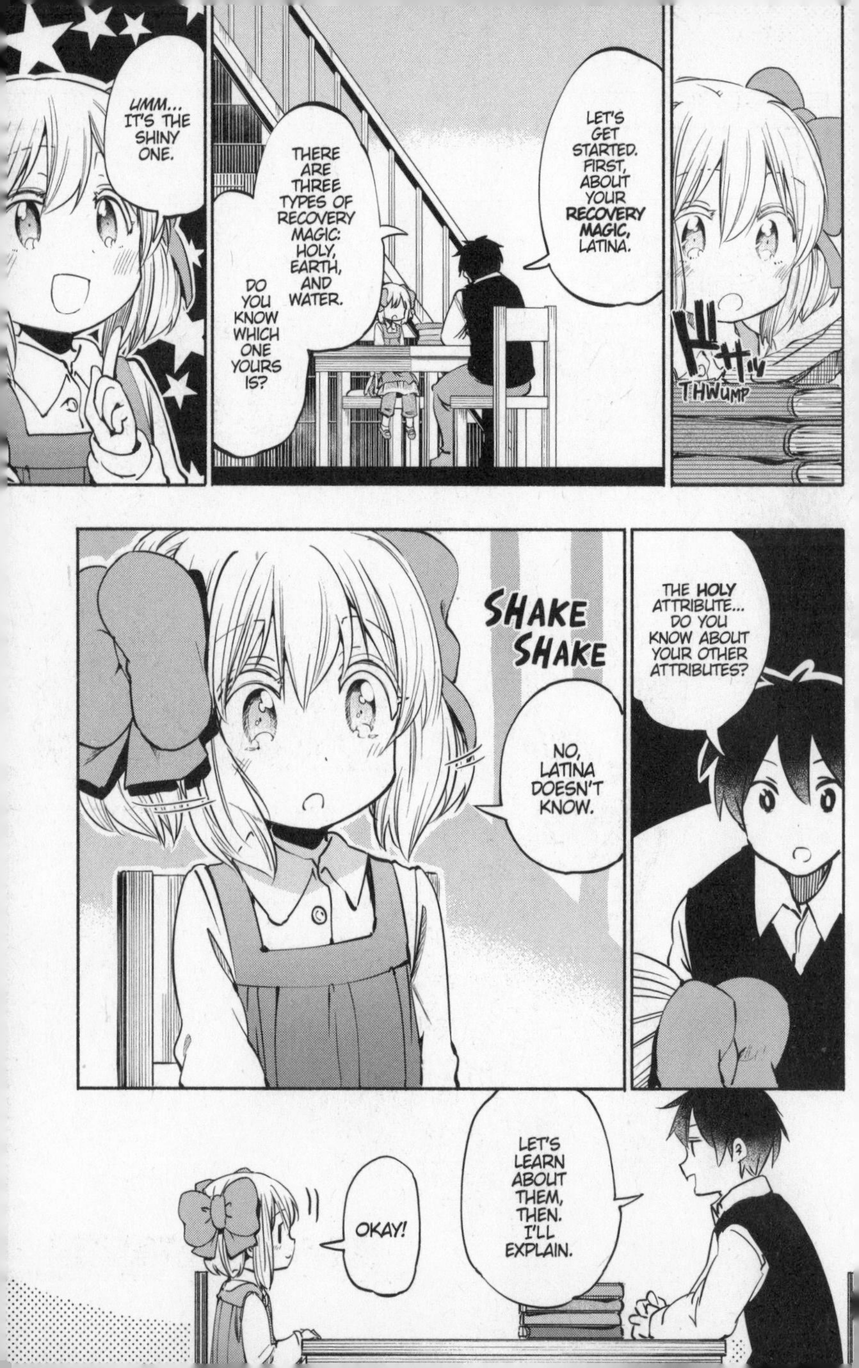
ドサッ
THWUMP
LET'S GET STARTED. FIRST, ABOUT YOUR RECOVERY MAGIC, LATINA.
THERE ARE THREE TYPES OF RECOVERY MAGIC: HOLY, EARTH, AND WATER.
DO YOU KNOW WHICH ONE YOURS IS?
UMM... IT'S THE SHINY ONE.
THE HOLY ATTRIBUTE... DO YOU KNOW ABOUT YOUR OTHER ATTRIBUTES?
SHAKE SHAKE
NO, LATINA DOESN'T KNOW.
LET'S LEARN ABOUT THEM, THEN. I'LL EXPLAIN.
OKAY!

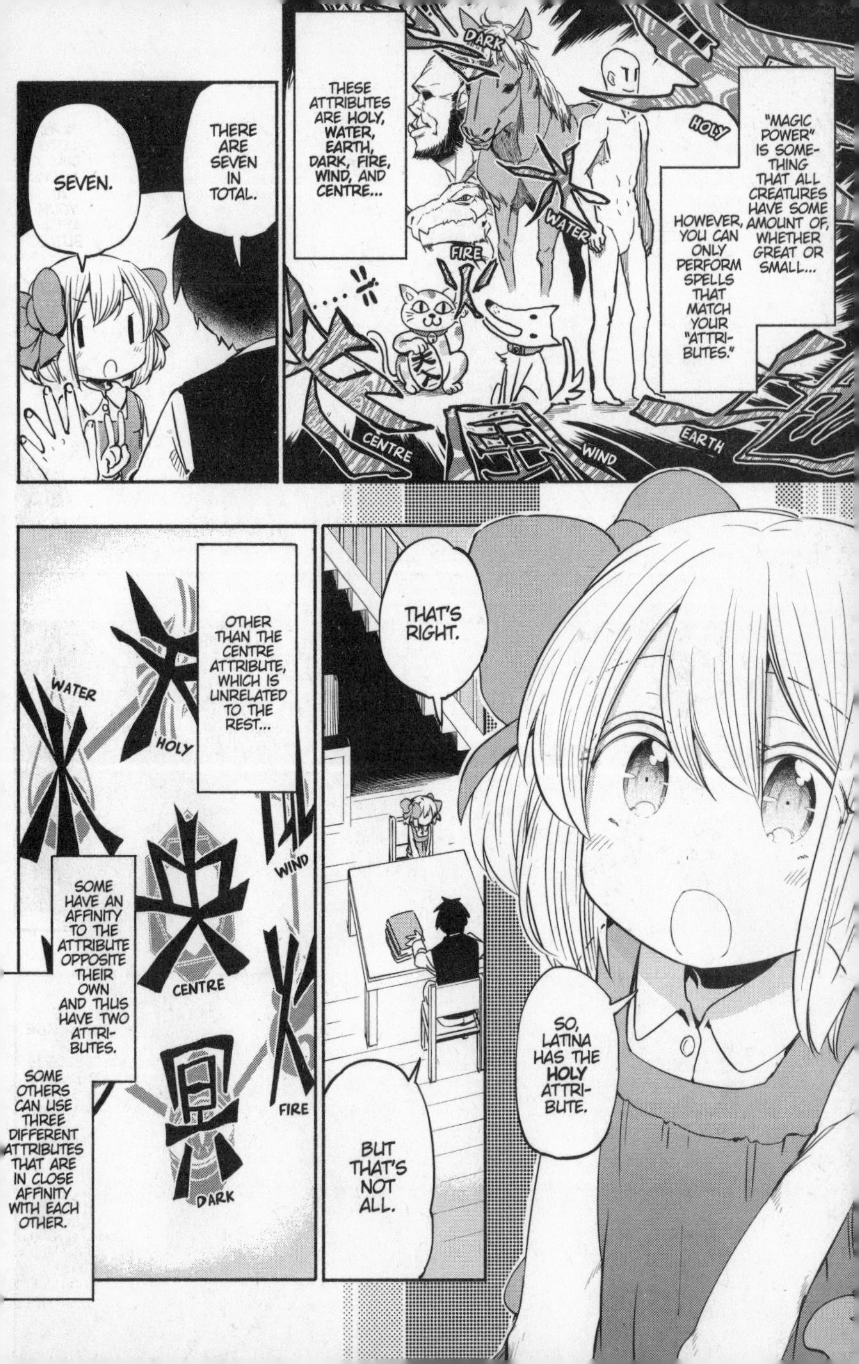
"MAGIC POWER" IS SOMETHING THAT ALL CREATURES HAVE SOME AMOUNT OF, WHETHER GREAT OR SMALL...
HOWEVER, YOU CAN ONLY PERFORM SPELLS THAT MATCH YOUR "ATTRIBUTES."
DARK
HOLY
THESE ATTRIBUTES ARE HOLY, WATER, EARTH, DARK, FIRE, WIND, AND CENTRE...
WATER
FIRE
EARTH
WIND
CENTRE
THERE ARE SEVEN IN TOTAL.
SEVEN.
SO, LATINA HAS THE HOLY ATTRIBUTE.
THAT'S RIGHT.
BUT THAT'S NOT ALL.
OTHER THAN THE CENTRE ATTRIBUTE, WHICH IS UNRELATED TO THE REST...
HOLY
WATER
WIND
SOME HAVE AN AFFINITY TO THE ATTRIBUTE OPPOSITE THEIR OWN AND THUS HAVE TWO ATTRIBUTES.
CENTRE
FIRE
DARK
SOME OTHERS CAN USE THREE DIFFERENT ATTRIBUTES THAT ARE IN CLOSE AFFINITY WITH EACH OTHER.

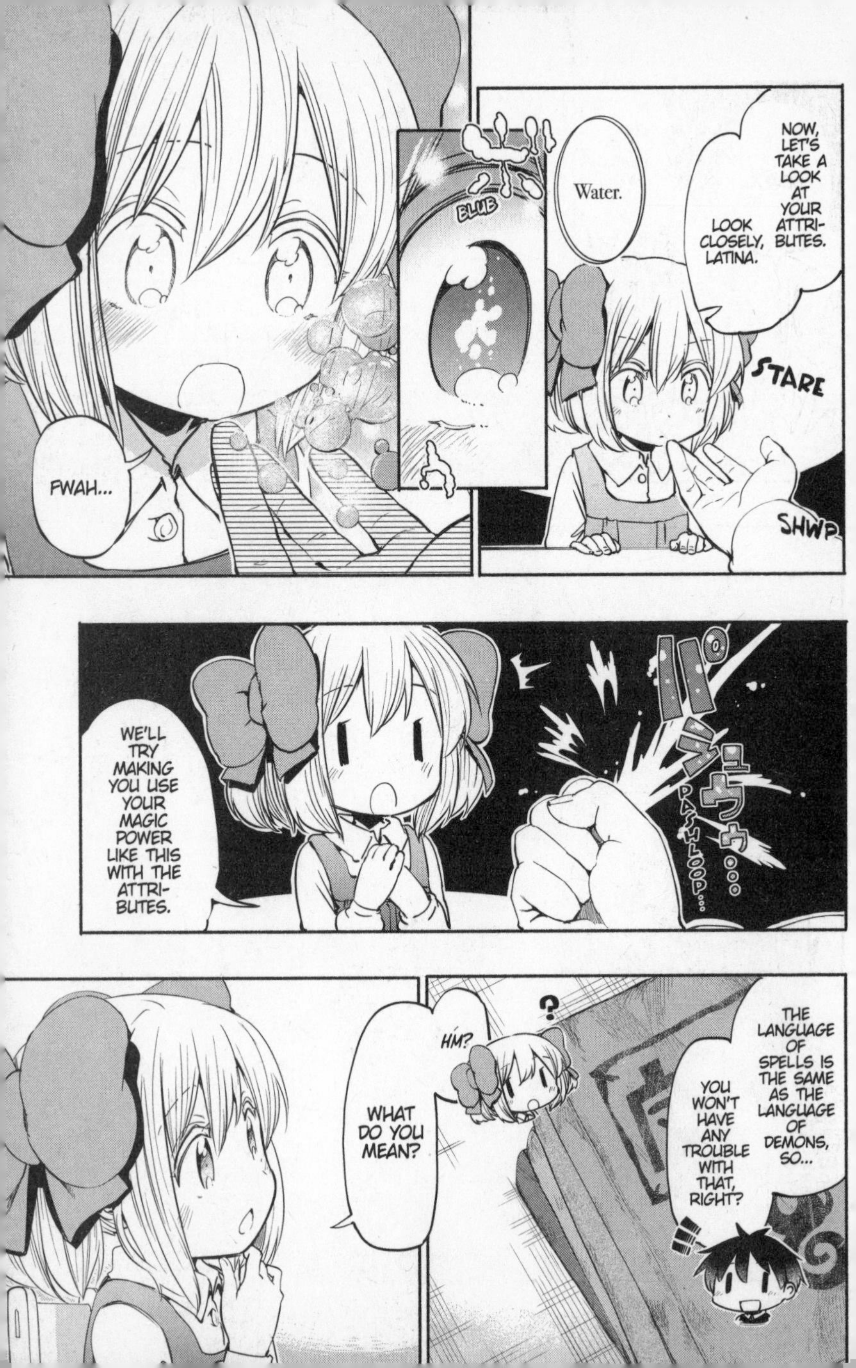
NOW, LET'S TAKE A LOOK AT YOUR ATTRIBUTES.
LOOK CLOSELY, LATINA.
STARE
SHWP
Water.
BLUB
FWAH...
PASHLOOP...
WE'LL TRY MAKING YOU USE YOUR MAGIC POWER LIKE THIS WITH THE ATTRIBUTES.
THE LANGUAGE OF SPELLS IS THE SAME AS THE LANGUAGE OF DEMONS, SO...
YOU WON'T HAVE ANY TROUBLE WITH THAT, RIGHT?
HM?
WHAT DO YOU MEAN?

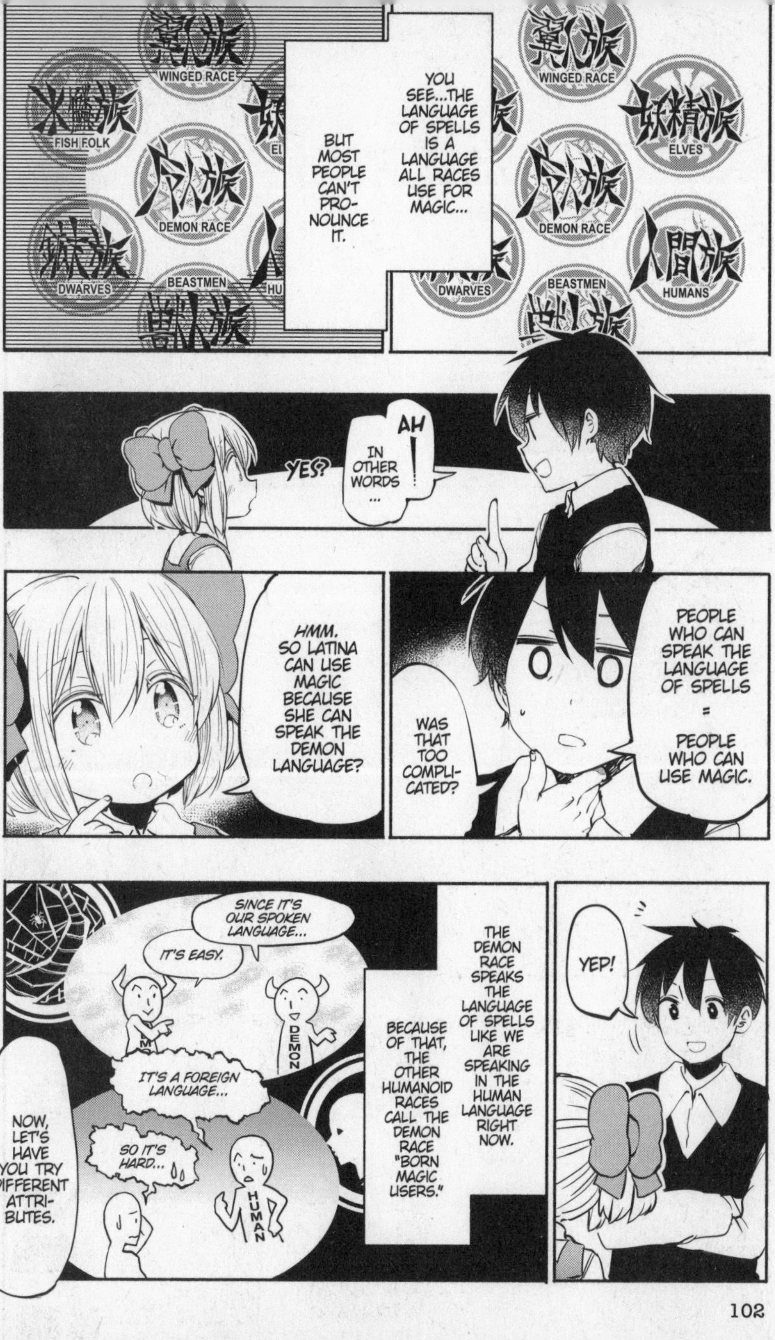
YOU SEE...THE LANGUAGE OF SPELLS IS A LANGUAGE ALL RACES USE FOR MAGIC...
WINGED RACE
ELVES
DEMON RACE
HUMANS
BEASTMEN
DWARVES
BUT MOST PEOPLE CAN'T PRO-NOUNCE IT.
WINGED RACE
FISH FOLK
DEMON RACE
DWARVES
BEASTMEN
AH! IN OTHER WORDS...
YES?
PEOPLE WHO CAN SPEAK THE LANGUAGE OF SPELLS = PEOPLE WHO CAN USE MAGIC.
WAS THAT TOO COMPLICATED?
HMM. SO LATINA CAN USE MAGIC BECAUSE SHE CAN SPEAK THE DEMON LANGUAGE?
YEP!
THE DEMON RACE SPEAKS THE LANGUAGE OF SPELLS LIKE WE ARE SPEAKING IN THE HUMAN LANGUAGE RIGHT NOW.
BECAUSE OF THAT, THE OTHER HUMANOID RACES CALL THE DEMON RACE "BORN MAGIC USERS."
SINCE IT'S OUR SPOKEN LANGUAGE...
IT'S EASY.
DEMON
IT'S A FOREIGN LANGUAGE...
SO IT'S HARD...
HUMAN
NOW, LET'S HAVE YOU TRY DIFFERENT ATTRI-BUTES.

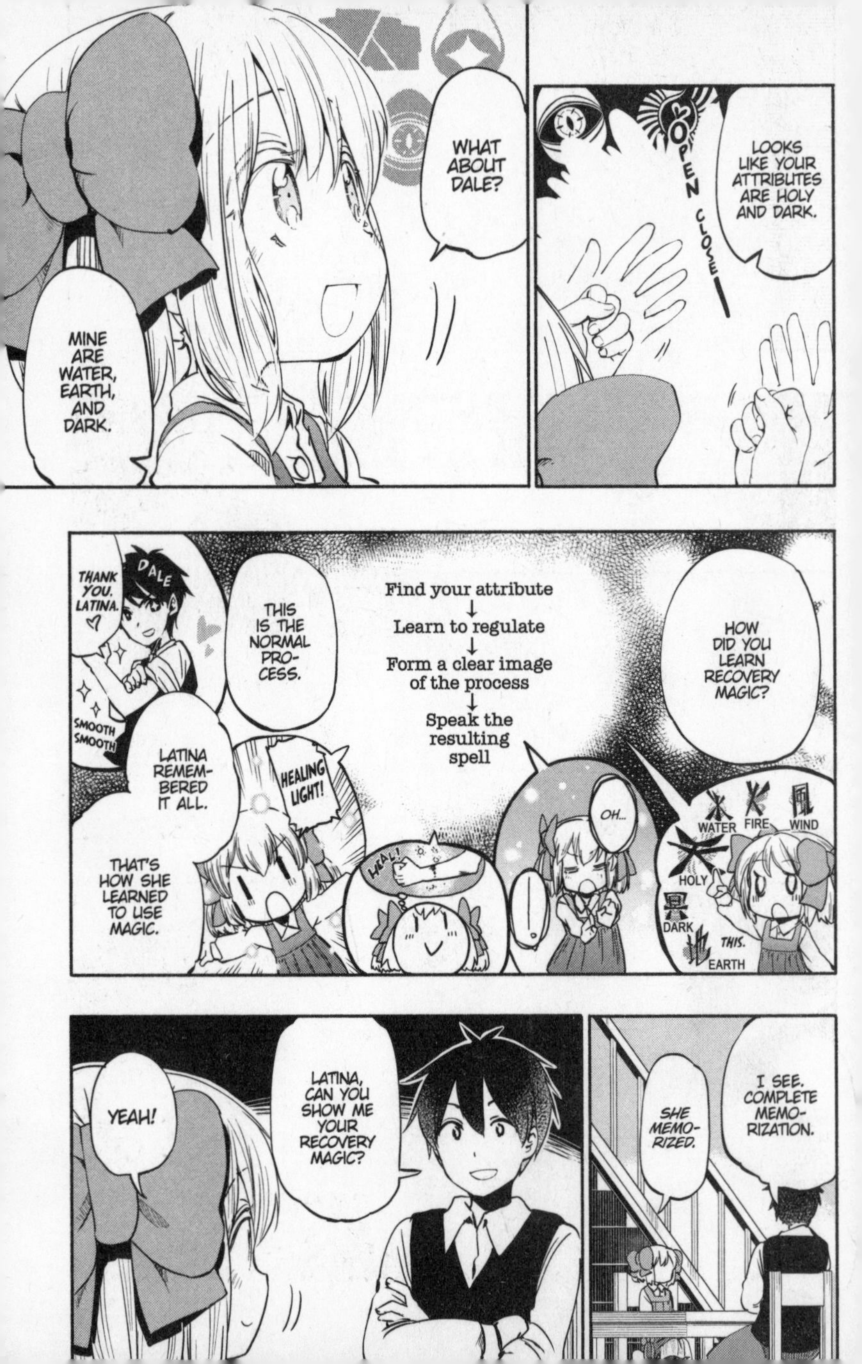
LOOKS LIKE YOUR ATTRIBUTES ARE HOLY AND DARK.
OPEN
CLOSE
WHAT ABOUT DALE?
MINE ARE WATER, EARTH, AND DARK.
HOW DID YOU LEARN RECOVERY MAGIC?
WATER
FIRE
WIND
HOLY
DARK
EARTH
THIS.
OH...
Find your attribute ↓ Learn to regulate ↓ Form a clear image of the process ↓ Speak the resulting spell
HEAL!
HEALING LIGHT!
THIS IS THE NORMAL PROCESS.
DALE
THANK YOU. LATINA.
SMOOTH SMOOTH
LATINA REMEMBERED IT ALL.
THAT'S HOW SHE LEARNED TO USE MAGIC.
I SEE. COMPLETE MEMORIZATION.
SHE MEMORIZED.
LATINA, CAN YOU SHOW ME YOUR RECOVERY MAGIC?
YEAH!

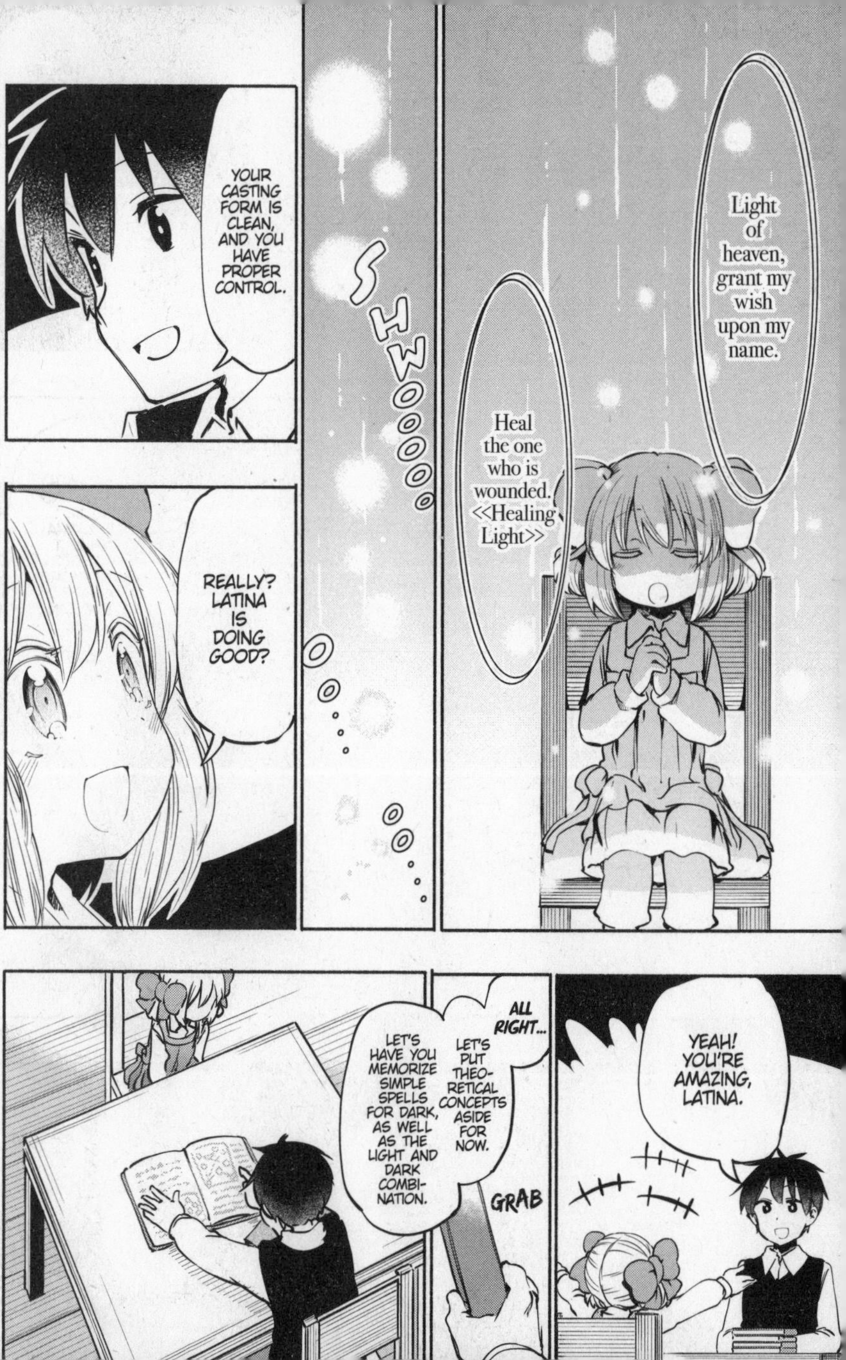
Light of heaven, grant my wish upon my name.
Heal the one who is wounded. <<Healing Light>>
SHWOOOOOO
YOUR CASTING FORM IS CLEAN, AND YOU HAVE PROPER CONTROL.
REALLY? LATINA IS DOING GOOD?
YEAH! YOU'RE AMAZING, LATINA.
ALL RIGHT...
LET'S PUT THEO-RETICAL CONCEPTS ASIDE FOR NOW.
LET'S HAVE YOU MEMORIZE SIMPLE SPELLS FOR DARK, AS WELL AS THE LIGHT AND DARK COMBI-NATION.
GRAB

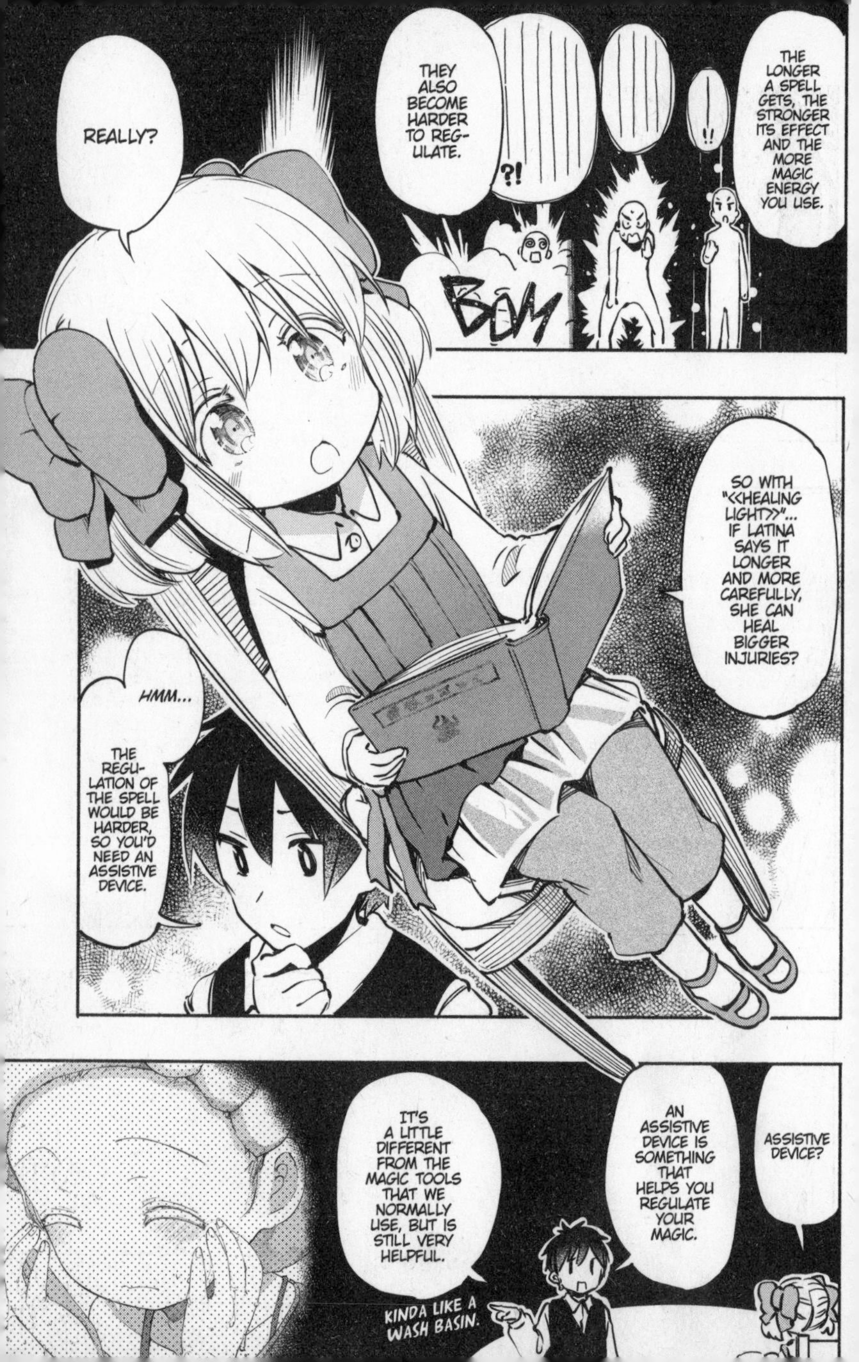
THE LONGER A SPELL GETS, THE STRONGER ITS EFFECT AND THE MORE MAGIC ENERGY YOU USE.
!!
?!
THEY ALSO BECOME HARDER TO REG-ULATE.
BOM
REALLY?
SO WITH "<<HEALING LIGHT>>"... IF LATINA SAYS IT LONGER AND MORE CAREFULLY, SHE CAN HEAL BIGGER INJURIES?
HMM...
THE REGU-LATION OF THE SPELL WOULD BE HARDER, SO YOU'D NEED AN ASSISTIVE DEVICE.
ASSISTIVE DEVICE?
AN ASSISTIVE DEVICE IS SOMETHING THAT HELPS YOU REGULATE YOUR MAGIC.
IT'S A LITTLE DIFFERENT FROM THE MAGIC TOOLS THAT WE NORMALLY USE, BUT IS STILL VERY HELPFUL.
KINDA LIKE A WASH BASIN.

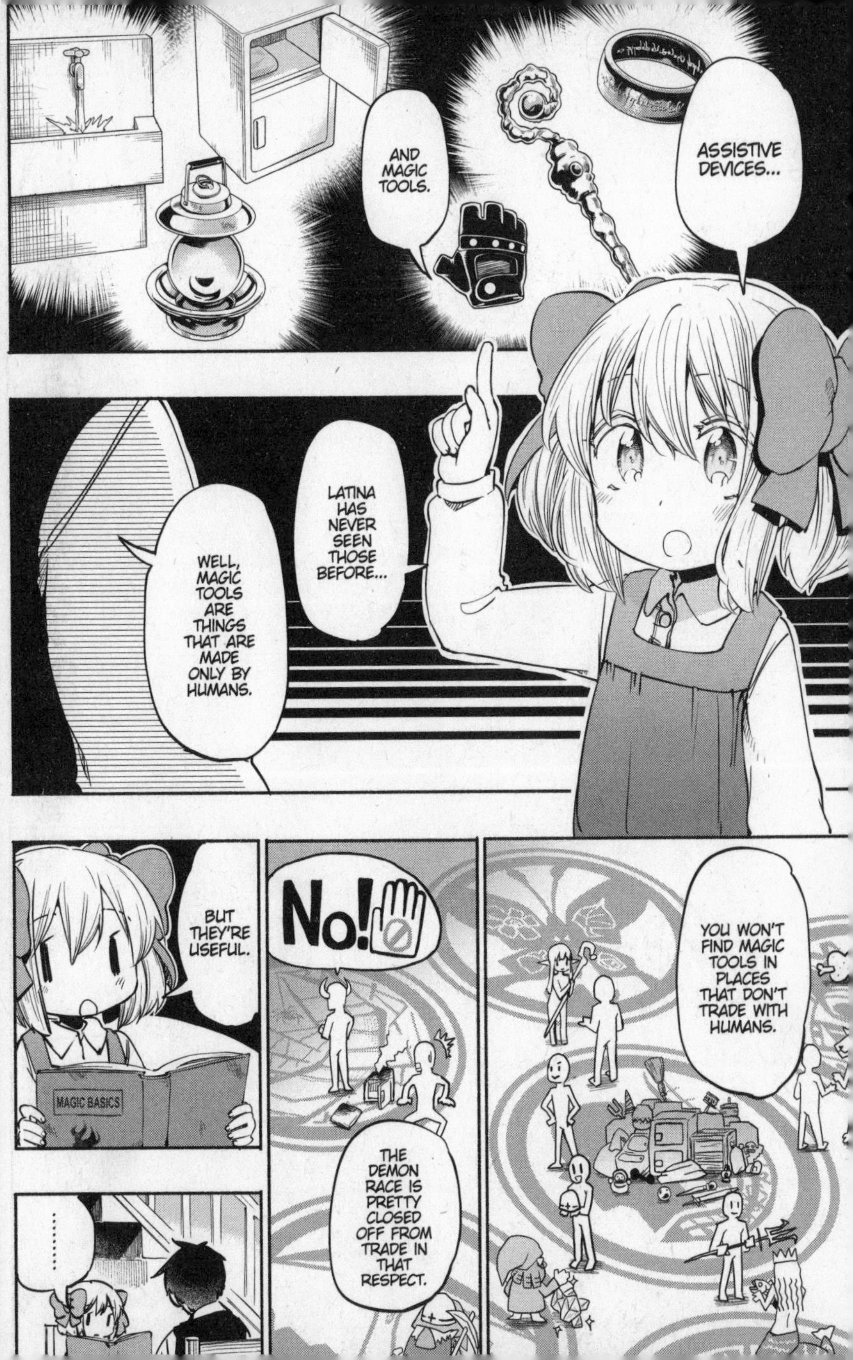
ASSISTIVE DEVICES...
AND MAGIC TOOLS.
LATINA HAS NEVER SEEN THOSE BEFORE...
WELL, MAGIC TOOLS ARE THINGS THAT ARE MADE ONLY BY HUMANS.
YOU WON'T FIND MAGIC TOOLS IN PLACES THAT DON'T TRADE WITH HUMANS.
No!
THE DEMON RACE IS PRETTY CLOSED OFF FROM TRADE IN THAT RESPECT.
BUT THEY'RE USEFUL.
MAGIC BASICS
......

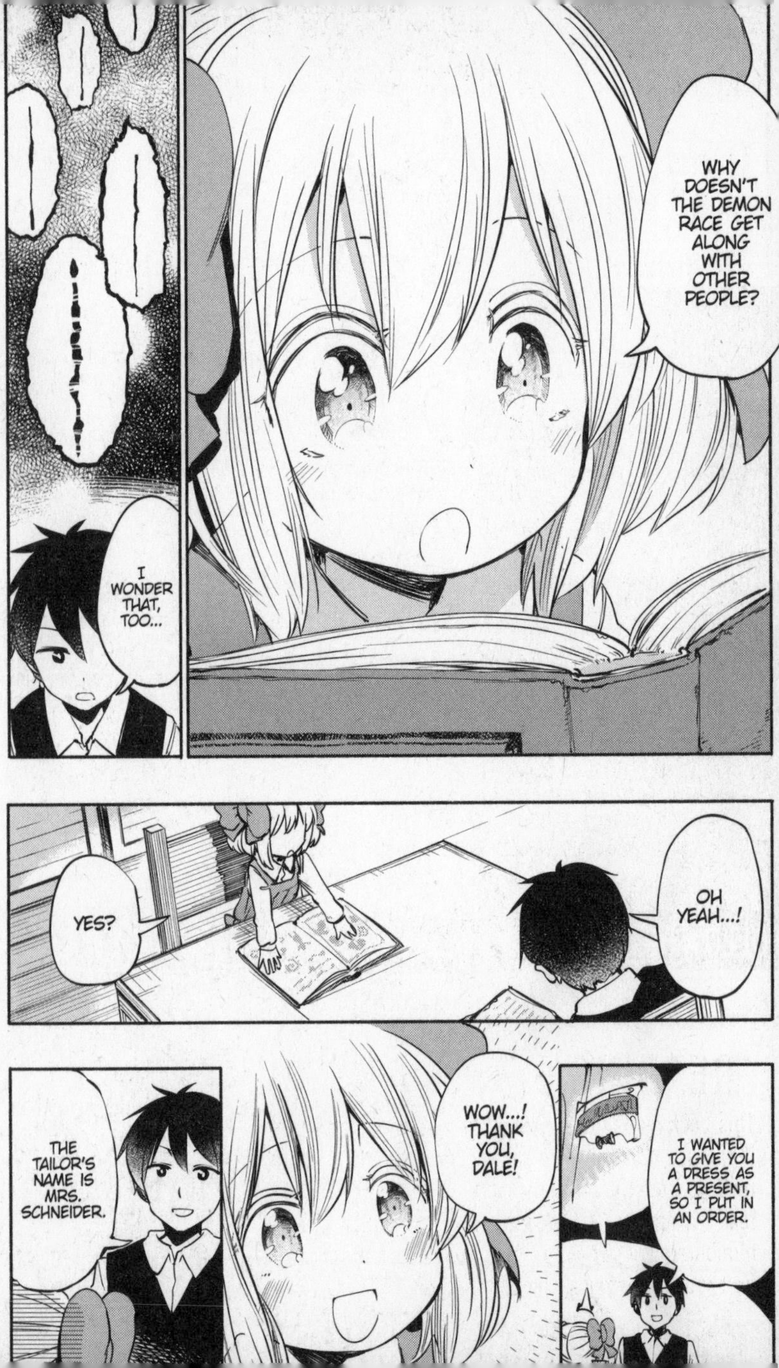
WHY DOESN'T THE DEMON RACE GET ALONG WITH OTHER PEOPLE?
I WONDER THAT, TOO...
OH YEAH...!
YES?
I WANTED TO GIVE YOU A DRESS AS A PRESENT, SO I PUT IN AN ORDER.
WOW...! THANK YOU, DALE!
THE TAILOR'S NAME IS MRS. SCHNEIDER.

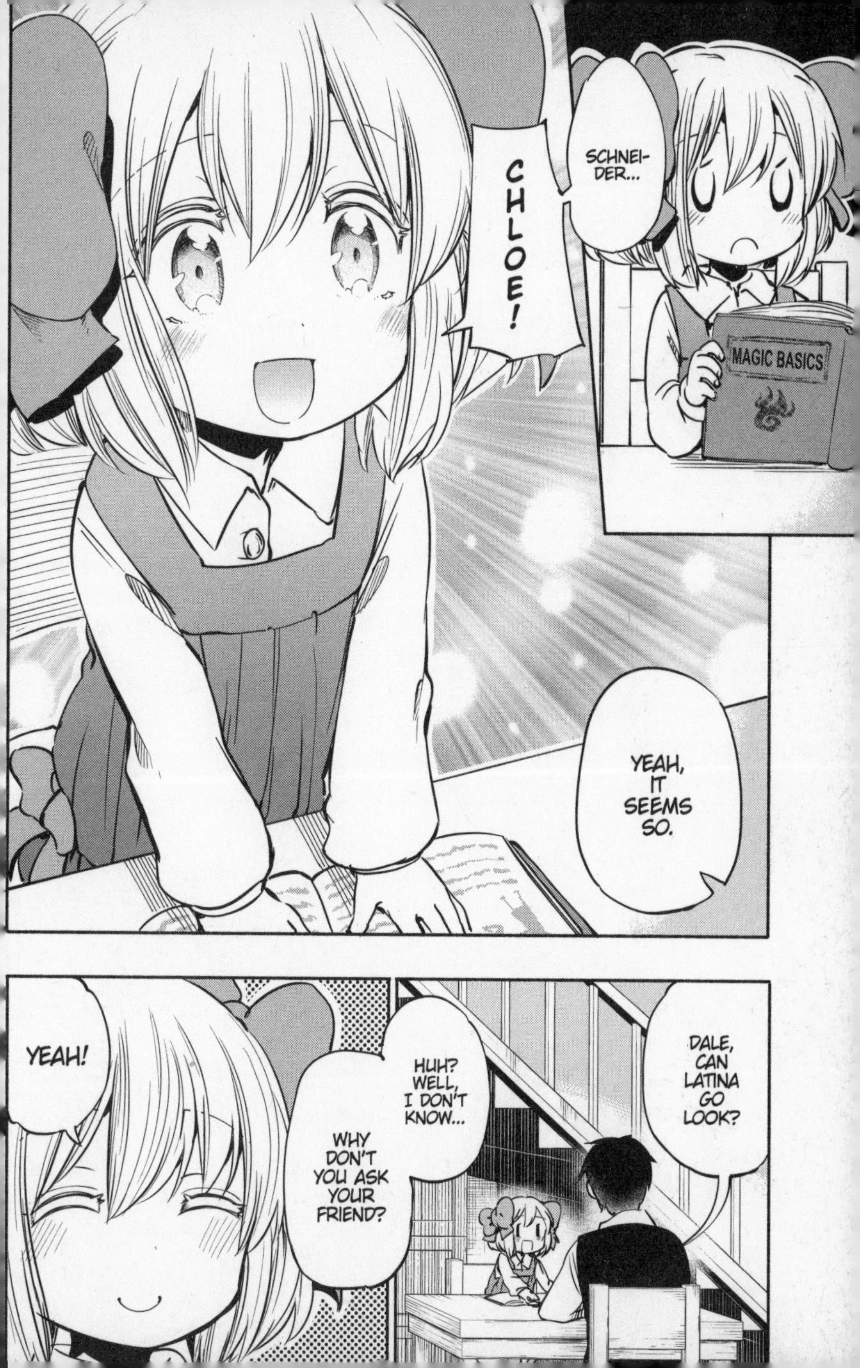
SCHNEI-DER...
MAGIC BASICS
CHLOE!
YEAH, IT SEEMS SO.
DALE, CAN LATINA GO LOOK?
HUH? WELL, I DON'T KNOW...
WHY DON'T YOU ASK YOUR FRIEND?
YEAH!

IF It's
For My
Daughter
I'd Even Defeat
a Demon
Lord

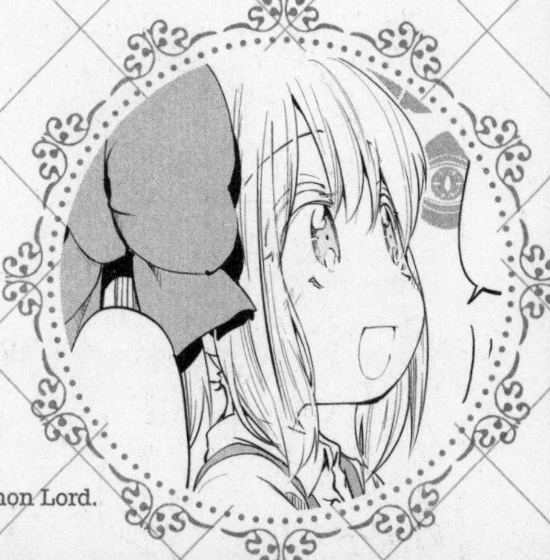

If It's For My Daughter, I'd Even Defeat a Demon Lord.

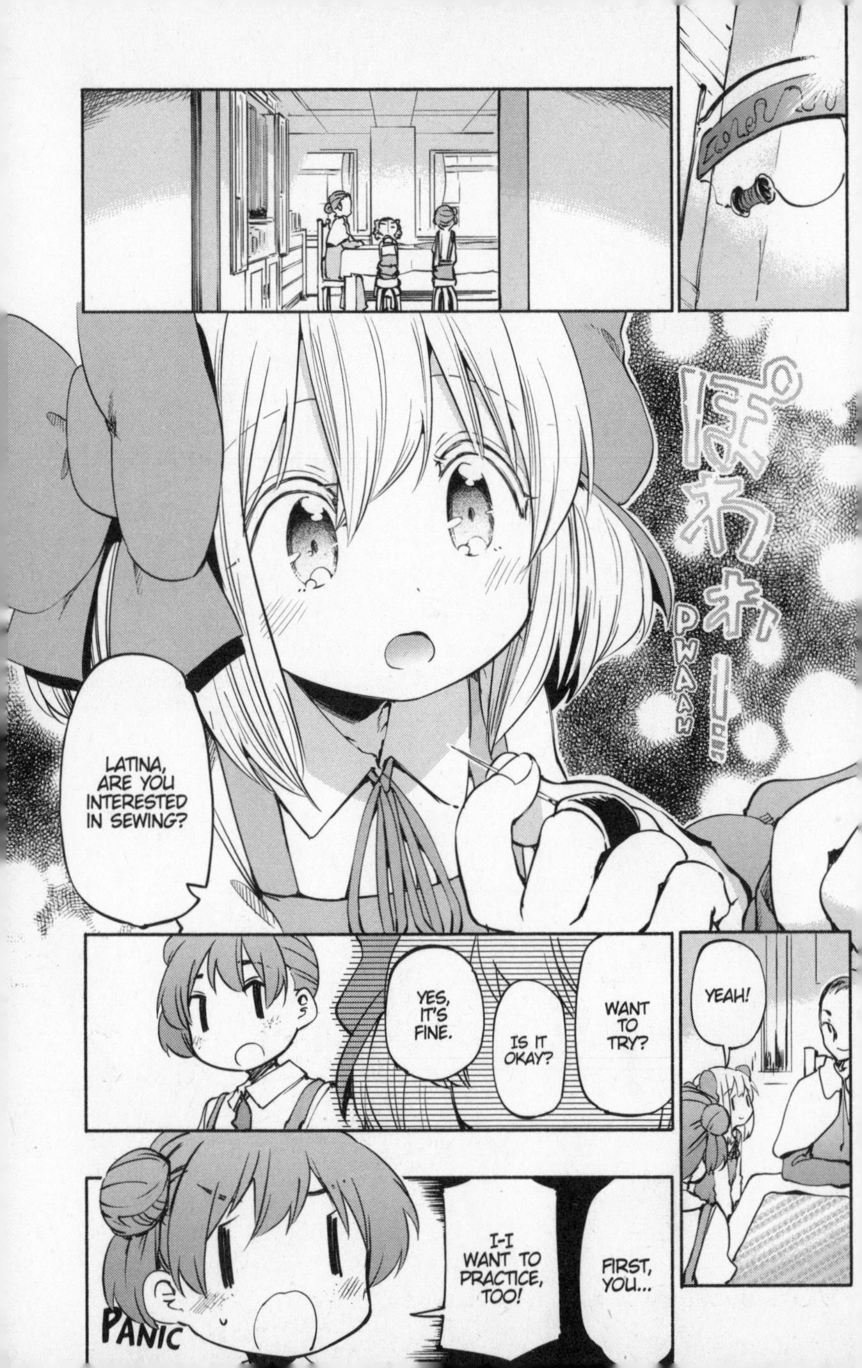
ぽあー!!!
PWAAH
LATINA, ARE YOU INTERESTED IN SEWING?
YEAH!
WANT TO TRY?
IS IT OKAY?
YES, IT'S FINE.
FIRST, YOU...
I-I WANT TO PRACTICE, TOO!
PANIC

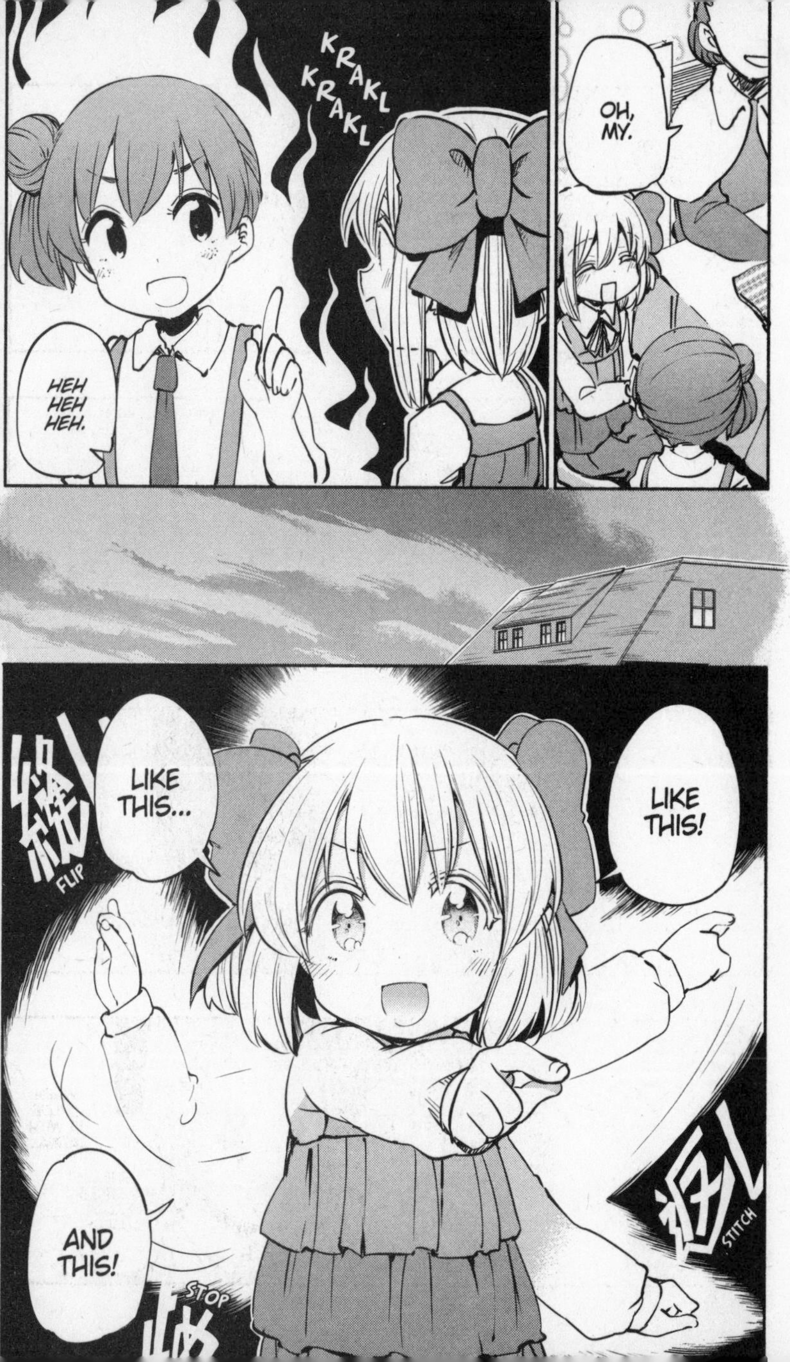
OH, MY.
KRAKL KRAKL
HEH HEH HEH.
LIKE THIS!
LIKE THIS...
FLIP
STITCH
AND THIS!
STOP

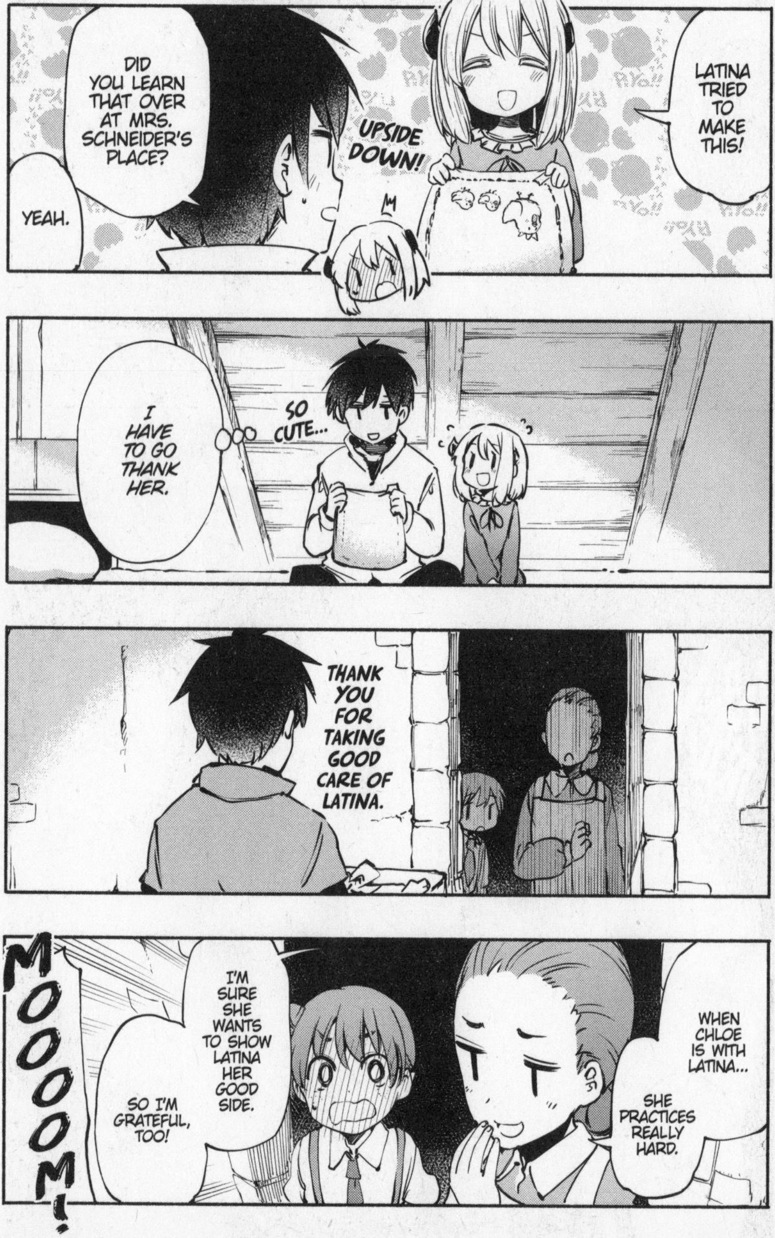
LATINA TRIED TO MAKE THIS!
UPSIDE DOWN!
DID YOU LEARN THAT OVER AT MRS. SCHNEIDER'S PLACE?
YEAH.
SO CUTE...
I HAVE TO GO THANK HER.
THANK YOU FOR TAKING GOOD CARE OF LATINA.
WHEN CHLOE IS WITH LATINA...
SHE PRACTICES REALLY HARD.
I'M SURE SHE WANTS TO SHOW LATINA HER GOOD SIDE.
SO I'M GRATEFUL, TOO!
MOOOOM!

12. Little Girl One Day in Summer

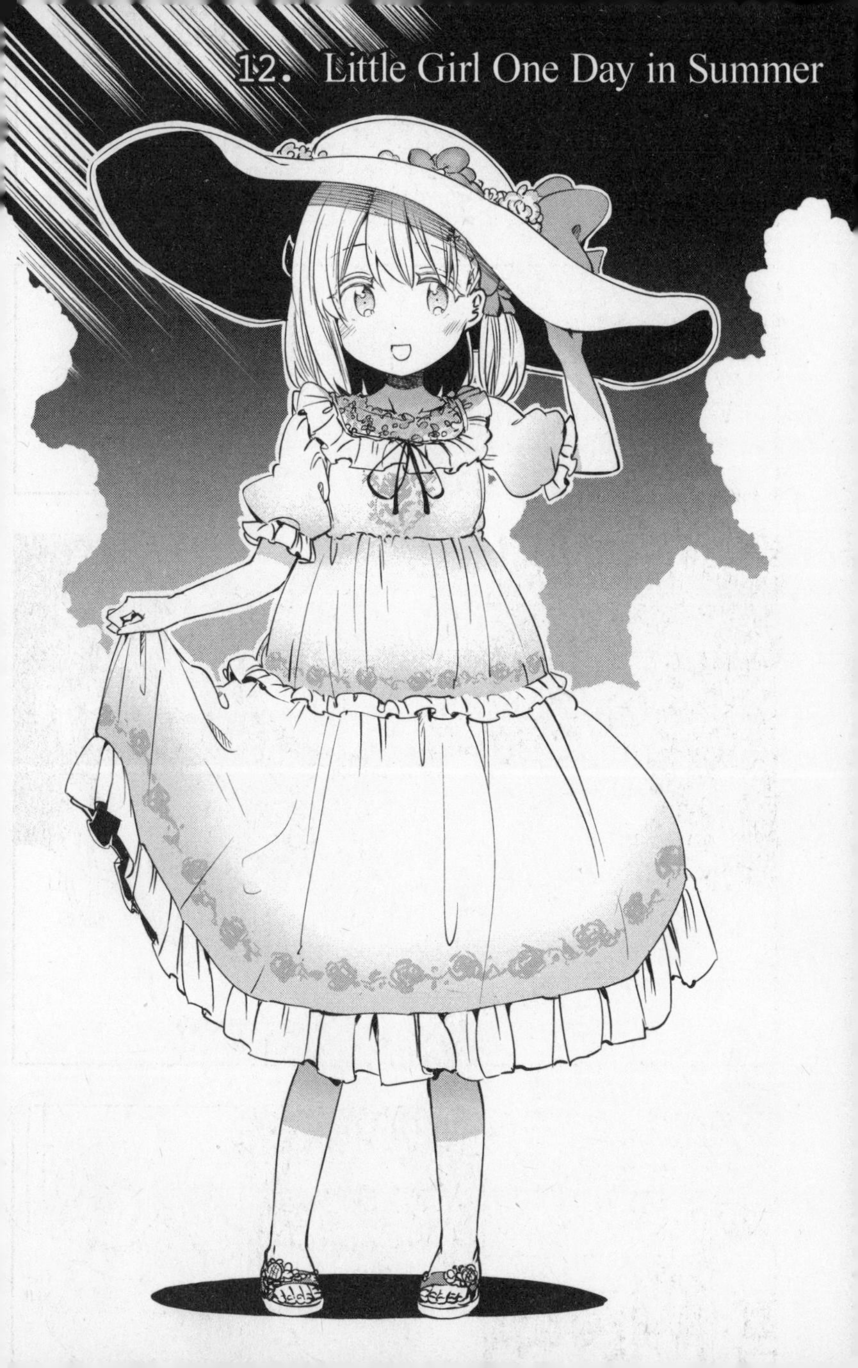

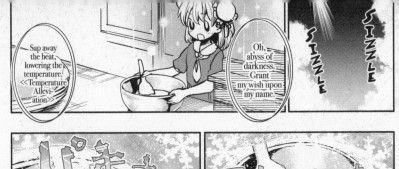

Sap away the heat, lowering the temperature! «Temperature Alleviation»

Oh, abyss of darkness. Grant my wish upon my name.

SIZZLE SIZZLE SIZZLE

PA-KRIK-KRIK

KOOOOO...

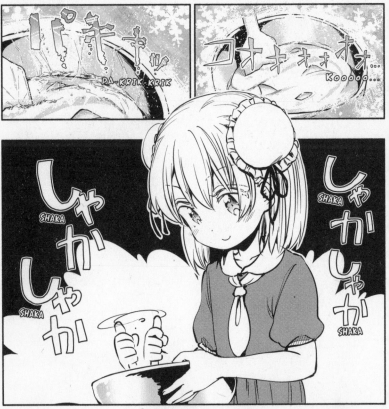

SHAKA SHAKA SHAKA SHAKA

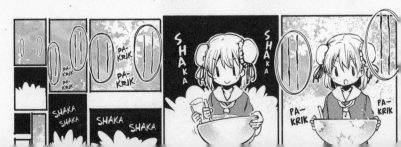

PA-KRIK PA-KRIK PA-KRIK

SHAKA SHAKA

SHAKA SHAKA SHAKA SHAKA

PA-KRIK PA-KRIK

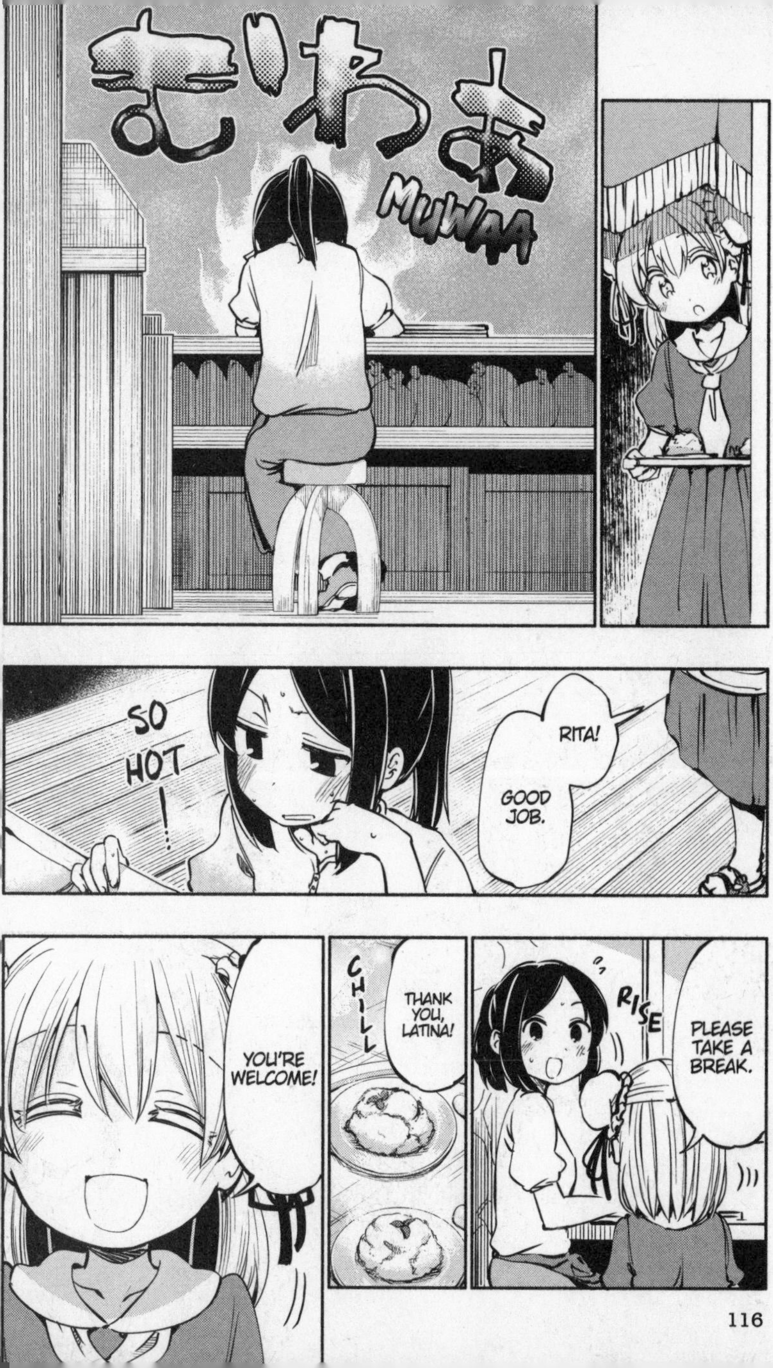
むわぁ
MUWAA
RITA!
GOOD JOB.
SO HOT !...
PLEASE TAKE A BREAK.
RISE
THANK YOU, LATINA!
CHILL
YOU'RE WELCOME!

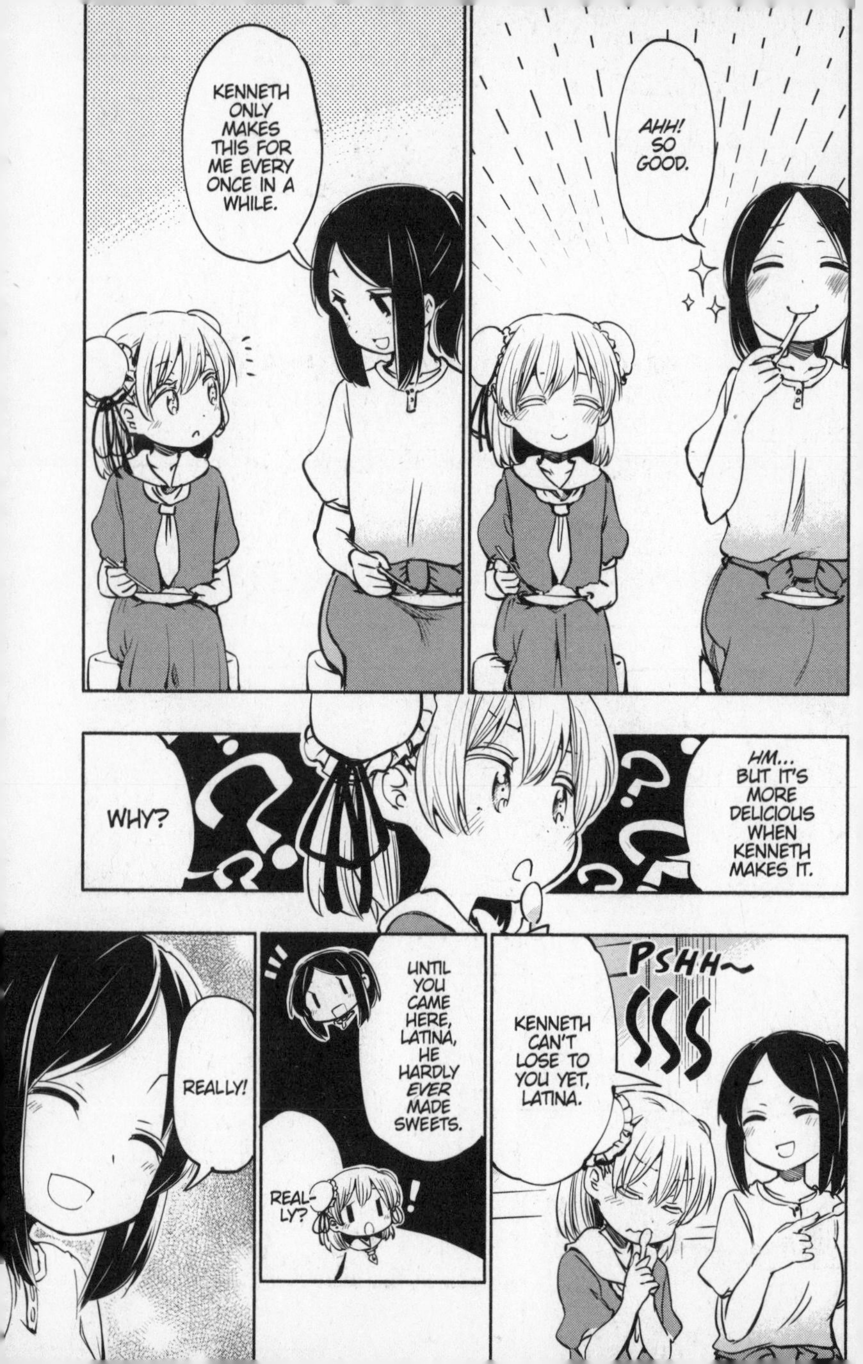
AHH! SO GOOD.
KENNETH ONLY MAKES THIS FOR ME EVERY ONCE IN A WHILE.
HM... BUT IT'S MORE DELICIOUS WHEN KENNETH MAKES IT.
WHY?
PSHH~
KENNETH CAN'T LOSE TO YOU YET, LATINA.
UNTIL YOU CAME HERE, LATINA, HE HARDLY EVER MADE SWEETS.
REAL-LY?
REALLY!

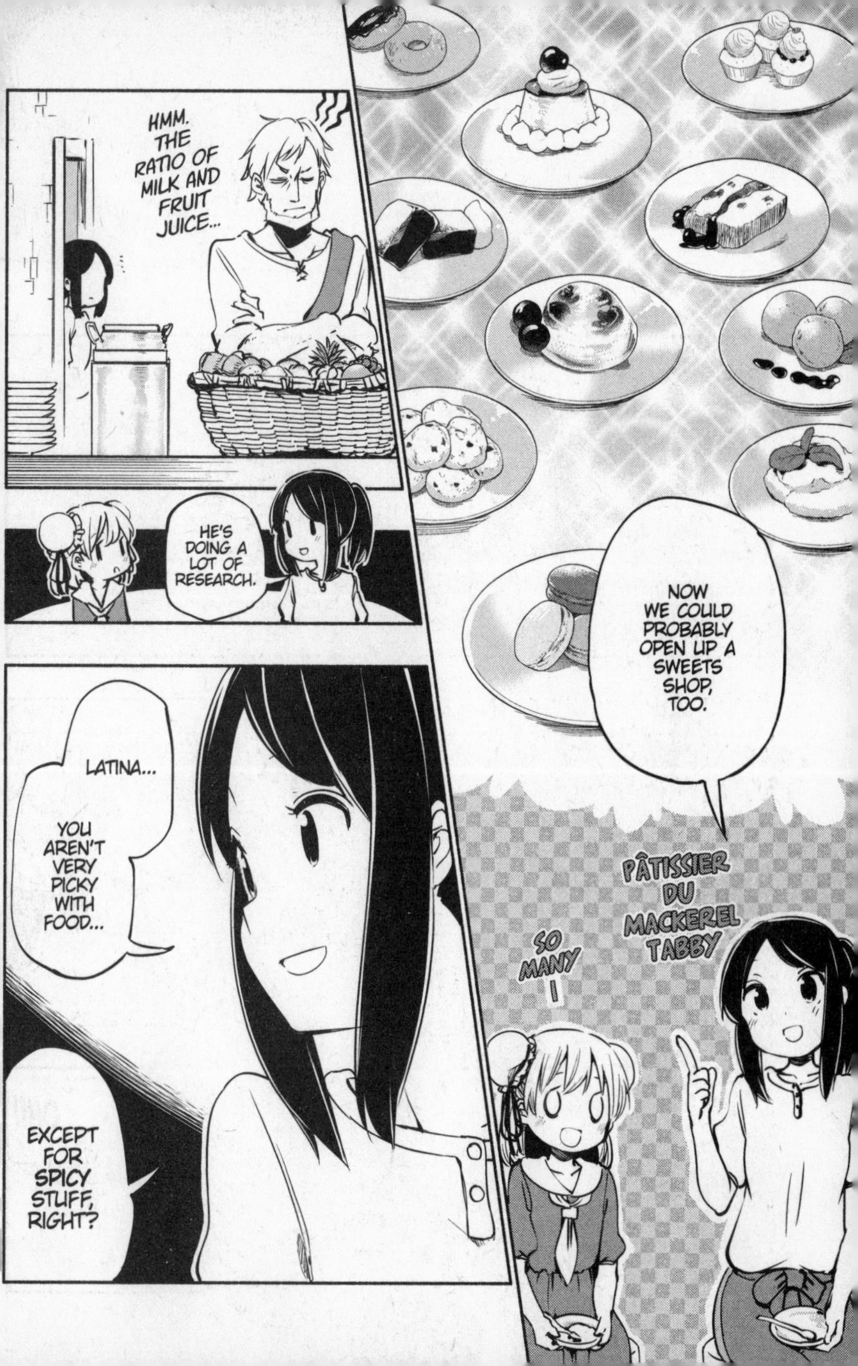
NOW WE COULD PROBABLY OPEN UP A SWEETS SHOP, TOO.
PÂTISSIER DU MACKEREL TABBY
SO MANY
HMM. THE RATIO OF MILK AND FRUIT JUICE...
HE'S DOING A LOT OF RESEARCH.
LATINA...
YOU AREN'T VERY PICKY WITH FOOD...
EXCEPT FOR SPICY STUFF, RIGHT?

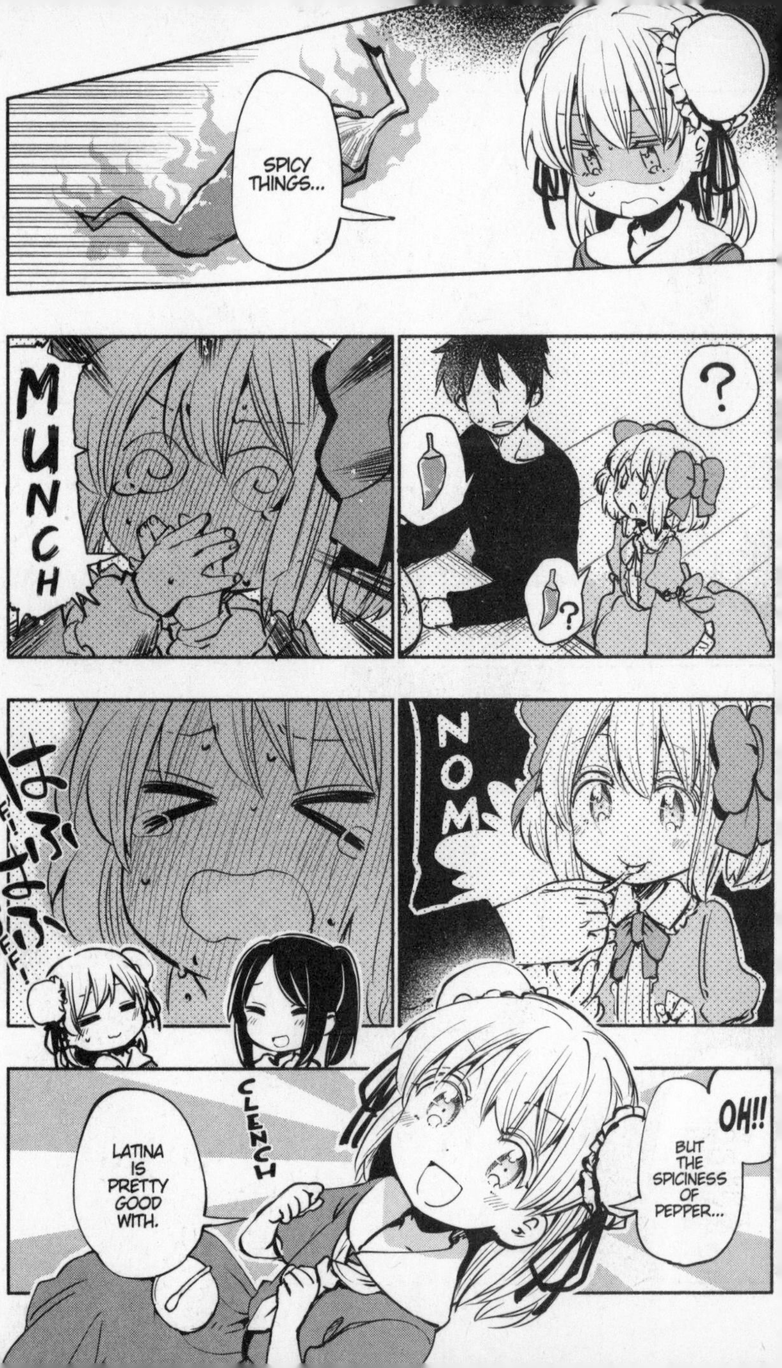
SPICY THINGS...
?
?
MUNCH
NOM
はふ HUFF!
はふ HUFF!
OH!!
BUT THE SPICINESS OF PEPPER...
CLENCH
LATINA IS PRETTY GOOD WITH.

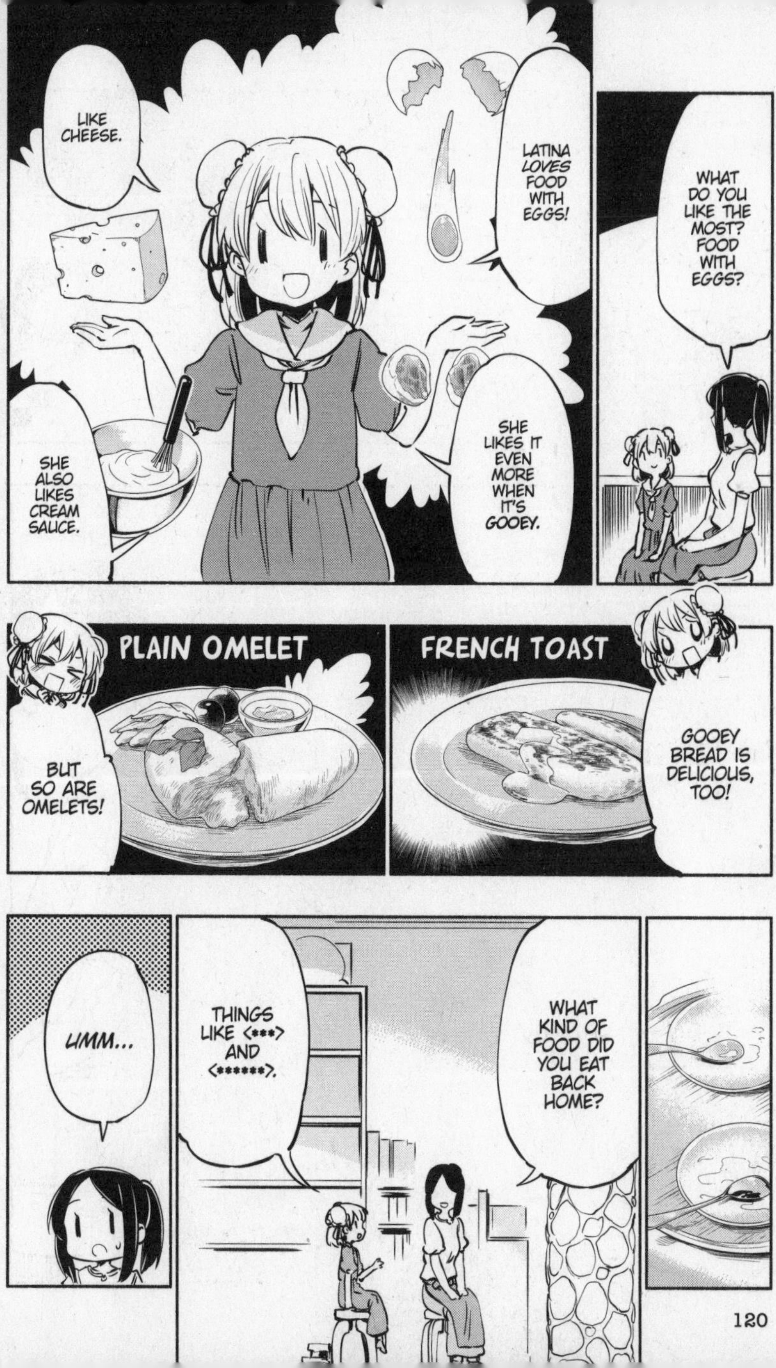
WHAT DO YOU LIKE THE MOST? FOOD WITH EGGS?
LATINA LOVES FOOD WITH EGGS!
SHE LIKES IT EVEN MORE WHEN IT'S GOOEY.
LIKE CHEESE.
SHE ALSO LIKES CREAM SAUCE.
FRENCH TOAST
GOOEY BREAD IS DELICIOUS, TOO!
PLAIN OMELET
BUT SO ARE OMELETS!
WHAT KIND OF FOOD DID YOU EAT BACK HOME?
THINGS LIKE <***> AND <******>.
UMM...

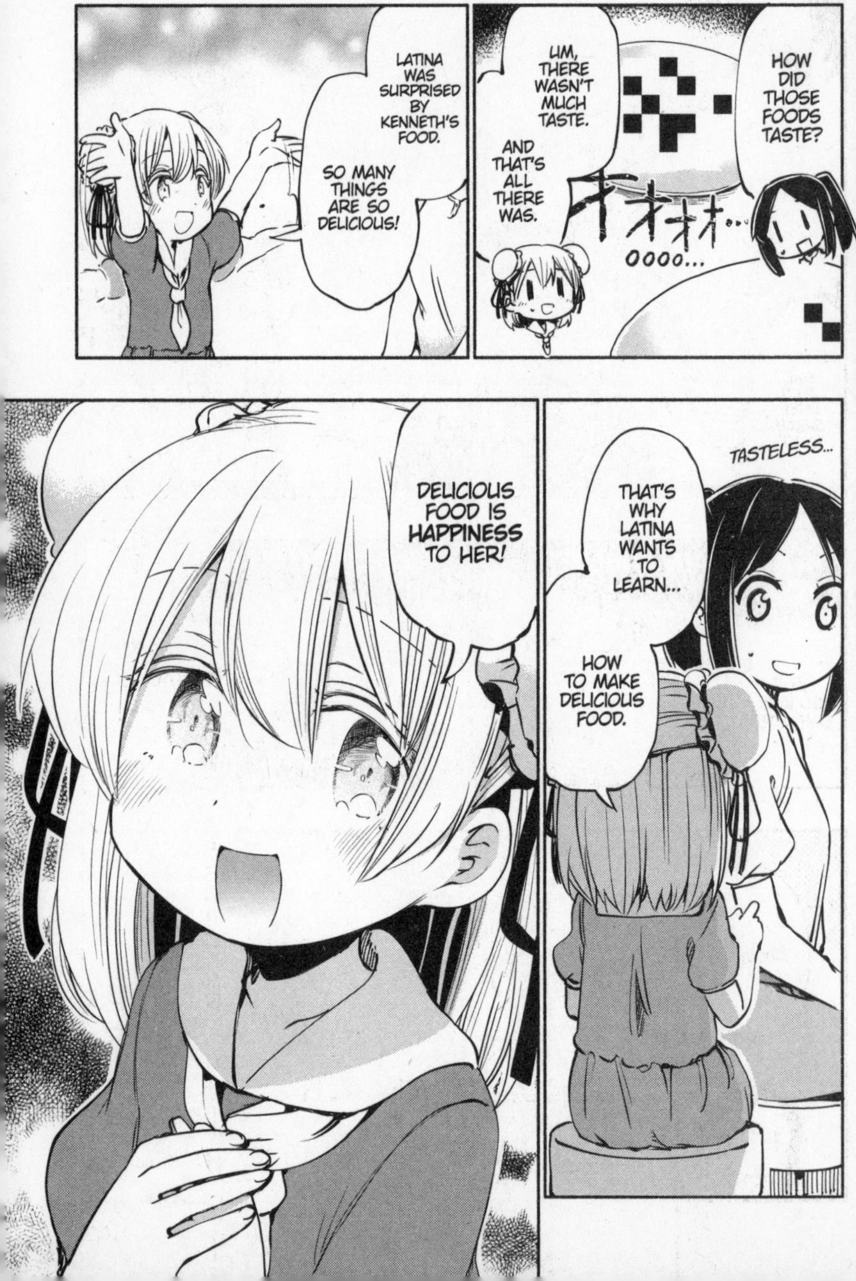
HOW DID THOSE FOODS TASTE?
UM, THERE WASN'T MUCH TASTE.
AND THAT'S ALL THERE WAS.
オオオオ…
OOOO...
LATINA WAS SURPRISED BY KENNETH'S FOOD.
SO MANY THINGS ARE SO DELICIOUS!
TASTELESS...
THAT'S WHY LATINA WANTS TO LEARN...
HOW TO MAKE DELICIOUS FOOD.
DELICIOUS FOOD IS HAPPINESS TO HER!

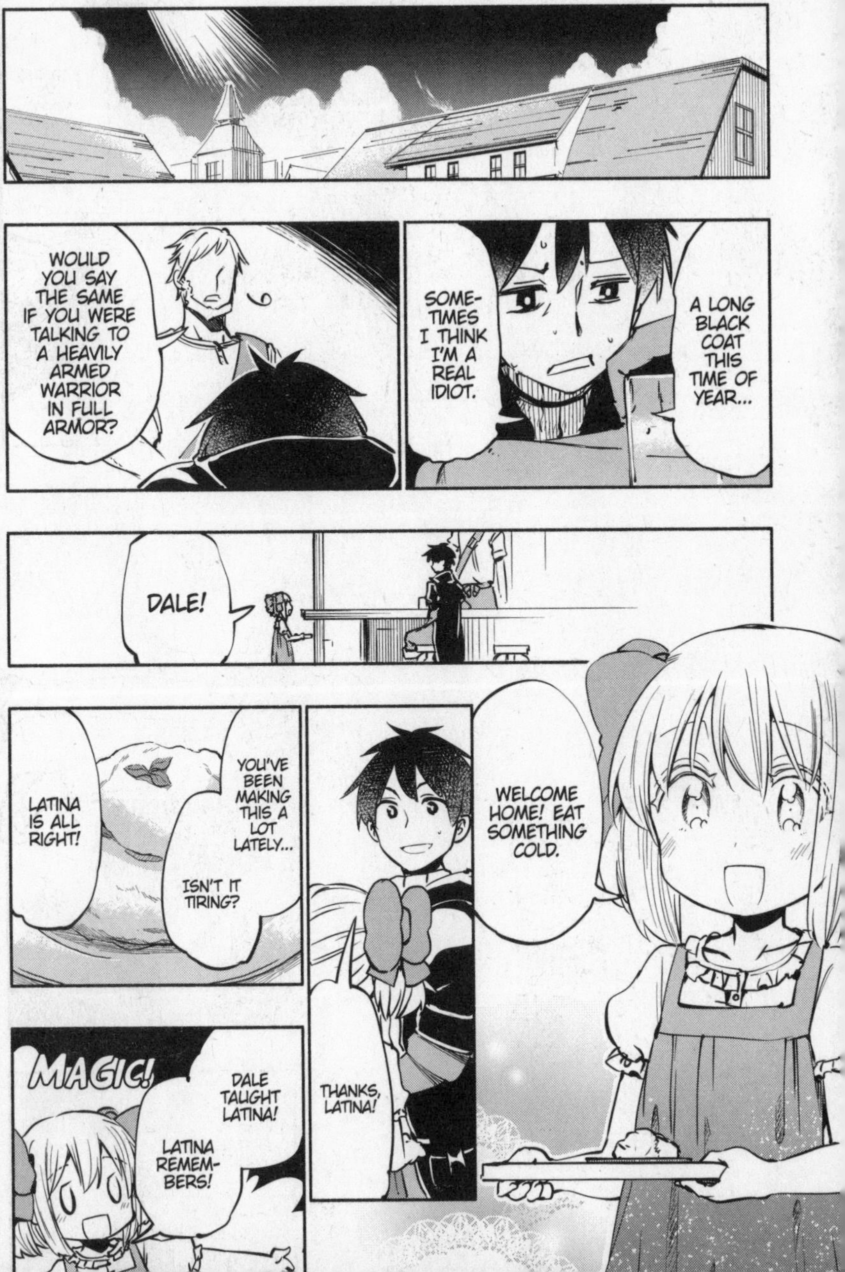
A LONG BLACK COAT THIS TIME OF YEAR...
SOME-TIMES I THINK I'M A REAL IDIOT.
WOULD YOU SAY THE SAME IF YOU WERE TALKING TO A HEAVILY ARMED WARRIOR IN FULL ARMOR?
DALE!
WELCOME HOME! EAT SOMETHING COLD.
THANKS, LATINA!
YOU'VE BEEN MAKING THIS A LOT LATELY...
ISN'T IT TIRING?
LATINA IS ALL RIGHT!
DALE TAUGHT LATINA!
LATINA REMEM-BERS!
MAGIC!

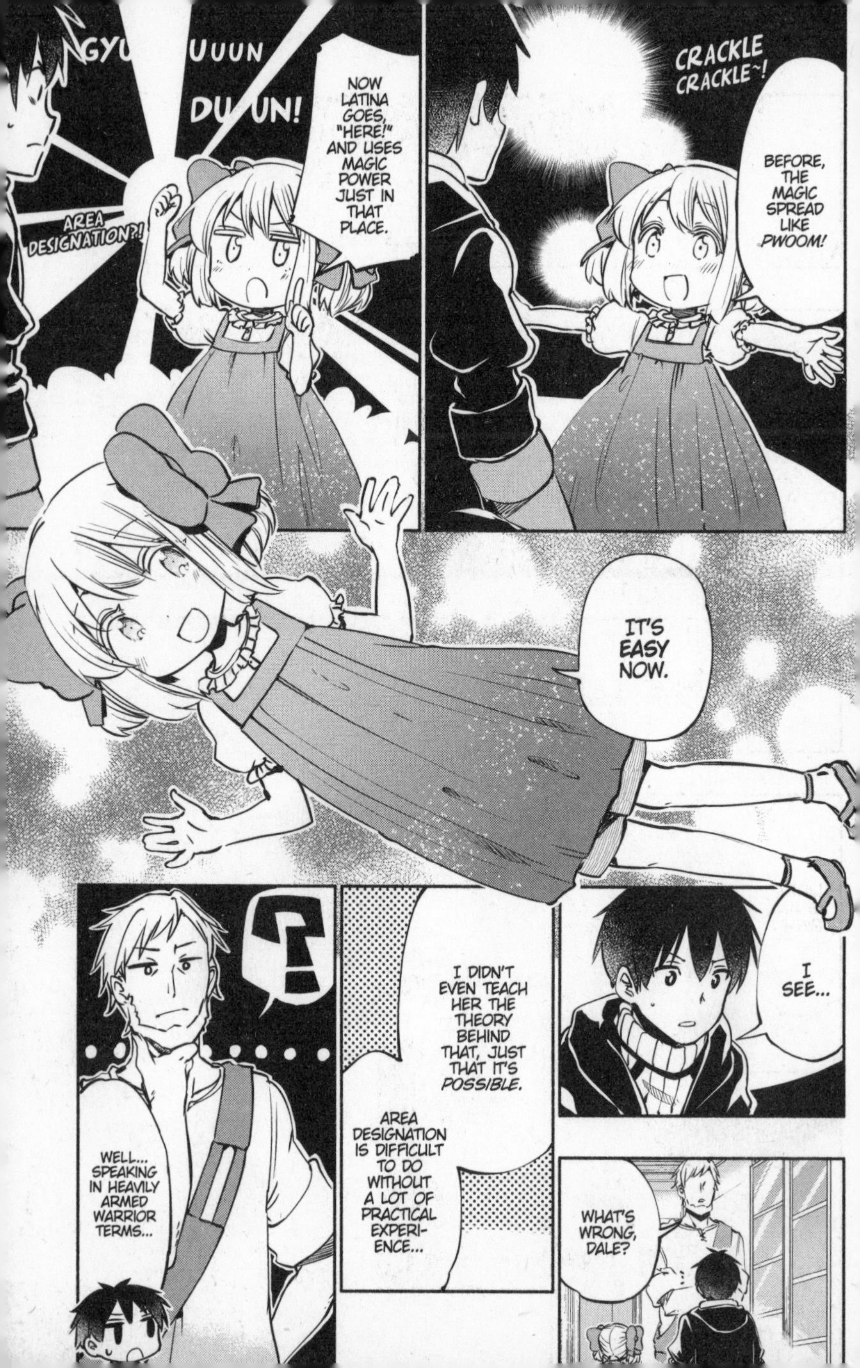
CRACKLE CRACKLE~!
BEFORE, THE MAGIC SPREAD LIKE *PWOOM!*
GYU UUUN
DU UN!
NOW LATINA GOES, "HERE!" AND USES MAGIC POWER JUST IN THAT PLACE.
AREA DESIGNATION?!
IT'S EASY NOW.
I SEE...
WHAT'S WRONG, DALE?
I DIDN'T EVEN TEACH HER THE THEORY BEHIND THAT, JUST THAT IT'S *POSSIBLE*.
AREA DESIGNATION IS DIFFICULT TO DO WITHOUT A LOT OF PRACTICAL EXPERI- ENCE...
?!
......
WELL... SPEAKING IN HEAVILY ARMED WARRIOR TERMS...

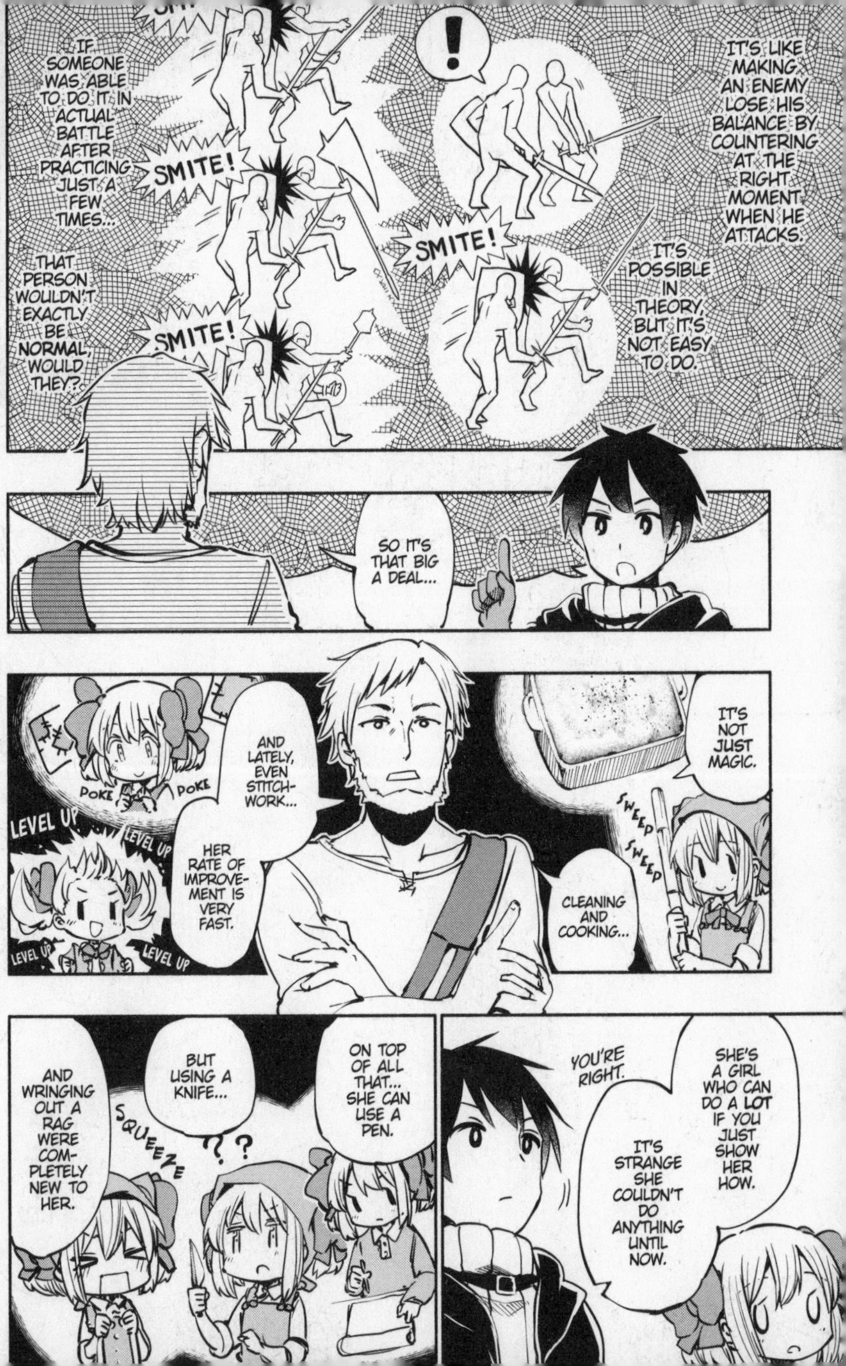
IT'S LIKE MAKING AN ENEMY LOSE HIS BALANCE BY COUNTERING AT THE RIGHT MOMENT WHEN HE ATTACKS.
!
IT'S POSSIBLE IN THEORY, BUT IT'S NOT EASY TO DO.
SMITE!
SMITE!
SMITE!
IF SOMEONE WAS ABLE TO DO IT IN ACTUAL BATTLE AFTER PRACTICING JUST A FEW TIMES...
THAT PERSON WOULDN'T EXACTLY BE NORMAL, WOULD THEY?
SO IT'S THAT BIG A DEAL...
IT'S NOT JUST MAGIC.
SWEEP SWEEP
CLEANING AND COOKING...
AND LATELY, EVEN STITCH-WORK...
HER RATE OF IMPROVEMENT IS VERY FAST.
POKE POKE
LEVEL UP
LEVEL UP
LEVEL UP
LEVEL UP
YOU'RE RIGHT.
SHE'S A GIRL WHO CAN DO A LOT IF YOU JUST SHOW HER HOW.
IT'S STRANGE SHE COULDN'T DO ANYTHING UNTIL NOW.
ON TOP OF ALL THAT... SHE CAN USE A PEN.
BUT USING A KNIFE...
??
AND WRINGING OUT A RAG WERE COMPLETELY NEW TO HER.
SQUEEZE

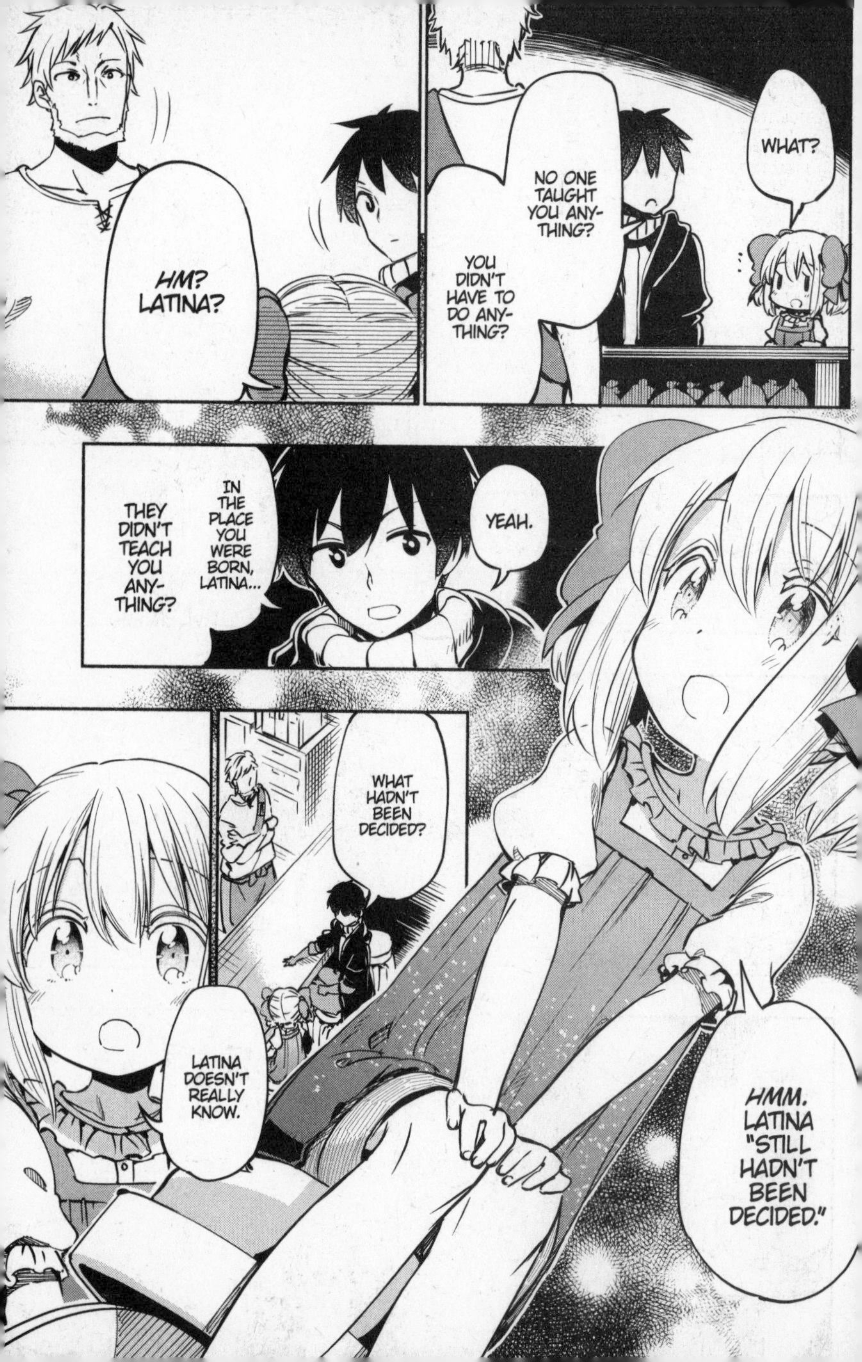
WHAT?
NO ONE TAUGHT YOU ANYTHING?
YOU DIDN'T HAVE TO DO ANYTHING?
HM? LATINA?
HMM. LATINA "STILL HADN'T BEEN DECIDED."
YEAH.
IN THE PLACE YOU WERE BORN, LATINA...
THEY DIDN'T TEACH YOU ANYTHING?
WHAT HADN'T BEEN DECIDED?
LATINA DOESN'T REALLY KNOW.

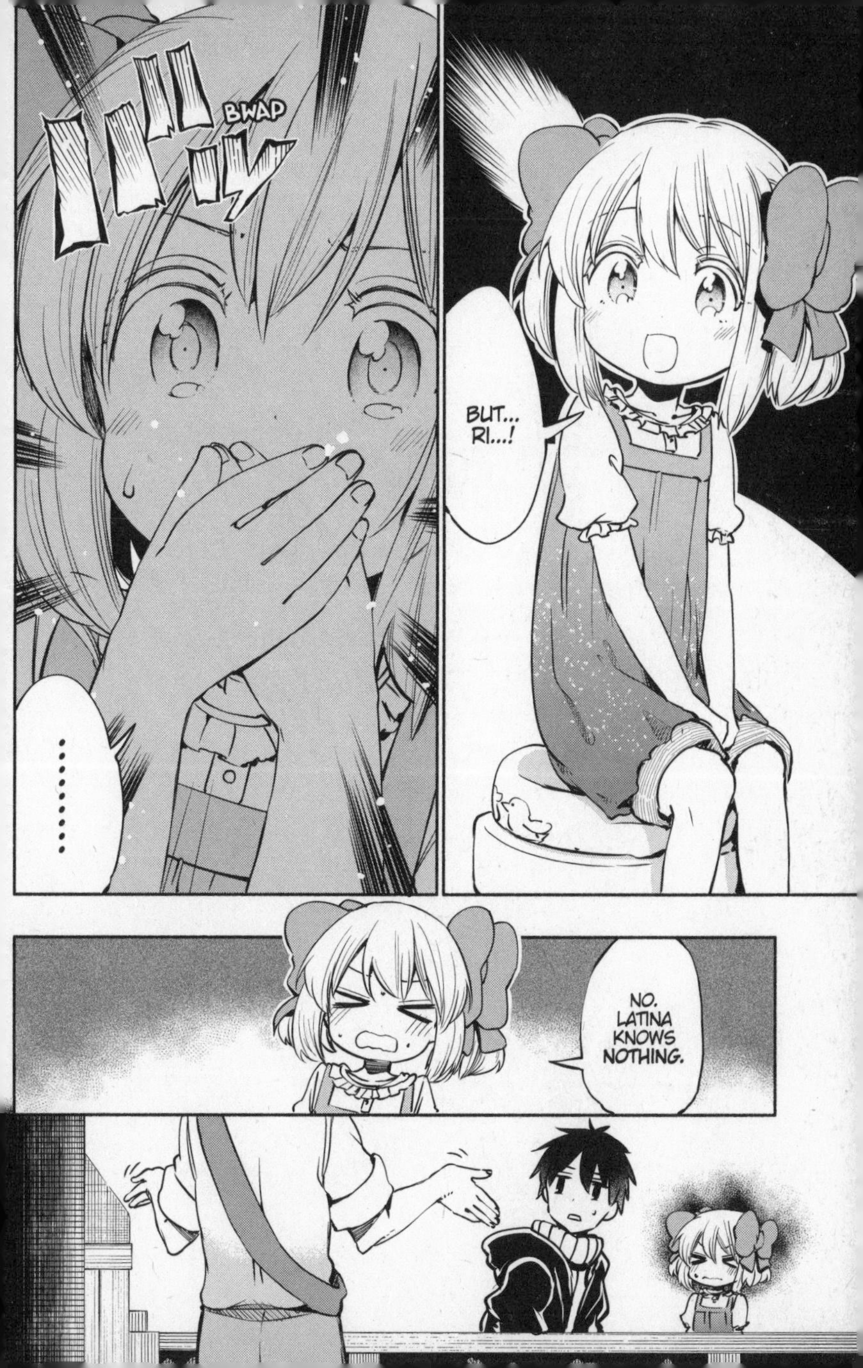
BUT... RI...!
BWAP
......
NO. LATINA KNOWS NOTHING.

IF It's
For My
Daughter
I'd Even Defeat
a Demon
Lord

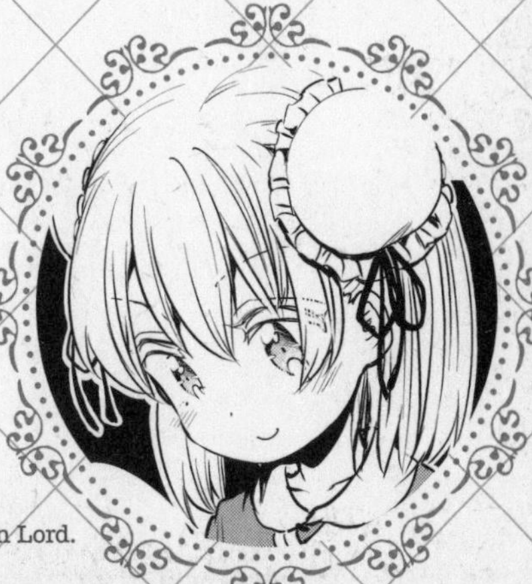

If It's For My Daughter, I'd Even Defeat a Demon Lord.

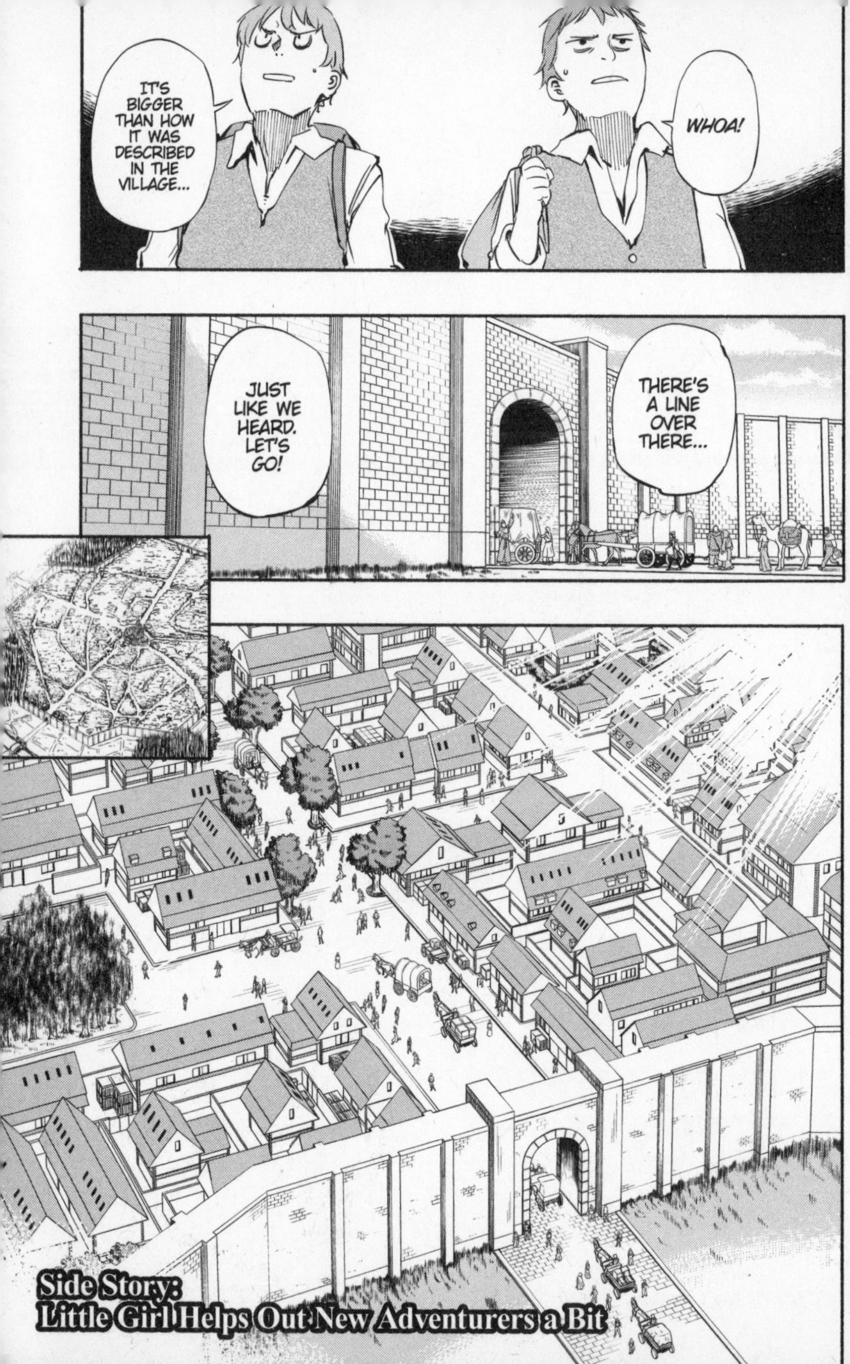
WHOA!
IT'S BIGGER THAN HOW IT WAS DESCRIBED IN THE VILLAGE...
THERE'S A LINE OVER THERE...
JUST LIKE WE HEARD. LET'S GO!
Side Story:
Little Girl Helps Out New Adventurers a Bit

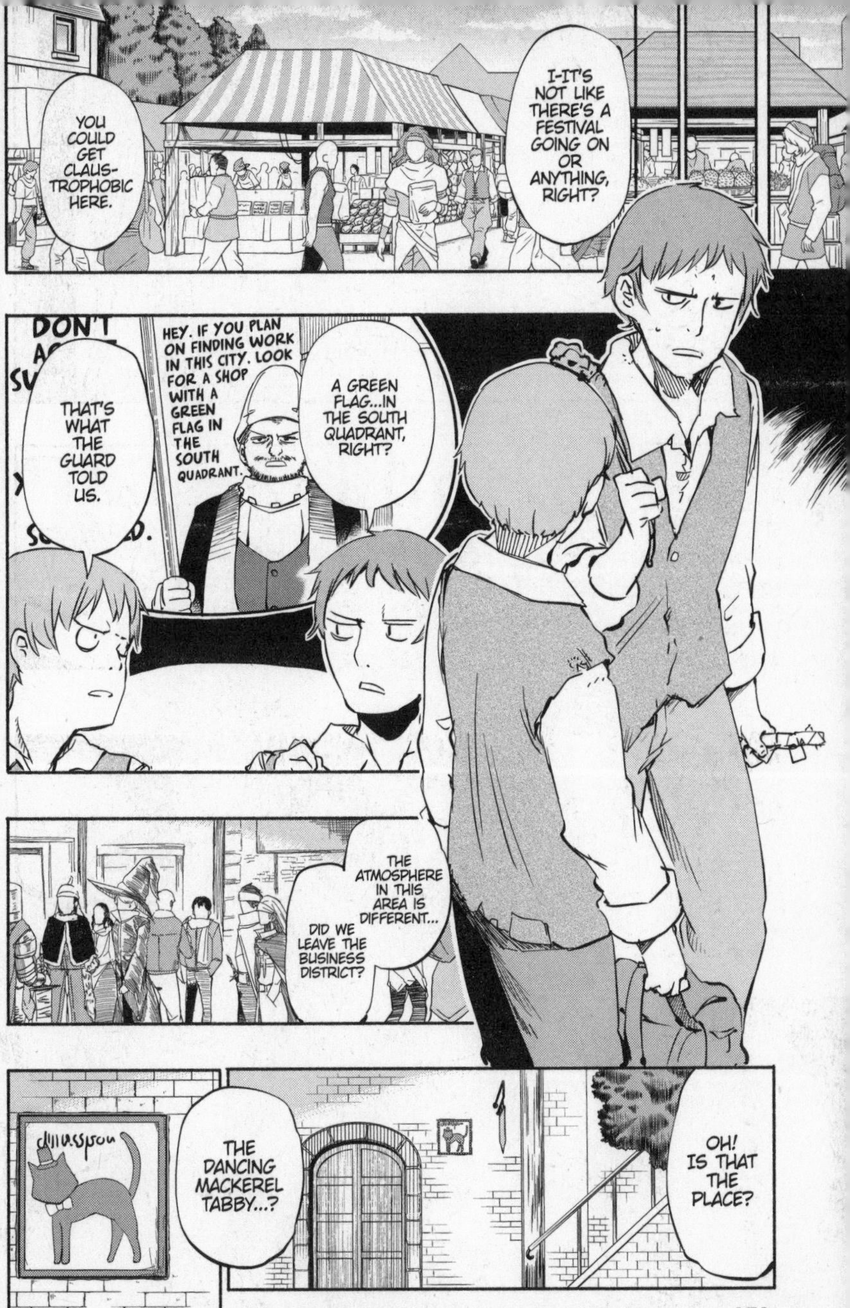
I-IT'S NOT LIKE THERE'S A FESTIVAL GOING ON OR ANYTHING, RIGHT?
YOU COULD GET CLAUS-TROPHOBIC HERE.
A GREEN FLAG...IN THE SOUTH QUADRANT, RIGHT?
HEY. IF YOU PLAN ON FINDING WORK IN THIS CITY. LOOK FOR A SHOP WITH A GREEN FLAG IN THE SOUTH QUADRANT.
THAT'S WHAT THE GUARD TOLD US.
THE ATMOSPHERE IN THIS AREA IS DIFFERENT...
DID WE LEAVE THE BUSINESS DISTRICT?
OH! IS THAT THE PLACE?
THE DANCING MACKEREL TABBY...?

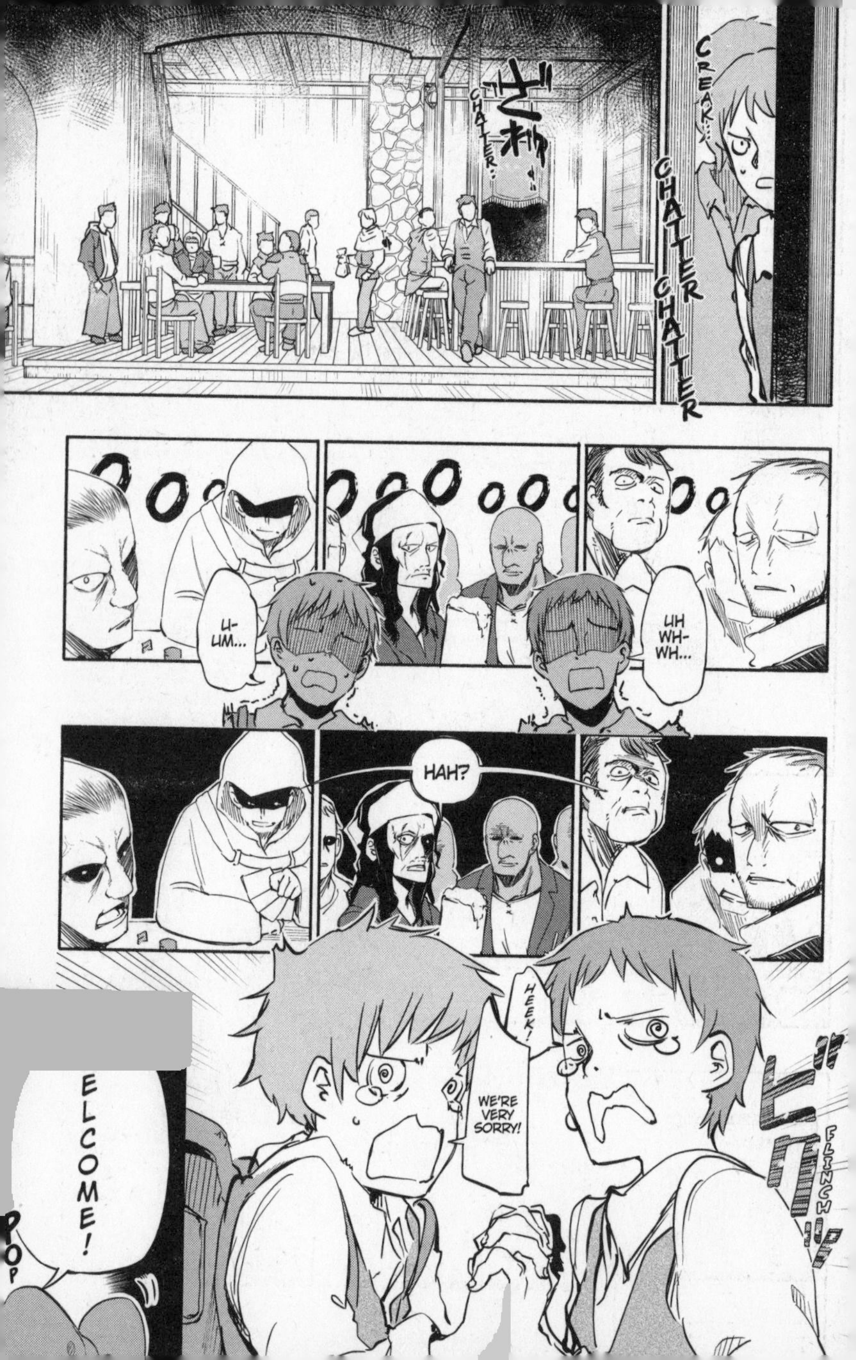
CREAK...
CHATTER CHATTER
CHATTER...
UH WH-WH...
U-UM...
HAH?
FLINCH
HEEK!
WE'RE VERY SORRY!
ELCOME!
POP

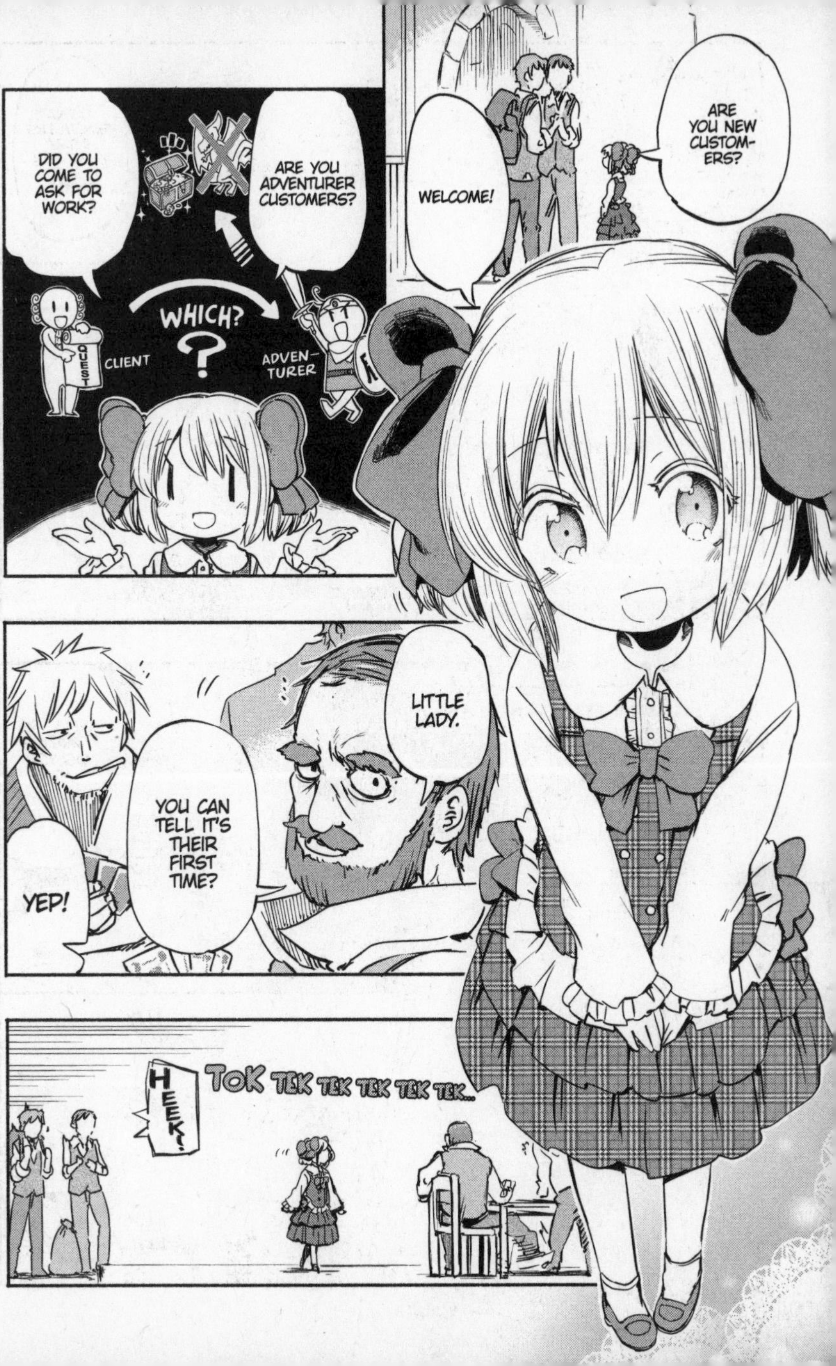
ARE YOU NEW CUSTOMERS?
WELCOME!
ARE YOU ADVENTURER CUSTOMERS?
DID YOU COME TO ASK FOR WORK?
WHICH?
ADVEN-TURER
QUEST
CLIENT
LITTLE LADY.
YOU CAN TELL IT'S THEIR FIRST TIME?
YEP!
TOK TEK TEK TEK TEK TEK...
HEEK!

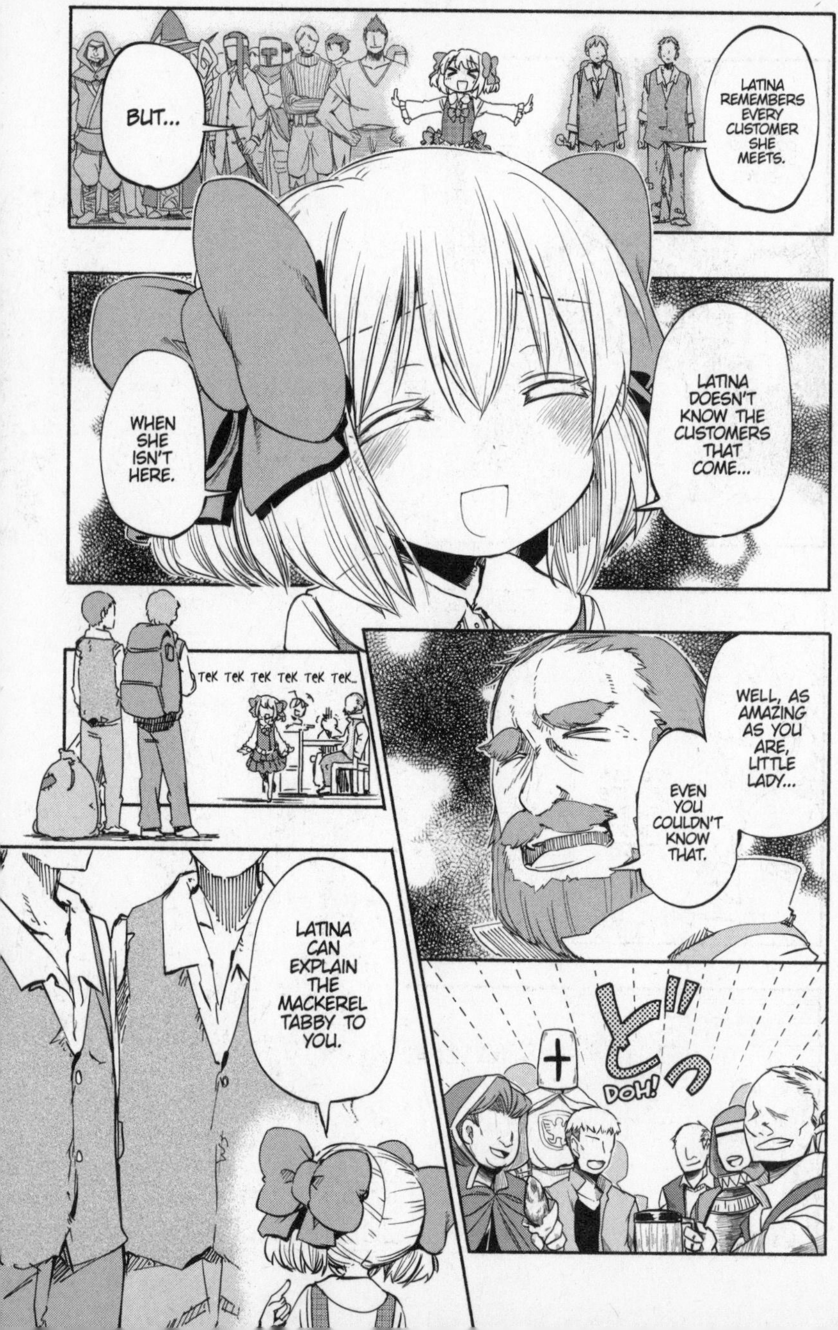
LATINA REMEMBERS EVERY CUSTOMER SHE MEETS.
BUT...
LATINA DOESN'T KNOW THE CUSTOMERS THAT COME...
WHEN SHE ISN'T HERE.
WELL, AS AMAZING AS YOU ARE, LITTLE LADY...
EVEN YOU COULDN'T KNOW THAT.
TEK TEK TEK TEK TEK TEK...
どっ
DOH!
LATINA CAN EXPLAIN THE MACKEREL TABBY TO YOU.

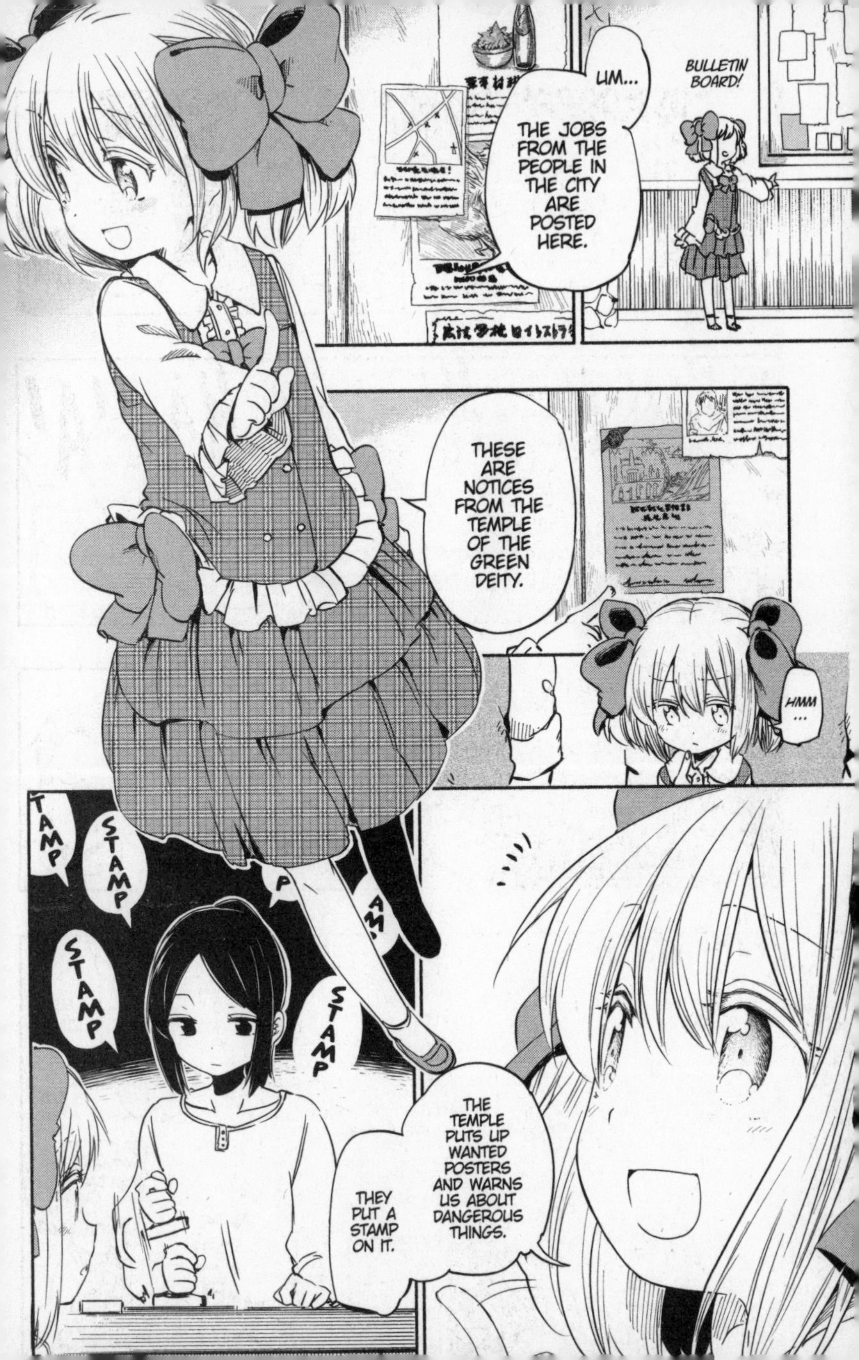
BULLETIN BOARD!
UM...
THE JOBS FROM THE PEOPLE IN THE CITY ARE POSTED HERE.
THESE ARE NOTICES FROM THE TEMPLE OF THE GREEN DEITY.
HMM ...
THE TEMPLE PUTS UP WANTED POSTERS AND WARNS US ABOUT DANGEROUS THINGS.
TAMP
STAMP
STAMP
STAMP
STAMP
THEY PUT A STAMP ON IT.

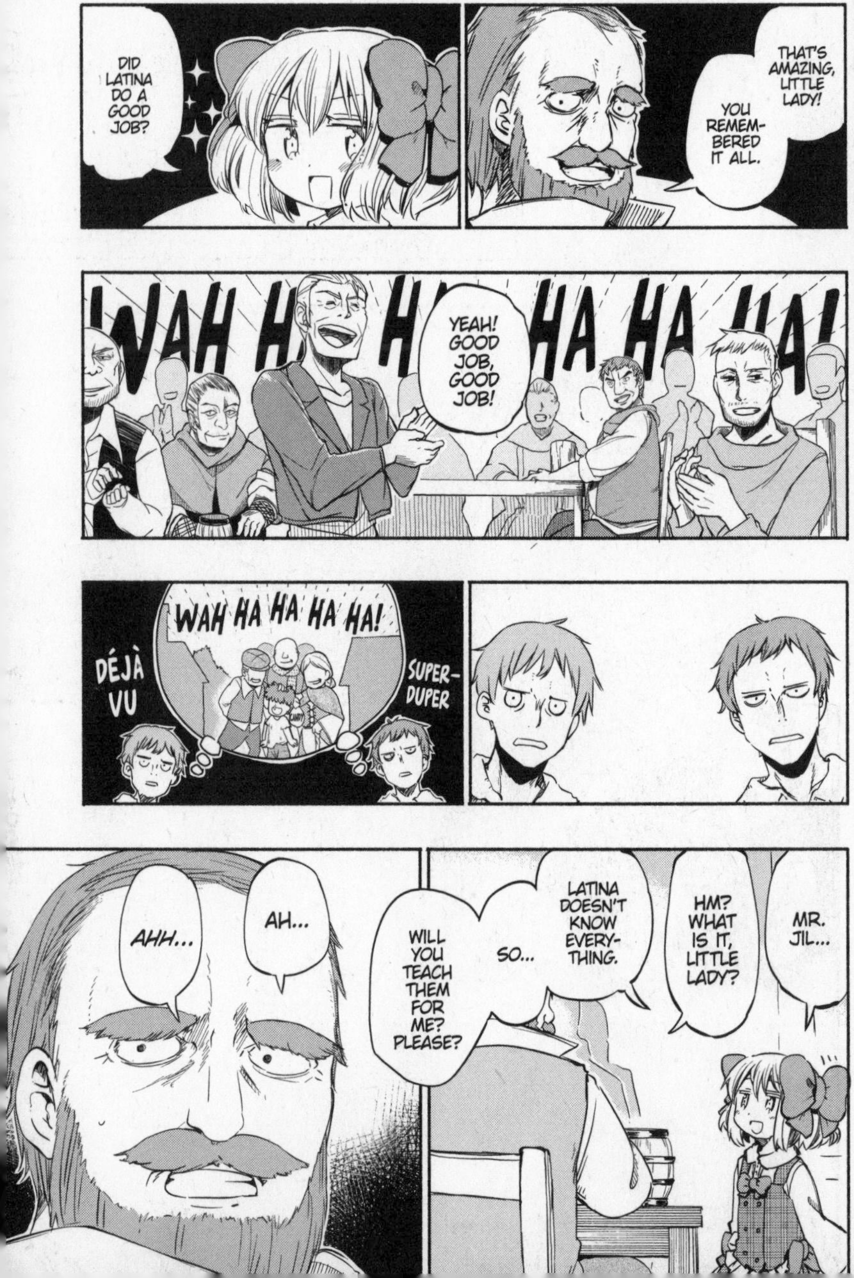
THAT'S AMAZING, LITTLE LADY!
YOU REMEMBERED IT ALL.
DID LATINA DO A GOOD JOB?
WAH HA HA HA HA HA!
YEAH! GOOD JOB, GOOD JOB!
WAH HA HA HA HA!
SUPER-DUPER
DÉJÀ VU
MR. JIL...
HM? WHAT IS IT, LITTLE LADY?
LATINA DOESN'T KNOW EVERYTHING.
SO...
WILL YOU TEACH THEM FOR ME? PLEASE?
AH...
AHH...

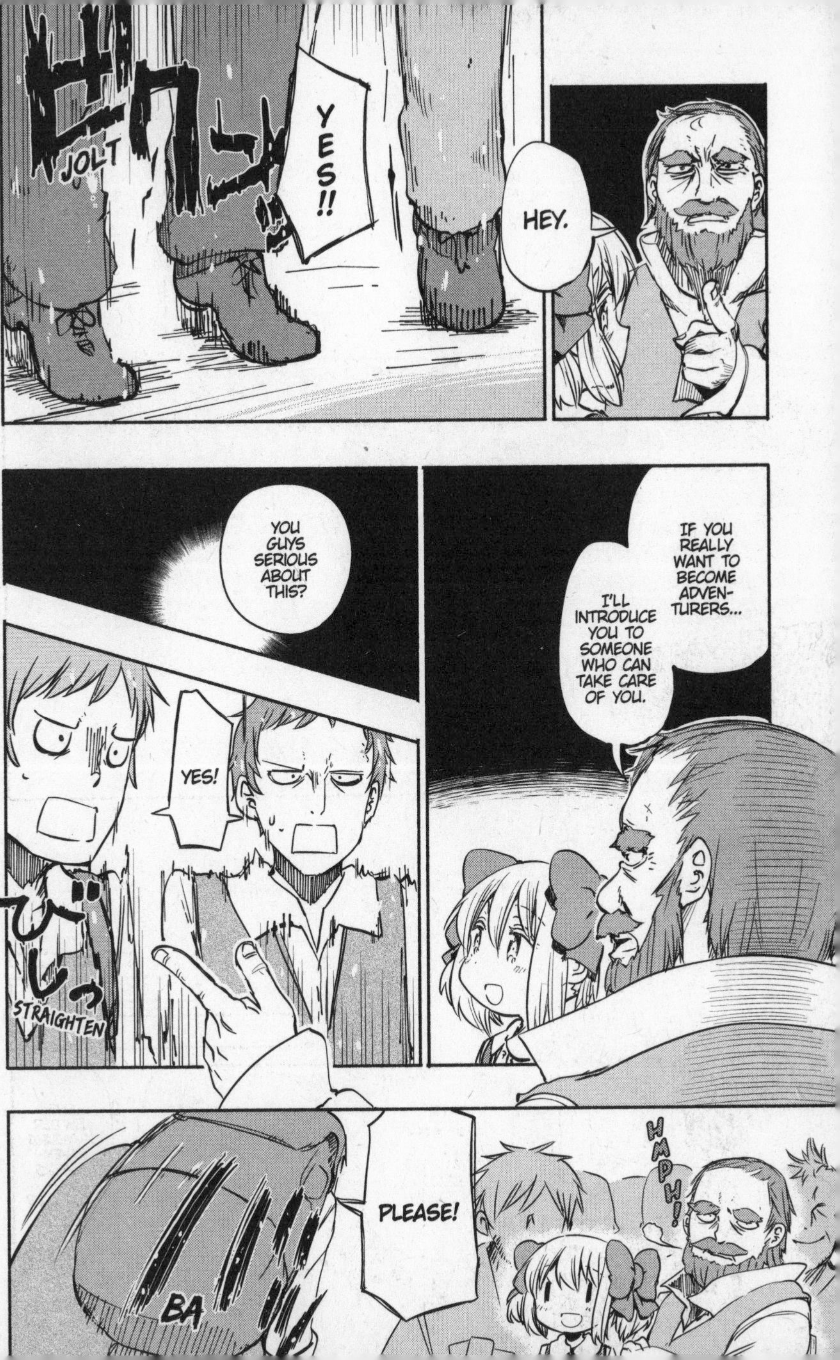
HEY.
JOLT
YES!!
IF YOU REALLY WANT TO BECOME ADVEN-TURERS...
I'LL INTRODUCE YOU TO SOMEONE WHO CAN TAKE CARE OF YOU.
YOU GUYS SERIOUS ABOUT THIS?
YES!
STRAIGHTEN
HMPH!
PLEASE!
BA

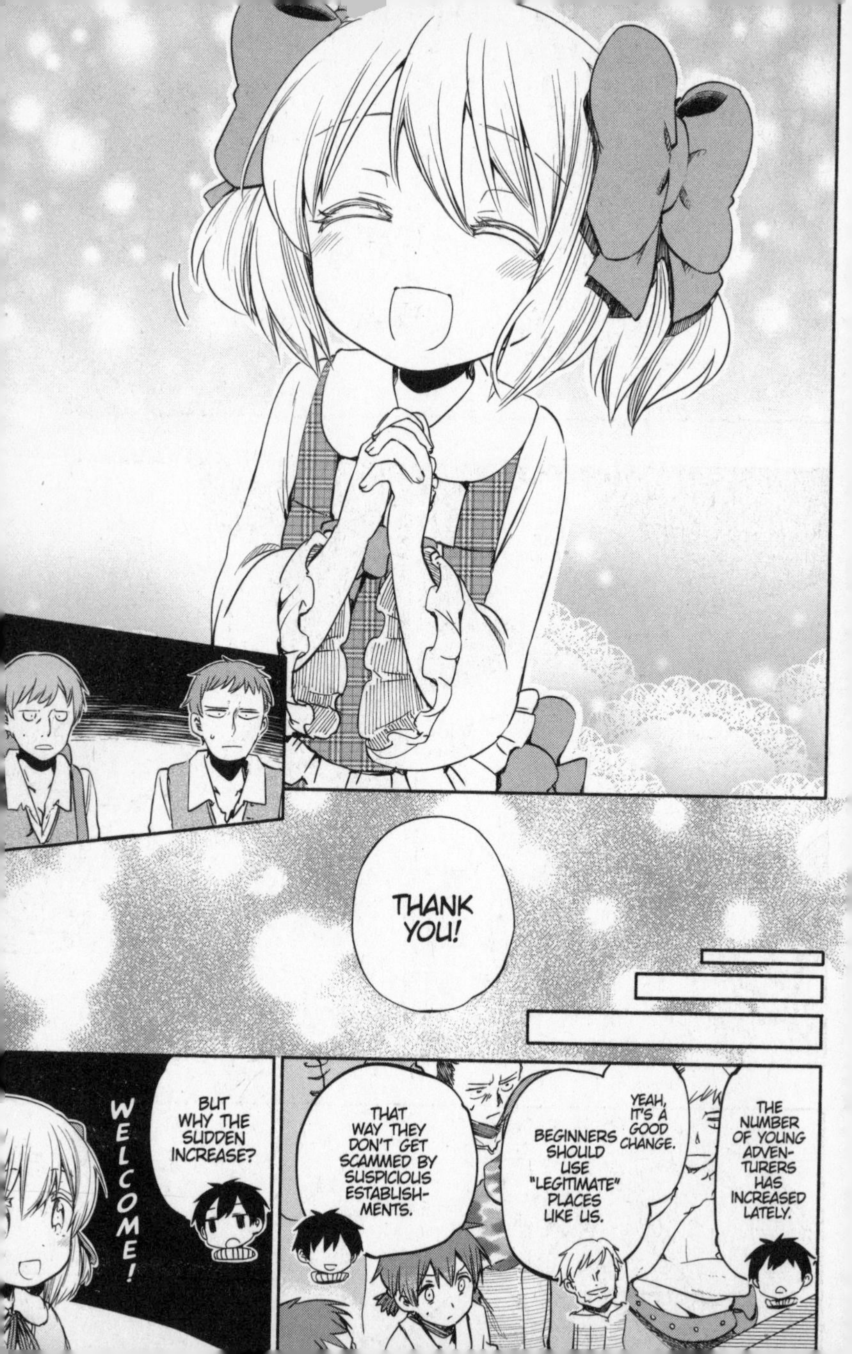
THANK YOU!
THE NUMBER OF YOUNG ADVENTURERS HAS INCREASED LATELY.
YEAH, IT'S A GOOD CHANGE.
BEGINNERS SHOULD USE "LEGITIMATE" PLACES LIKE US.
THAT WAY THEY DON'T GET SCAMMED BY SUSPICIOUS ESTABLISHMENTS.
BUT WHY THE SUDDEN INCREASE?
WELCOME!

IF It's
For My
Daughter,
I'd Even Defeat
a Demon
Lord

To be continued...!

If It's For My Daughter, I'd Even Defeat a Demon Lord

SHORT STORY

CHIROLU

Little Girl Causes a Local Boom Among Adventurers

The origin of the term "adventurer" is not clearly recounted in history. Most districts believe people who were not soldiers or hunters but were instead interested in exploring the unknown lands that were not yet split into domains—much less kingdoms—began to refer to themselves in such a way.

In other words, it is a "self-appointed" profession, so the details of the job are not really set in stone.

Even so, the reason youths continue to admire and desire such a position is probably due to the fact that it is the closest job you can get to being a hero. At the same time, it is a job where underdogs can dream about the possibility of obtaining fame and fortune.

Of course, not all the people calling themselves adventurers are skilled and strong, so their personalities and abilities vary drastically. This is something that the clients of adventurers know all too well.

Because of their work, most adventurers do not

commonly settle into a home and instead choose to stay at the various inns found in their area of choice. Though magical tools have made things a lot more convenient, there is still a need for housework and laundry. At a certain point, any reasonably large home would need to hire a servant. Because of this, the idea of just renting a single room at an inn became very attractive.

The temple of the Blue Deity, Azrac, greatly supports such a lifestyle by managing the finances of these travelers. In exchange for an administration fee, anyone can deposit their valuables at the temple, which is protected by a powerful private defense force, far safer than leaving any valuables in a room at an inn. On top of that, money that is deposited at the temple of the Blue Deity is input in financial numbers, allowing the depositor to withdraw the money at any temple of the Blue Deity in any town. In this way, travelers don't need to carry their valuables with them as they travel.

Even though adventurers are considered drifters that travel from place to place, they can only do so because of the system that supports them.

The establishments that give out work to adventurers are places that carry the flag of the Green Deity. They hang the flag of the Green Deity of Information, Akudaru, and collect and give out information to adventurers and travelers. The kingdom posts bounties or hunt requests for large, magical beasts through the temple. The aforementioned establishments also deal with other work orders and requests.

Naturally, such locations become a gathering place for adventurers and in turn gather many clients. In order to find the rate of pay and detailed requirements, one must find the

client listed on the request and ask them directly.

"Hmm..."

"What should we do...?"

The two men looking at the bulletin board in the Dancing Mackerel Tabby, reading the various requests from the citizens of Kreutz, were two such adventurers. They were still more "self-appointed" adventurers than they were adventurers. They had just left their hometowns to begin their lives as adventurers in Kreutz. They were still "novice" adventurers who were far removed from being accepted by the general public.

"This request...is definitely impossible."

"Right."

Near Kreutz was a forest where many magical beasts lived. They were bigger than regular beasts and had magical abilities. To keep them from overpopulating the area and to collect their valuable parts for magical tools, hunting quests were often available for these kinds of beasts.

But for the weak and inexperienced, such jobs were suicidal. Because of this, most self-appointed adventurers commonly took jobs not much different than regular manual labor.

"Looks like we're going to transport goods again."

"I thought adventurers would do more flashy kinda jobs."

The two young men gave a simultaneous sigh, disappointed with the gap between dream and reality.

"Good morning." An innocent, young voice swept away their somber mood.

The young men looked over toward the origin of the voice, making eye contact with an adorable girl whose platinum

hair was tied up in pigtails. The poster girl of the shop smiled brightly, holding a round tray that looked too big for her against her chest. They couldn't help but smile back.

"Transporting goods?"

"Yeah."

"That's right."

The little girl knew what the young men were looking at and only asked to confirm, not delving much further. She nodded at their replies.

"Today, a big boat will come into the port. Latina heard it's going to be a lot of work."

"Is that so?"

"Yeah. Latina overheard some customers." She looked upward in thoughtful contemplation as she spoke. "Latina has never seen a boat. She's only seen them in picture books."

She smiled again and turned her gaze back to the two young men, looking at them with pure gray eyes that lacked even a shadow of negativity. "But Latina knows that the things the boat brings in are very important to the city of Kreutz," she said emphatically.

She hardly ever held feelings of uncertainty toward others. She disliked hurtful words and never spoke aggressively. Because of that, the youth who acted as her guardian said she was "well-raised." Because of that, she only spoke words of decency and goodness to those around her.

"Thank you for all your hard work," Latina said.

"I... I see."

"Well, we better work hard today, too."

"But please don't push yourselves overmuch or get hurt," she added.

"We thought we saw a certain request here before."

"This request?"

One of the men nodded, then asked, "Was the request removed because the cat was found?"

"No, that's not the reason I took it down."

Both men looked at the wooden box they were carrying. From the rattling and scratching inside, it was easy to guess what it held.

"You found it?" Kenneth asked.

"At the place where we were working today."

"We thought we'd seen a request for this somewhere, so we caught it."

The exaggerated excitement of accomplishment in their voices was palpable. Suddenly, an odd change of atmosphere spread throughout the shop. Dale glanced around and realized the regulars had started to rise up in anticipation. "What's going on...?"

Everyone had their eyes on the two young men.

"Latina is almost back from playing outside," Kenneth said to them. "Can you wait until then?"

"Yes!"

"Of course."

"Hey!" Dale perked up at Kenneth's mention of Latina's name. "Why did Latina's name come up?"

"Latina is responsible for this quest."

"Huh?"

"Latina is the one who got the information from the client and knows the most about it. So, she is the one who will decide whether the cat is the one from the quest or not."

"Isn't that...a little much...?"

Though Dale didn't seem to realize it, Kenneth knew that there was another benefit to her drawings. The clients who normally brought in such quests were children, women and the elderly, who usually got nervous at the idea of even entering a place full of rowdy adventurers. Latina's presence gave those types of clients a calming effect. Sometimes she helped them when Rita was too busy, patiently listening and thoroughly asking them for details. She was quite skilled.

"Normally," Kenneth said, "we only put up a notice of the existence of such a quest, allowing the client and adventurer to discuss the details and negotiate the price amongst themselves. But these quests are different."

"Hm?"

"The people who do these kinds of quests usually don't like the idea of having rowdy adventurers where they live. It's hard for 'normal' people to even talk to adventurers, who usually appear gruff-looking."

It was difficult for citizens who had never been involved in any sort of combat to interact with rowdy adventurers.

"The typical reward amount is already set for this type of quest, so the client doesn't have to do any difficult negotiations. When we find the missing cat, the shop contacts the client. In exchange for the reward money, we return their cat to them."

As Kenneth explained, Dale opened his mouth with a question. "So why is such child's play becoming so popul..." But his question trailed off as his eyes turned toward the two young men who had just entered the shop. They rushed over to the bulletin board, then looked frantically to the flyer in Kenneth's hand.

Her caring words flowed naturally. Through these little daily interactions, she was building quite a large fan base. Indeed, it was because the little poster girl of the Dancing Mackerel Tabby had such support from the regulars that many fought over a certain type of quest.

When Dale, the guardian of said poster girl, found out exactly what type of quest it was, he stared back at the shopkeeper, Kenneth, in complete surprise.

"Why in the world is such a child's errand so popular?"

"Well, the reason is obvious," Kenneth said. The reason was so obvious that he made no effort to hide his surprise. He took the quest that Dale was looking at off of the bulletin board and shook it back and forth. "It's a quest to look for a lost cat."

"A cat," Dale said. "There're always looking-for-pet quests, but no one's ever given them a second glance till now! No matter how desperate they are, adventurers...wouldn't bother searching for a lost cat... It'd be one thing if the cat were found while doing another job, but..."

"Well, Latina has been the one drawing up the images of these cats," Kenneth said.

"As expected of Latina! Not only can she explain things in a way that's easy to understand, she has the creative skills to back it up!" Dale's constant lavishing of praise was, at this point, quite normal.

Kenneth looked down at the flyer in his hand. It wasn't perfectly realistic, but the picture accurately captured the hue and length of the hair, as well as the eye color. Latina had even added the red string collar around the neck that the owner had described.

It wasn't so difficult a quest and for the final decisions to really be fair, the client needed to confirm the animal themselves.

Because of that, Dale's look of suspicion was to be expected.

"Well, it's just a front, really," Kenneth said and didn't explain any further. Just then, everyone heard an adorable little voice from the entrance.

"I'm home!"

"Welcome home, Latina!"

"Hi Dale!"

The moment he heard her voice, Dale had spun around in his seat and opened his arms wide to welcome her. She ran over to him for a hug, but Kenneth's voice made her stop short.

"Latina, do you want to confirm a possible lost cat?"

"Cat?!"

Her face lit up and she ran over to Kenneth.

"La...Latina...?" Dale said, but she didn't notice his sad cry of protest.

Instead, she hopped up and down in front of Kenneth in excitement, making her skirt and platinum hair sway. "Cat? You found a cat?"

"We think so." The young men lowered the box and tilted it toward her. Her smile widened as she looked at the cat inside. Latina loved essentially all animals.

"Cat... So fluffy and cute...! It's so cute!"

Dale wasn't alone in thinking that she was far cuter.

Latina's guardian was unbelievably sweet to his adopted child, but he was a boarder of the Dancing Mackerel Tabby,

which also ran a restaurant. This meant he couldn't adopt a pet for her—not that Latina would ever ask for something in such a selfish manner or even bring up such a request.

"Wooow...! Can Latina pet it?"

"Be careful not to get scratched," one of the young men warned her as she slowly stuck her hand into the box. The brown, tiger-striped cat with a round face meowed in suspicion but gave up and grew quiet once Latina touched it.

"Wow...! Wow...! Cat!"

She was completely absorbed in petting it.

The two young men leaned over next to her, a special vantage point, and looked on with blissful expressions.

"......"

Dale watched the three of them for a bit, then turned to Kenneth. "In other words, it's to make Latina happy."

"Latina likes cats, but it seems the cats in town run away from her," Kenneth said. Latina's love of cats always overexcited her, making the cats in town stay away and meaning she didn't often get a chance to touch one.

The lost cat requests were a great and sensible way to let her interact with cats as much as she wanted. As for the people who completed the quest, getting to fawn over her as she fawned over the cat was a reward in and of itself.

As Latina looked up at the young men who had brought in the cat, giggling with an expression completely unlike her normal one, the two quest completers looked as if their hearts had been stolen away.

Dale understood that feeling all too well. It was reasonable to believe that all people would be easily captivated by a smile like that. Latina's adorableness was just that strong.

"W...well, if Latina is happy, I don't mind it," he said, though it was just a bit frustrating that the glowing smile wasn't directed at him.

"You never bother to hide how you're really feeling," Kenneth said.

Dale crossed his arms, pretending to be unaffected as he watched from a distance as Latina continued petting the cat. Kenneth sighed at his complete inability to guard his expression as the adventurer walked over to the counter to get a quest completed stamp on the flyer in his hand.

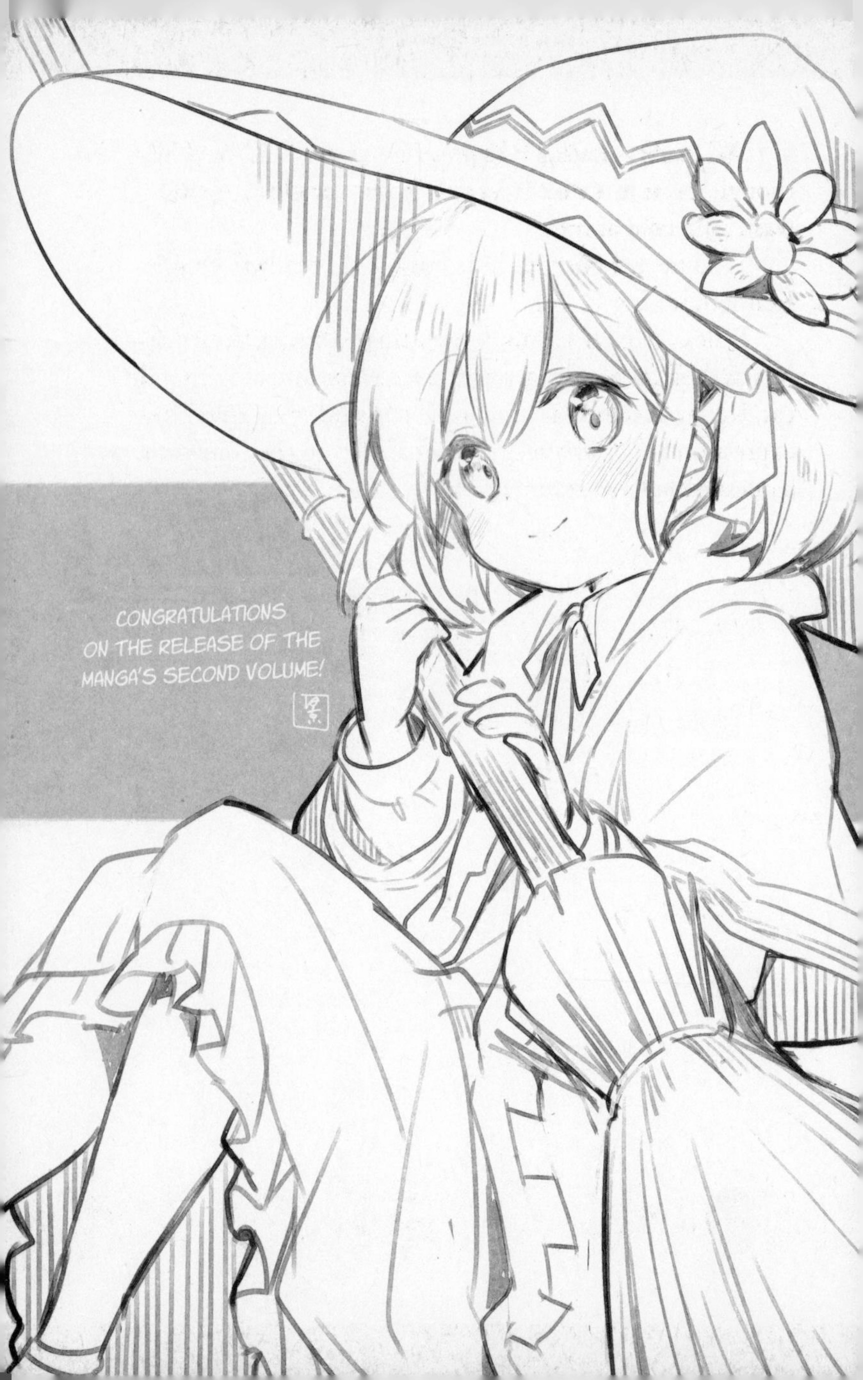
CONGRATULATIONS
ON THE RELEASE OF THE
MANGA'S SECOND VOLUME!

Afterword

Nice to meet you again!
This is Hota.

I hope you enjoyed the manga version of *If It's for My Daughter, I'd Even Defeat a Demon Lord.*

I really liked drawing various expressions this time. I am enjoying the original author's wonderfulness all over again. *Uwee hee hee!*

We are about to start school for Latina, and there--oops! Looks like I'm going to run out of space. Well, I hope to see you again soon!

Special Thanks
Mei-san
Masami-san
Doi-san
Mikagebaku-san

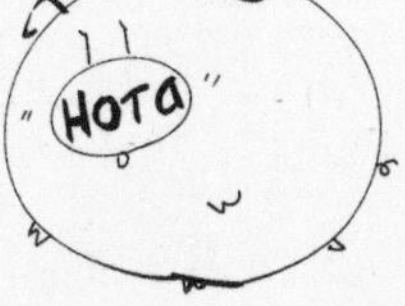
HOTA

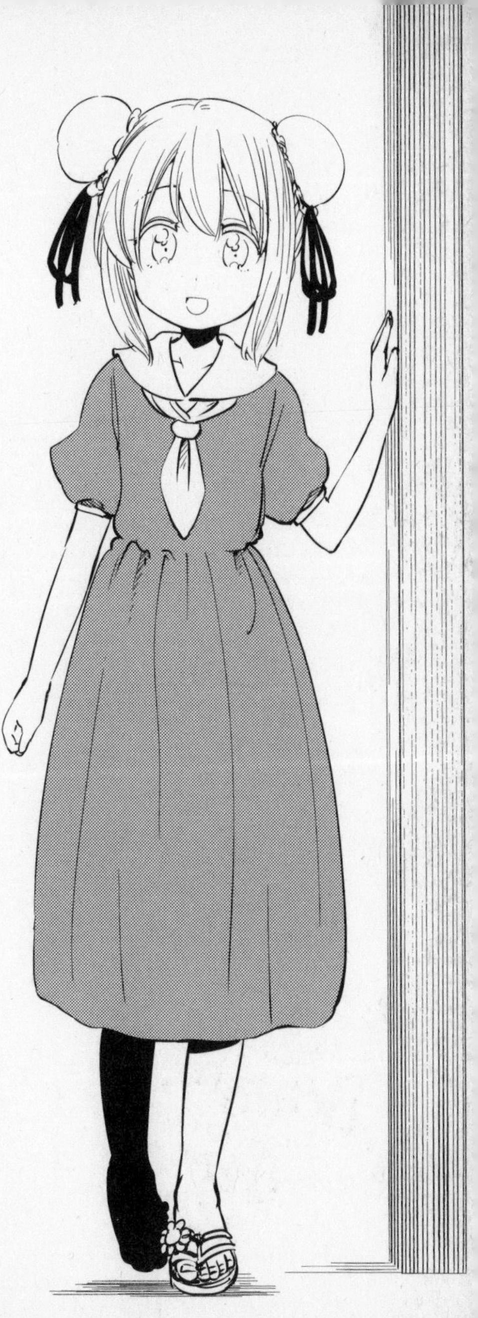

IF It's
For My
Daughter,
I'd Even Defeat
a Demon
Lord

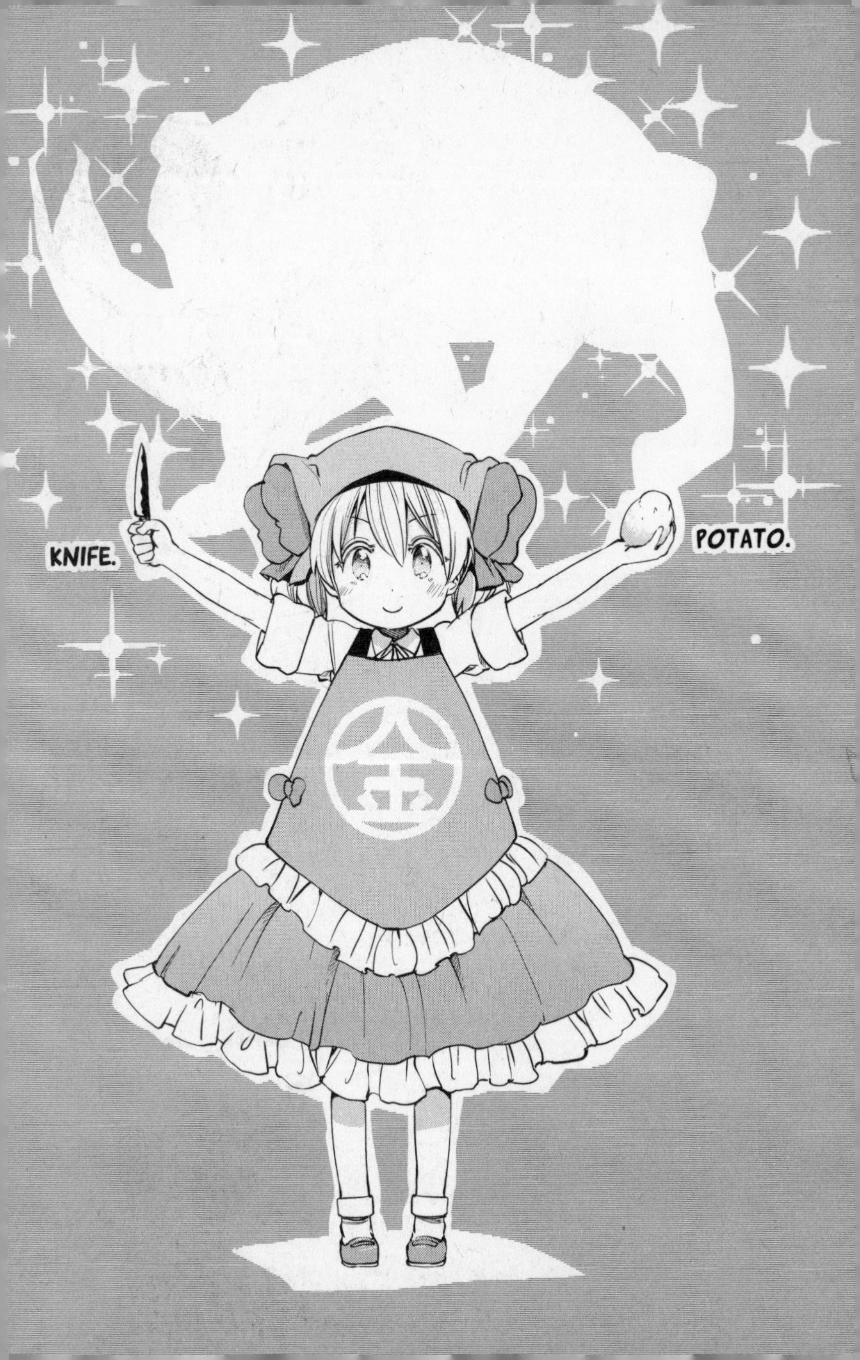
POTATO.
KNIFE.

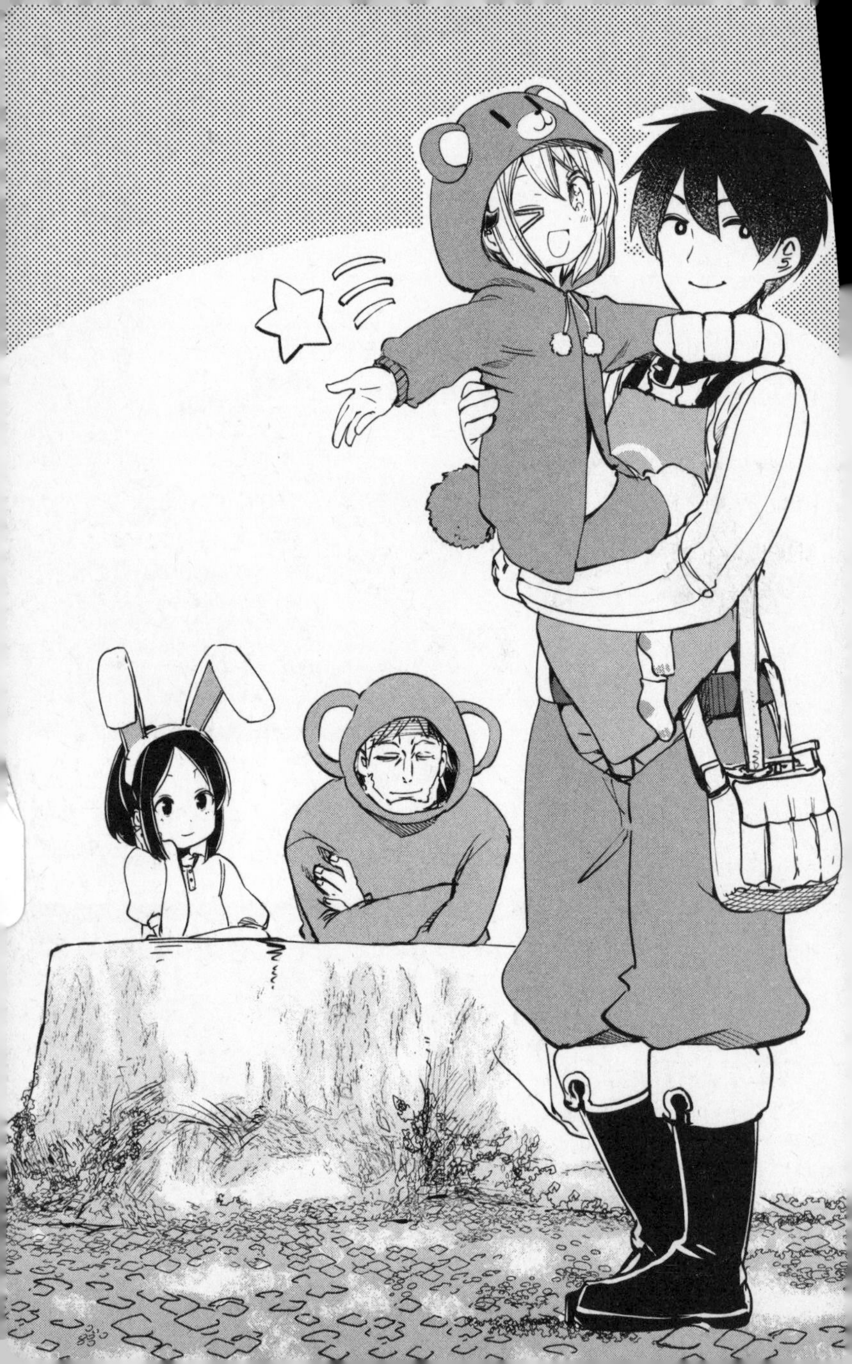

SEVEN SEAS ENTERTAINMENT PRESENTS

IF It's FOR My Daughter, I'd Even DeFeat a Demon Lord vol.2

story by **CHIROLU**   art by **Hota.**   character design by **KEI・TRUFFLE**

TRANSLATION
Angela Liu

ADAPTATION
Julia Kinsman

LETTERING
Ochie Caraan

COVER DESIGN
KC Fabellon

PROOFREADER
Kurestin Armada
Janet Houck

EDITOR
Jenn Grunigen

PRODUCTION ASSISTANT
CK Russell

PRODUCTION MANAGER
Lissa Pattillo

EDITOR-IN-CHIEF
Adam Arnold

PUBLISHER
Jason DeAngelis

UCHINOKO NO TAMENARABA, ORE HA MOSHIKASHITARA MAOU MO
TAOSERU KAMOSHIRENAI VOL. 2
©Hota. 2017
©CHIROLU 2017
First published in Japan in 2017 by KADOKAWA CORPORATION, Tokyo.
English translation rights arranged with KADOKAWA CORPORATION, Tokyo.

Seven Seas books may be purchased in bulk for promotional, educational, or
business use. Please contact your local bookseller or the Macmillan Corporate
and Premium Sales Department at 1-800-221-7945, extension 5442, or by
e-mail at MacmillanSpecialMarkets@macmillan.com.

Seven Seas and the Seven Seas logo are trademarks of
Seven Seas Entertainment, LLC. All rights reserved.

ISBN: 978-1-626929-18-0

Printed in Canada

First Printing: October 2018

10 9 8 7 6 5 4 3 2 1

FOLLOW US ONLINE: *www.sevenseasentertainment.com*

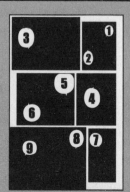

READING DIRECTIONS

This book reads from *right to left*, Japanese style.
If this is your first time reading manga, you start
reading from the top right panel on each page and
take it from there. If you get lost, just follow the
numbered diagram here. It may seem backwards at
first, but you'll get the hang of it! Have fun!!